OPERA AND DRAMA IN
EIGHTEENTH-CENTURY LONDON
The King's Theatre, Garrick and the Business of Performance

In this study, Ian Woodfield explores the cultural and commercial
life of Italian opera in late eighteenth-century London. It was a
period when theatre and opera worlds mixed, venues were shared
and agents and managers collaborated and competed. Through
primary sources, many analysed for the first time, Woodfield
examines such issues as finances, recruitment policy, the handling of
singers and composers, links with Paris and Italy, and the role of
women in opera management. These key topics are also placed
within the context of a personal dispute between two of the most
important managers of the day, the woman writer Frances Brooke
and the actor David Garrick, which influenced the running of the
major venues, the King's Theatre, Drury Lane and Covent Garden.
Woodfield has also uncovered new information concerning the
influential role of the eighteenth-century music historian and critic
Charles Burney, as artistic adviser to the King's Theatre.

Ian Woodfield is Professor of Historical Musicology at Queen's
University Belfast. His current research interests include Mozart,
and he has recently been awarded an Arts and Humanities Research
Board grant to study the autograph score of *Cosi fan tutte*. His
published books include *The Early History of the Viol* (Cambridge
University Press, 1984), *English Musicians in the Age of Exploration*
(Pendragon, 1995) and *Music of the Raj: A Social and Economic History
of Music in Late Eighteenth-Century Anglo-Indian Society* (Oxford
University Press, 2000).

Opera and Drama in Eighteenth-Century London

The King's Theatre, Garrick and the Business of Performance

Ian Woodfield

CAMBRIDGE
UNIVERSITY PRESS

PUBLISHED BY THE PRESS SYNDICATE OF THE UNIVERSITY OF CAMBRIDGE
The Pitt Building, Trumpington Street, Cambridge, United Kingdom

CAMBRIDGE UNIVERSITY PRESS
The Edinburgh Building, Cambridge CB2 2RU, UK
40 West 20th Street, New York, NY 10011-4211, USA
10 Stamford Road, Oakleigh, VIC 3166, Australia
Ruiz de Alarcón 13, 28014 Madrid, Spain
Dock House, The Waterfront, Cape Town 8001, South Africa

http://www.cambridge.org

First published 2001

Printed in the United Kingdom at the University Press, Cambridge

Typeface Monotype Dante 10.75/14 pt.   *System* QuarkXPress™   [SE]

A catalogue record for this book is available from the British Library

ISBN 0 521 80012 9 hardback

To Thérèse

CONTENTS

TABLES

MUSICAL EXAMPLES

ACKNOWLEDGEMENTS

My main debt of gratitude is to the archivists of three commercial banks, which hold records of the accounts of several figures of significance to this study. Victoria Hutchings of C. Hoare & Co. kindly facilitated my visit to transcribe the ledgers relating to the Brooke–Yates opera management in the mid 1770s. I benefited considerably from the expert assistance of Philip Winterbottom of Drummonds Bank (records held in the Royal Bank of Scotland Archives, London) in locating and transcribing the 1778–9 opera account of Sheridan and Harris and that of their associate Jonathan Garton. Tracey Earl of Coutts & Co. was kind enough to make a transcription of the banking records of the castrato Pacchierotti.

Prompt replies to requests for information are acknowledged from librarians working in the following institutions: the British Library; the London Theatre Museum; the Royal Academy of Arts at Burlington, Piccadilly; Cambridge University Library; the Bodleian Library; the William Salt Library at Stafford; the National Library of Wales at Aberystwyth; the New York Public Library; the Huntington Library; the Beinecke Library at Yale; the Widener Library at Harvard; Duke University Special Collections.

I acknowledge with gratitude assistance in obtaining material or in providing helpful commentary on earlier drafts from Donald Burrows, Patricia Howard, Robert Hume, Simon McVeigh, Judith Milhous, Curtis Price and John Rutledge. I am also indebted to Mr and Mrs John Comyn for providing me with transcripts of several Burney letters in their collection, and to the Hyde Collection, Four Oaks, New Jersey, for permission to reproduce a letter in their archive. Readers for Cambridge University Press made many helpful suggestions.

Finally, it is a pleasure to acknowledge the generous financial assistance of Queen's University Belfast in support of numerous visits to London and one research trip to various libraries in the USA. The School of Music at Queen's, as always, has been a stimulating and supportive environment in which to work.

A NOTE ON CONVENTIONS

The *manager* or *impresario*: the person with ultimate responsibility for the management of a season, often called the *proprietor* in contemporary sources.

The *recruiter*: a person (usually a musician or composer) engaged to make a European tour to sign up leading Italian singers on behalf of the London management.

The *emissary*: someone (not necessarily connected with opera) employed to deliver a specific commission (a letter, a verbal proposal or a contract) to a singer, dancer or composer.

The *agent*: a long-term resident in Italy, paid or unpaid, acting on behalf of the London management.

The *representative*: a person acting on behalf of an opera singer.

Introduction

In the 1750s, the King's Theatre in London was in a state of near collapse. A shifting series of alliances between performer-impresarios, aristocratic amateurs and bankers kept it afloat, but the venture was plagued by financial instability and managerial incompetence. Its artistic decline was even more spectacular. The days when Handel was the resident opera impresario were by now little more than a memory. Since that august era, no other composer of stature had stayed long enough in London to make an impact, and repertoire was of depressingly low quality. Perhaps only one factor ensured the survival of the theatre at all: the unchallenged place of Italian opera at the heart of the social and musical world of the English aristocracy. In the 1760s, there were some signs that the worst period was over. High-quality singers, always central to the success of Italian opera in London, began to appear more regularly, with the castrati Manzuoli and Elisi enjoying popular successes. More significant in the long term was the establishment of *opera buffa* as a regular part of the London season. Comic opera was cheaper to stage, gave variety to the season, and in due course produced its own lineage of stars with the charisma to attract audiences. Mixed seasons of *opera seria* and *opera buffa* afforded some protection against failure in either genre, and a further spreading of the risk was provided by ballet. To judge by the salaries paid to leading dancers from Paris, their contribution to the financial stability of the opera house became ever more essential as time went on. After four seasons in London, feted by society, Pacchierotti, one of the leading castrato singers of the late eighteenth century, retained a sense of realism on this issue. He was well aware that people frequented the King's Theatre because of the dancing, and he expressed the view that if this taste were to cease, the 'melancholy consequence' would be the 'indispensible ruin' of the place.[1]

The contrast between the fortunes of the King's Theatre in the mid century and in the 1780s could hardly be greater. The authors of a recent study of this later period, the managements of Sheridan, Taylor and Gallini, have presented an exciting portrait of the London opera house during some exceptionally turbulent years. Competing teams of managers fought fiercely for control of what was now seen as a highly prestigious cultural asset. Audiences were increasing in size, and the auditorium was periodically enlarged to cope with the rising demand. Seasons with top castrati like Pacchierotti and Marchesi were becoming the norm rather than the exception, and during Gallini's management the quality of the Italian repertoire in Vienna was finally recognised. A potent symbol of this renaissance is the fact that in late 1790, London came close to recruiting both Haydn and Mozart as rival opera composers.[2]

The decade before this 'Golden Age', perhaps the least studied period in the history of the King's Theatre, is the subject of this book. It coincides broadly with Sacchini's tenure of the position of house composer in the 1770s. Rightly judged by posterity to be several classes below Handel as an opera composer, Sacchini was nonetheless an important and influential figure in his day, and he was to play a central role in the revival of the fortunes of the King's Theatre. He was recruited by George Hobart, an aristocratic amateur, who, through a combination of poor management and bad luck, was unable to translate imaginative ideas into a successful programme. Even though for his last season he hired not only Sacchini but also the famous castrato Millico, his management ended in failure, perhaps because he simply ran out of resources. In the event, he left a valuable legacy for his successors, the team who took over the opera house in 1773, and who were to bring both stability and prosperity. The new managers came from a very different background – the London literary and theatrical world. There were five partners, but only three active managers: Frances Brooke, the novelist, translator, critic and would-be dramatist; and two actors of considerable renown, Mary Ann Yates and her husband Richard. Brooke was undoubtedly the driving force behind the partnership, quickly proving herself an exceptionally capable manager. Having from the start assumed overall responsibility for policy, she demonstrated so sound a grasp of artistic planning and financial control that the King's Theatre began to prosper to a hitherto unprecedented degree. A much more influential figure in the history of Italian opera in London than has hitherto been recognised, her role in the revitalisation of the King's Theatre lies at the heart of this study. Sacchini remained in London during Sheridan's management. It is not my intention to go over ground covered in the recent study of this later period, but in the light of newly discovered documentation a revised interpretation will be proposed in three significant areas: the theatrical politics underlying the seminal 1778 sale of the opera house; the finances of the King's Theatre during Sheridan's management; and the salary paid to Pacchierotti.

It will be useful to outline the main themes of this study, which are as follows:

(1) Theatre politics

In the 1770s, the affairs of the Italian opera house became deeply entangled with the world of the London theatres and in particular with the interests of two major figures of the English stage, David Garrick and Richard Brinsley Sheridan. Theatre in London was regulated by the Licensing Act of 1737, which restricted performances to the two 'patent' theatres at Drury Lane and Covent Garden. Despite a small breach of the act in 1766 when a limited patent for summer performances was granted to Samuel Foote at the Little Theatre, it was still very much in force in the 1770s. Permission to stage Italian opera performances at the King's Theatre was not subject to the 1737 Act, but was granted through an annual licence, issued by the Lord Chamberlain's office once the financial viability of the proposed season had been secured.[3]

The effective monopoly on spoken dramatic performances enjoyed by the proprietors of Drury Lane and Covent Garden greatly enhanced the commercial profitability of their theatres, and it also conferred considerable artistic power on the managements, both in the hiring and firing of actors and in the selection of plays to be performed. Garrick, manager at Drury Lane, was inundated with offers of plays, meritorious and otherwise. His necessary rejection of most of these scripts not infrequently led to the breakdown of hitherto cordial relationships. A significant factor in the entanglement of the Italian opera house in London theatrical politics of the 1770s was one such rejection. The author Frances Brooke had submitted a play to Garrick entitled *Virginia*, which had been rejected because he had already accepted another play on the same subject by Samuel Crisp. This rebuff rankled deeply, and, rightly or wrongly, she believed that her play had not been given a fair hearing by the actor simply because she was a woman. Modern critics do not see in Brooke's plays unjustly neglected works, nor does her personal charge against Garrick seem particularly well founded. He presented a range of new plays by women authors, sometimes taking great pains to ensure their success. When Brooke's views became public, he received strong support from other women writers. Nonetheless, that the famous actor had behaved in what in the modern era would be termed a 'sexist' fashion was Brooke's unshakeable conviction. After a period in Canada, she returned to London where she conceived a remarkably bold plan: this was to attempt to mount a direct challenge to Garrick by staging her own plays. In the light of the restrictions imposed by the 1737 Act, it would have been difficult to raise capital for a new building with no guarantee that a new patent would be issued by the authorities. Her attention thus turned to the King's Theatre, already a focus of some opposition to the existing monopoly. The opera house had many advantages, occupying an attractive site close to the fashionable areas of West London, with a loyal, wealthy and aristocratic audience, and a licence, albeit granted only for public performances of Italian opera. Moreover, the King's Theatre was manifestly under-used, lying vacant for four to five months each year, and even during the season staging only two operatic performances a week. The idea began to gain currency that an application to stage theatrical performances out of the opera season or on intervening nights during it, might win favour with the authorities as a controlled further breach of the 1737 Act.

With this as her avowed aim, Brooke put together a small consortium to take over the opera house when it came up for sale in 1773. Had she succeeded in gaining the desired permission, she would not only have been in a position to attempt to demonstrate to the world at large the fallibility of Garrick's artistic judgement by staging successful productions of her own rejected works, much more significantly she would have further undermined some of the monopolistic influence enjoyed by the established theatre managers. At that point, the public ramifications of what had started as a private dispute began to cause alarm in wider theatrical circles, Brooke's bold move in effect claiming for the King's Theatre the much desired but elusive status as London's third winter theatre. The adverse consequences of such a change were well understood by the proprietors of the two established theatres, and they resisted it with all the means at their disposal. Brooke, however, a woman of extraordinary tenacity in the pursuit of her ambitions, was a formidable adversary, and the issue dominated London theatre politics for much of the decade, during which repeated applications for a licence were rejected by the Lord Chamberlain, who appeared anxious at all costs to preserve the *status quo*, even though some of the arguments in favour of a relaxation, notably the increase in London's population since 1737, were beginning to seem compelling. On a personal level, the old quarrel between Garrick and Brooke simmered on, flaring up in 1778, when satirical attacks were published by both sides.

During Brooke's five years as manager, the commercial and artistic prospects of the King's Theatre as an opera house were transformed. Even though permission to stage plays on alternate nights had not yet been granted, the prospect of a successful application to the Lord Chamberlain was now a serious concern for the managers of the two established theatres. When, late in 1777, it became apparent that Brooke was considering her next career move, Sheridan, who had taken over Drury Lane after Garrick's retirement, felt he had to put in a pre-emptive bid with the support of Thomas Harris at

Covent Garden. The 1778 sale amounted to a remarkable coup on the part of the theatre establishment. The previous defensive strategy, which was to fight off Brooke's applications for permission to stage plays at the King's Theatre, had become dangerously exposed, and, in what might perhaps be termed a hostile take-over, that is, one in which the interests of the acquired organisation were not the chief concern of the purchasers, Sheridan and Harris achieved their immediate aim, but it was a hugely rash gamble, given that they could put up hardly any of the £22,000 selling price from cash in hand. As a result of this coup, the orderly system of finance established by Brooke at the Italian opera house was utterly shattered, and the mess was still being sorted out a decade later.

(2) Opera management

The failure to achieve her primary objective, the public demonstration of the injustice of Garrick's rejection of her works, left Brooke with an opera house to run, and this she did with notable success. Throughout her period at the King's Theatre, she displayed strength of purpose and clarity of vision, both useful attributes for an eighteenth-century opera manager, but it was her ability to cope with an unforseen crisis that was to prove decisive. In her second year as artistic director, she was confronted with a very serious problem. A rival place of entertainment, the Pantheon, began to develop an alternative strategy for presenting major opera stars in London. Situated in a more fashionable locality and free from the crush of coaches that so irked opera patrons, the Pantheon could offer almost all the ancillary elements of a night at the opera: elegant surroundings; a tea room; tables for cards; and facilities for staging dances and masques. When its proprietors took the decision to hire Agujari, a major star of Italian opera, there was consternation at the King's Theatre. It seemed likely that the traditional loyalty of the English aristocracy to Italian opera was about to be put to a severe test. With considerable verve, Brooke elected to meet the threat head on. Her choice of Gabrielli to counter Agujari was an inspired one, and the singer's debut at the King's Theatre was an operatic event of high drama, which provoked intense debate.

A detailed account of the administration of the King's Theatre at this period will be given, and new information on a range of topics concerning the business of opera performance will be discussed: banking arrangements; finances; salary levels; recruitment policy; and the use of agents. Particular attention will be paid to the links between London and Rome and Naples, and the role of the English artistic community in Italy in sending up-to-date information about singers, composers and scores back to London. There were several well-established sources of repertoire. Music for the season could be provided by a 'house' composer, as was the case with Sacchini, and it could be commissioned directly from an independent composer, but it was just as important to keep in touch with what was going on in Italy. Through her contacts with Ozias Humphry and other English artists, Brooke remained very well informed about which operas were proving most successful in Florence, Rome and Naples, and popular scores were regularly purchased and sent back to London for use in new productions. The connection with Rome was especially important in the supply of recent *opere buffe*, and works by Piccinni, Paisiello and Anfossi were sent to Brooke to be adapted for the King's Theatre.

(3) Opera criticism

The fierce debates that raged in Paris over opera, between advocates of tradition and reform, found only a muted echo in London. The most substantial critique to be published in London was an English translation of Algarotti, *An Essay on the Opera* (1767), but there was hardly any original commentary from indigenous writers. One important source, however, has been overlooked. Le Texier, a reciter, theatrical impresario and would-be opera director, spent several decades of his life in London, attempting to establish for himself an influential position in the King's Theatre management. For two seasons in the late 1770s, he published a periodical entitled *Journal*

Etranger, which included substantial reviews of King's Theatre productions. Signed opera criticism is rare in late eighteenth-century London, and it is useful to be able to evaluate the Frenchman's critique against the background of his career and known views. Given the warmth of his relationship with Garrick, it is quite likely that the *Journal Etranger* reviews reflect ideas on acting in opera espoused by the great actor, whose indirect influence on eighteenth-century reform movements on the Continent was profound, and who now perhaps had a more personal interest in supporting an attack upon Italian opera at the King's Theatre.[4] Although much of what Le Texier had to say was the common currency of opera criticism, his priorities, as an actor, were different from those of the poet Algarotti. He is especially severe on acting deficiencies in the King's Theatre casts, their routine use of stereotyped gestures and exaggerated caricature. He deplores the lax attitude to production management, the use of inappropriate costumes and scenery, and ludicrous gaffes, such as the refusal to ensure the inaudibility of the prompter. Following Algarotti, he even criticises audience behaviour, which he deems excessively indulgent of all these vices. His ideals certainly seem close to those associated with Garrick, notably the insistence on preserving the dramatic illusion, and the natural portrayal of character. Musical issues are of less concern, but, as might be expected, Le Texier approves the use of the chorus in *opera seria* and the action finale in *opera buffa*, and he condemns the excessive reliance on *da capo* arias. A bizarre character, he was thoroughly despised by the opera fraternity, and in consequence he failed to influence the conduct of Italian opera at the King's Theatre in any lasting way, yet his critique of London's failures is interesting in itself, and his journal amounts to a rare manifesto for opera reform in an English context.

(4) Careers of singers

The King's Theatre maintained and indeed enhanced its reputation as a leader in the market place for the leading stars of Italian opera.

During the period of this study, the major figures to appear in London were Guadagni, Millico, Agujari (at the Pantheon), Gabrielli and Pacchierotti. Much new information will be presented concerning the London years of these performers, in some cases hitherto unknown financial details of their salaries, in others unpublished accounts of their reception. In general, the 1770s saw the position of castrati as the top earners being challenged by women superstars, while at a rather lower level the position of the *basso buffo* began to develop its own distinctive star status.

(5) Music

The early months of 1773 seem in retrospect a critical turning point for Italian opera in London. In the preface to the libretto of his first London opera *Il Cid*, Sacchini is clearly identified with some of the central ideals of Parisian reform opera, notably as a lover of 'bella semplicità'. In the opera itself, prominent use is made of chorus and dance. A few weeks after the première of *Il Cid*, London had its first taste of Parisian reform opera itself, when Millico starred in two performances of *Orfeo*. Only two months later, however, this production was abandoned in favour of the pasticcio version originally given in London in 1770, and the brief flirtation with authentic Gluck appeared to be over. Although elements of reform opera remained in Sacchini's subsequent London operas (and those of Traetta) with their emphasis on spectacle, prominent use of chorus and orchestrally accompanied recitative, and occasional attempts to integrate ballet, there was no decisive shift in the nature of Italian opera in London.

Throughout this period in London, Sacchini was the dominant figure. His work was the unquestioned touchstone by which other composers, at least in *opera seria*, were judged. In describing him as a musical 'deity', the author of *ABC Dario Musico* was reflecting a view widely held in England. Although in retrospect these were not especially distinguished years for Italian opera in London, there was a growing recognition, evident in the recruitment policy of both

Hobart and Brooke, of the value of employing a good composer to provide original work of quality. The scale of Sacchini's success in 1773 demonstrated that a composer, in support of a leading castrato, could contribute much to the artistic and financial success of the opera house. The culture of the pasticcio, dominant in the 1750s and 1760s, for a time suffered a decline, as Brooke, a writer herself, began to seek out original works from the best available opera composers on the Continent. The list of composers who wrote, or were approached to write for London during her management, is impressive: Sacchini, Piccinni, Paisiello, Traetta, and J. C. Bach. In support of this policy, salary levels for composers rose, although not to the level enjoyed by leading singers. The agreed fee of £150 paid to Sacchini for each opera he composed in the mid 1770s far exceeded the payment that Mozart could expect from the Burgtheater for an opera in the 1780s. It might fairly be said that artistic policy was well conceived, but that it promised rather more than was actually achieved. A particular disappointment was the failure of negotiations that might have attracted the two leading Neapolitan opera composers to London. Piccinni refused an offer from Hobart, and his only original commission from Brooke, *Vittorina*, was a flop; Paisiello was on the verge of coming to London, when he received a better offer from St Petersburg. Despite these setbacks, the quality of repertoire was certainly improving. The recent evaluation of Brooke's last season as 'one of the most successful artistically in the later history of the King's Theatre' seems well merited, ending, as it did, with the most important opera to receive a London première during this period, J. C. Bach's *La clemenza di Scipione*.[5] No attempt will be made in this study to add to the recently published commentaries on operas from Sacchini's last years in London between 1777 and 1782, nor to assess the most popular *opera buffa* to be given during this period, a revival of Piccinni's well-known classic *La buona figliuola*, but there will be brief discussions of musical issues raised by Sacchini's *Il Cid*, *Perseo*, *Motezuma* and *Creso*, and by *Didone abandonata*, the pasticcio in which Gabrielli made such an impression. All that survives of Sacchini's music for King's Theatre productions at this period are published collections of selected 'favourite' airs. The loss of the full scores places severe limitations on what can be said about the overall dramatic effectiveness of these works.

(6) The role of Charles Burney

Burney is justly celebrated as a historian and critic of Italian opera in late eighteenth-century London, but less well known is his role as artistic adviser to the King's Theatre. This study will consider this aspect of his career, and it will be suggested that during the managements of Hobart and Brooke, he was an influential figure in the development of artistic policy. With the first-hand knowledge gained during his extended tours of the Continent, he was well placed to assist with advice on the recruitment of singers and the choice of repertoire. A number of questions remain unanswered. How he reconciled his formal responsibilities at the Pantheon with this informal role at the King's Theatre is especially unclear, and the possibility of a conflict of interest is obvious. It is also evident that when he came to assess this period for his *General History*, he found himself reviewing singers whose recruitment he had suggested and perhaps actively assisted. Again, there is the possibility that this might have affected his objectivity.

(7) A woman in management

Even though singers like Mingotti had been involved briefly in the running of the King's Theatre on several previous occasions, Brooke's period of five seasons as artistic director at the King's Theatre marked a new departure, an unusual example of a woman in a very high-profile management position. The only comparable example in the London concert world is that of Theresa Cornelys. It is a paradox that although her decision to take on this responsibility was the direct consequence of a dispute in which she assumed that her gender was a key factor, her general management of the opera house seems hardly to have been affected by her sex. In the biography by Lorraine McMullen, Brooke's tenure at the King's Theatre is presented as a brief managerial interlude in a career in which her most distinguished achievements were in the fields of the novel and the libretto.[6] The present study follows McMullen's account of the origins of the quarrel, but proposes a new interpretation of its conclusion. In particular, it will be suggested that the hitherto baffling *Queen of Quavers* satire was in fact the final pro-Garrick shot in the public war of words between the two sides.[7] In view of the possibility that Le Texier's fierce reviews of King's Theatre productions might also have been encouraged by Garrick, it will be argued that the great actor's dispute with Brooke was a more significant episode in the conduct of the opera management at this period than has hitherto been realised.

SOURCES

Italian opera in London during the second half of the eighteenth century has recently attracted a good deal of scholarly attention.[8] The discovery of papers relating to the Giardini–Leone dispute has illuminated the precarious world of a mid-century impresario and his recruiter as they struggled to put together a cast. The friendship between the two men is seen declining rapidly into mutual distrust, acrimony and legal wrangling.[9] The publication of the King's Theatre bank accounts at Drummonds has shed further light on the shaky finances of the 1750s and 1760s.[10] For the later period, a wealth of newly discovered material in the Bedford Papers and in the Public Record Office has enabled the tangled history of Italian opera in London during the 1780s and 1790s to be told in great detail. Recent studies include: an account of Earl Cowper's role as a recruiting agent in Florence;[11] an investigation into the circumstances surrounding the Pantheon fire;[12] and a wide-ranging survey of opera salaries in eighteenth-century England.[13] All this work has culminated in the first volume of a major study of Italian opera in England from 1778, a richly documented and fascinating account of the turbulent but exciting legacy of the Sheridan sale.[14] The period 1770–8 has received less attention. Terry's classic study of J. C. Bach is rich in detail about composers and singers active at the King's Theatre during these years,[15] while Petty's published thesis gives a season-by-season account of the repertoire and its reception by critics.[16] The best account of the Brooke–Yates partnership as a whole is in McMullen's literary biography of Brooke.[17] There have been several accounts of the activities of major singers of this period, notably Millico, Guadagni and Pacchierotti.[18] A valuable account of Sacchini's first London opera appears in Dennis Libby's introduction to the facsimile edition of *Il Cid*.[19]

For primary sources, research into Italian opera in London during the 1770s relies heavily on the Burney family. Charles Burney's comprehensive survey of King's Theatre productions includes the whole of this period.[20] His critical focus is on the star singers, their vocal qualities, their musicality and acting abilities, but a secondary subject of interest is opera reception; especially if a singer failed to live up to his or her reputation, he was anxious to provide an explanation. A certain coyness affects some of his evaluations, perhaps because of his own role in suggesting the original recruitment. Additional comments on opera are to be found in his private letters[21] and those of his friend Thomas Twining, who, although not a regular opera-goer, held decided views on some opera-related matters.[22] Fanny Burney depicts the social world of the opera stars in London society, a richly comic mix of adulation and friendship, benevolence and backbiting.[23] There are brief descriptions of Brooke and the Yates couple, but the best-known musical passages are the vivid portrayals of Millico, Sacchini, Agujari, Davies and Gabrielli. Susan Burney's unpublished journal for 1779–80 is devoted almost exclusively to opera, providing details of singers such as Danzi, Roncaglia and Trebbi, who were first recruited by Brooke.[24]

Newspaper coverage of opera-related matters during the 1770s is

sporadic but useful, even though factual reporting is sometimes manifestly inaccurate. The day after the lawsuit brought by Cecilia Davies
against the opera management was settled, three accounts appeared
in the morning press which disagree over every detail – the identity of
the judge, the name of the court, the reason the action was brought
and the damages awarded. As the reputation of the King's Theatre
recovered, so the volume of gossip about its affairs increased. Much
of it is highly partisan and probably unreliable, but it at least demonstrates the extent to which star singers remained the focus of attention. Newspaper criticism of opera productions at the King's Theatre
appears from time to time during the 1770s, and becomes fairly
regular by the end of the decade. The anonymous London critics in
general reflected the high esteem in which Sacchini was held; operas
by composers who might be regarded as rivals (Anfossi and Traetta)
were coolly received. Adverse criticism in a newspaper, however,
could not stop a winner. After the first London performance of
Paisiello's *La frascatana*, a critic savaged it: 'There never was an Opera
more heavy and tedious than *La Fraschetana*. The music does nothing
but roar and thunder; it makes noise to no purpose.'[25] With fifty performances by 1800, it proved the most popular comic opera of the
century after *La buona figliuola*.

The well-known published writings of three regular opera-goers,
Horace Walpole,[26] Lady Mary Coke[27] and Mrs Harris,[28] provide
much useful coverage of the 1770s. Walpole was well informed about
opera politics but, when commenting on singers or productions, was
censorious to such a degree that his views can rarely be considered
representative of mainstream opinion. Even so universally praised a
debut as that of Manzuoli in 1764 gained from him only qualified
approval.[29] Lady Mary Coke was a frequent visitor to the King's
Theatre. Her diary is often vacuous and is usually concerned with
society gossip, yet it occasionally includes important pieces of information, and she gives a particularly good impression of the impact of
La buona figliuola in 1767. Mrs Harris, an altogether more lively writer,
was a shrewd observer, whose comments on opera at the King's
Theatre always seem pertinent.

A number of sources not hitherto consulted by opera historians have been especially useful in this study:

The Althorpe manuscripts

Lord Spencer and his wife were opera-goers as were several of their correspondents. Letters from Hans Stanley MP, Sir William Jones, Mrs Howe, George Bussy Villiers (Fourth Earl of Jersey) and General Cunningham contain references to Italian opera singers in London.[30] Not surprisingly, the comments concern the star performers and their doings. Useful snippets of information on recruitment are sometimes reported, but the most interesting passages are those which give on-the-spot reactions to the debuts of leading singers. Comparisons with Burney's supposedly considered judgements are sometimes instructive. George Bussy Villiers is a particularly useful informant. We learn from him of the new stage boxes added to increase the capacity of the King's Theatre in 1773, and he briefly reports London reactions to the first two singers of the title-role of Gluck's *Orfeo*. The views expressed by the Spencer circle of acquaintances may be considered typical of those of the aristocratic clientele upon whose support the King's Theatre relied.

The Ozias Humphry manuscripts

Valuable information on the recruitment of opera singers is to be found in a series of letters in the Ozias Humphry correspondence in the Royal Academy of Arts, Burlington House, Piccadilly.[31] Other letters from Brooke to Humphry in the Bodleian Library[32] and in the Donald Hyde Collection[33] also contain references to opera matters. The detention in quarantine and the subsequent death of James Butler, the man entrusted with the urgent task of recruiting a leading comic man for the 1774–5 season, left his friend Humphry, then resident in Rome, with the job of completing the commission. The letters relating to this episode shed light on the activities of the network of singers' representatives, agents, bankers, lawyers and diplomats upon whose knowledge and good-will the London opera house had to rely. There has never been much doubt as to the kinds of individuals involved: the Humphry letters confirm what has long been surmised about the role of diplomatic establishments such as that of Sir William Hamilton in Naples, of long-term English residents and their meeting places such as the English Coffee House in Rome, and of the large, but essentially transient population of fashionable noblemen and gentry making the Grand Tour.

The diary of Edward Pigott

Between 1772 and 1776, Pigott reported a few visits to productions at the King's Theatre, and on one occasion to the Pantheon and a Bach–Abel concert. His descriptions are vivid, and he gives an excellent impression of the Pantheon as a fashionable society resort, and of Gabrielli's stage presence.[34]

The Hoare & Co. opera accounts

For four years between 1773 and 1777, the King's Theatre managers held an opera account at Henry Hoare & Co. in Fleet Street, which they used to make payments to singers, musicians and dancers. It forms a valuable addition to the already published ledgers from Drummonds. From the Hoare account, it is possible to calculate the salary scales paid to leading singers and dancers, and hitherto unknown details, such as who led the orchestra during the early seasons of this management, are revealed.

The Drummonds account of Sheridan and Harris

The opera account of Sheridan and Harris for the 1778–9 season was not known to the authors of *Italian Opera in Late Eighteenth-Century London*. Together with the account of Jonathan Garton, who had some financial role in the King's Theatre that season, it gives some useful insights into the extraordinarily tangled finances of this short-lived partnership. Other details can be supplied from Pacchierotti's Coutts account, and from a single page of opera accounts from 1780 in the Salt manuscripts. Amusing comments on this singer's predicament appear in his own letters to Charles and Fanny Burney.[35] The contrast between the orderly Hoare accounts and the chaotic financial arrangements of Sheridan is striking.

Journal Etranger

Le Texier's periodical is now scarce. The June 1777 issue, which contains an extended review of the 1776–7 season, is in the British Library. Duke University Library (special collections) holds a run, but the last three issues have been reported as being missing. The only complete set appears to be in the Widener Library at Harvard.

The Remarkable Trial of the Queen of Quavers

Published satires provide partisan but useful insights into what was going on at the King's Theatre during the last years of the Brooke era. She renewed her attack on Garrick in the summer of 1777 with the publication of a novel, *The Excursion*, in which the actor's artistic judgement is satirised.[36] In response, 'A Téte-à-Téte [*sic*] between the King of Quavers and the Heroine of Romance' appeared, a tiny three-scene playlet which pokes fun at the three managers of the King's Theatre.[37] Far more savage in tone, however, is *The Remarkable Trial of the Queen of Quavers*, published by J. Bew early in 1778. This satire has been interpreted as a diatribe against Italian opera, but its target is in fact the trio of opera managers, whose personal shortcomings are ruthlessly pilloried. Many conventional themes of Italian opera satire are worked in, but the generous absolution granted to a distinguished list of singers and composers (a few of the closest associates of the managers are pointedly omitted) is sufficient to demonstrate that Italian opera itself is not the target.

From all these various sources, private letters and diaries, financial records, newspaper reportage and published satires, a picture emerges of the resurrection of one of Europe's leading opera houses, the transformation over the course of a single decade of an enterprise precariously balanced on the edge of viability, into one of London's leading cultural institutions. At the same time, this is the story of a personal triumph, of one woman's bold challenge to the London theatrical establishment.

Charles Burney's melancholy account of the state of the King's
Theatre in the 1750s leaves the reader in no doubt that Italian opera in
London was in a state of very serious disarray, following a sequence
of schisms, failures, bankruptcies and imprisoned or absconding
managers. So bad had matters become that the spectre of imminent
collapse seemed to hang over the opera house at the start of each
new regime. Earl Cowper's second wife wrote to him on 24 January
1757: 'I don't like ye new Opera so well as ye last, but there was a very
full House on Satturday, to ye great joy of Giardini and Mingotti. I
begin to think that ye operas will go on.'[1] It was apparently something of a surprise to her that the season was likely to continue at all.
Burney thought that these two musicians had set themselves up for
'the chance of speedy ruin' by daring to take on the management of
this problematic theatre.[2] Managerial shortcomings were more than
matched by the sense of artistic decline. Indifferent performers and
an over-reliance on the pasticcio had become perennial problems.
Until the arrival of Cocchi, there was not even a resident composer at
this period. A good sense of how depressingly low standards had
become is conveyed in an account, again by Earl Cowper's wife, of a
pasticcio *Solimano* given in 1758:

> The Opera went off very well last night. I think all the Mattei's songs
> were very pretty, & I never heard her sing better than she did last night.
> Signor Potenza was very often horribly out of tune, but very few of y^e
> audience were sensible of that. I thought Omfra cara suited his voice
> very well & ye accompaniment kept him in tune, & ye little Duetto of
> Handel's. They sang in tune & it was encored by ye English, but y^e
> Foreign *Princes* & especially *Midas* seem'd to hold Handel's Musick very
> cheap, & y^e *ingenious* Mr Ward shook his heavy Head at it. It was ye best
> Tuesday, Vaneschi has had.[3]

No one seemed to care, even about poor tuning. Burney was deeply unimpressed by Signor Potenza, 'an uncertain singer, and an affected actor, with more taste than voice'.[4] The incorporation of Handel's music into this pasticcio (in this case a duet from *Amadigi*) made little difference.

Although the London opera house took many years to recover from this low point, a growing number of individual successes began to point the way towards a more viable future. It is clear from Burney's account that there was an increasing audience at least for *opera buffa*, symbolised by the success of Galuppi's *Il filosofo di campagna*, which in 1761 scored a hit with a run of fifteen performances. At a benefit for the *prima buffa* that year, 'not one third of the company that presented themselves at the Opera-house doors were able to obtain admission'.[5] This success was followed in 1763 by another, when audiences flocked to see Anna de Amicis. According to Burney, her figure and gestures had been 'in the highest degree elegant and graceful' and her voice and manner of singing 'exquisitely polished and sweet'.[6] Others were similarly impressed:

16 November 1762   Jones to Lady Spencer

> I was at the new Burletta last Saturday, La Signora Amicis a very agreable voice, with taste, great humour, her person genteel & easy, bien degagée, and tho' her face is very bad, yet she pleases much, the first man is also very well & has a good deal of humour, the other two men & two women have nothing bad in their voices, their persons very well, so that upon the whole I think the Burletta will do very well this winter.[7]

Gray also noted the popularity of De Amicis, and such was her success that Bach requested her as his leading woman in *Orione*.[8] The time was clearly now right for the formal establishment of a regular *opera buffa* troupe, whose performances could alternate with those of the serious company. Such an arrangement did indeed come into force in the summer of 1766, and it rapidly paid dividends, following the recruitment of Lovattini.[9]

Another pointer to where the future prosperity of the King's Theatre might lie was provided by an event of major significance in

the history of Italian opera in London. The recruitment of the castrato Manzuoli for the season 1764–5 has been much discussed,
largely as a result of his possible contact with the Mozart family, but
his arrival in London signalled an important turning point in the fortunes of the opera house.[10] London had long valued castrato singers,
but there was the obvious danger that in response to the problems
encountered during the 1750s, King's Theatre managers would start
to recruit cheaper, less distinguished singers, and thus be trapped in a
downwards spiral of diminishing returns. The reception accorded to
Manzuoli put an end to any prospect of that. He demanded and
received a massive salary of £1,500, a rate unmatched by any singer
until Gabrielli, over a decade later, and his debut caused a major sensation. Burney recalled: 'There was such a crowd assembled at all the
avenues, that it was with very great difficulty I obtained a place, after
waiting two hours at the door.'[11] No other singer so impressed him:
'the sensations he excited seem to have been more irresistible and
universal, than I have ever been witness to in any theatre'. The lesson
was obvious; the outlay of a huge salary for a singer of superstar charisma might seem risky, but such a policy was in fact liable to produce
a much better financial outcome than a less ambitious recruitment.
Time and again, money spent this way, for example on Gabrielli,
Pacchierotti and Marchesi, proved money well spent.

When in 1769 the King's Theatre came under the management of
the Honourable George Hobart, the future Third Earl of Buckinghamshire, the outlines of the strategy most likely to succeed were by
now very evident. The new manager's initial appraisal of the state of
the opera house would have focused on Lovattini's recent triumph in
La buona figliuola, which was so great that the previous season there
had been only *opera buffa* productions. Hobart, however, would have
been in no doubt that *opera seria* with a star castrato still lay at the
heart of the English aristocratic audience's interest in Italian opera,
and he accordingly laid plans for its re-introduction.[12] His decision to
recruit Guadagni was a shrewd one, as the castrato was already
known in London, having performed with De Crosa's troupe in the
1748–9 and 1749–50 seasons, and he was by now a *seria* singer of

acknowledged quality.[13] Hobart's first choice as a partner for the castrato, Anna de Amicis, was also a well-conceived selection. After her
success in London as *prima buffa*, she had gone to Italy, where her
career as a serious singer looked promising.[14] The pairing of
Guadagni with De Amicis in *opera seria* had obvious potential, but in
the event Hobart was only able to recruit the castrato.

Impressions formed at the start of a new managerial regime could
be hard to overturn, and from Hobart's point of view, it was unfortunate that he made a complete hash of the start of his first season. As
so often in the world of eighteenth-century opera, personal relationships interfered with musical decisions. While in Italy the previous
year, he had taken the singer Zamperini as his mistress, and she now
won the position of 'first' woman over Guadagni's sister.[15] The supporters of the latter made their feelings plain on the opening night,
and Hobart over-reacted ludicrously:

29 November 1769   George Bussy Villiers to Lady Spencer

> I hear from the Crewes, who have more Macaroni intelligence, that
> there has been a riot at the Operas the Galleries chusing to hiss the
> Zamperini. Mr Hobart took fire, carried the Guards up, & made a most
> agreable fracas: The whole Event of which I suppose is that she is now
> sure of meeting with the same reception everytime she appears. We
> shall hear more of it, I dare say; if such is Mr Hobart's method of
> acquiescing with the Voice of the Public.[16]

The management of cabals, groups of supporters of rival singers,
required a good deal of diplomacy on the part of an opera impresario, and it was always made more difficult when there was a personal
involvement. Walpole noted gleefully the activities of the two parties
supporting the rival singers 'who alternately encore both in every
song' so that 'the operas last to almost midnight'.[17] More significantly, the dispute meant that Hobart was from the start at odds with
his *primo uomo*, whose sister was widely felt to have been slighted.

To add to Hobart's problems, audiences were at first poor.
Walpole, as always ready with a pithy put-down, observed: 'The

operas are commended and deserted. I desert but cannot commend them.'[18] George Bussy Villiers informed Lady Spencer on 23 December that the house was 'quite thin'.[19] The pessimism was not entirely justified; attendance was often indifferent around Christmas before picking up in the New Year, and Guadagni's performances were soon attracting praise.[20] It was not long, however, before the castrato began to run into problems. According to Burney, he was a difficult character with 'strong resentments and high notions of his own importance', which 'revolted many of his warmest friends, and augmented the malice of his enemies'. It was not so much these personal shortcomings (if indeed they existed) that got Guadagni into trouble, as his approach to acting. His insistence on preserving the 'dignity and propriety' of the dramatic character led him to adopt practices which began to antagonise his audiences. Especially unpopular was his refusal to perform encores, and this gave his enemies the chance to exploit his predicament by calling repeatedly and vociferously for them. As we shall see later, Guadagni's calculated challenge to the long-established conventions of audience behaviour at the King's Theatre which underpinned the relationship between the aristocratic audience and the star singers, stemmed ultimately from ideas about the presentation of drama espoused by Garrick.

Although Guadagni enjoyed the support of a fiercely partisan clique, his reputation with the wider opera-going public began to suffer, and he was also unable to reach agreement with Hobart over the size of his fee for the next season. The *London Magazine* stated that he had received £1,150 for his first year, the going rate in London for a castrato of his stature, but he was now demanding £1,600, with £1,000 to be paid in July and £50 a month thereafter. Hobart refused to trust his singer with so large a sum before the season had even begun, but he apparently offered him the choice of receiving the fee in the usual way or at £30 a week.[21]

The outcome of these accumulating disputes was a serious schism; Guadagni abandoned Hobart at the King's Theatre and agreed to join Giardini in an unlicensed opera sponsored by Mrs

Cornelys.[22] The personal animosity that led to this action is easy to understand, but its rationale is less obvious. It was a near impossibility to make money out of Italian opera in London at this period, and there was never the remotest likelihood of two houses co-existing profitably. The purpose of the rival venture can only have been to damage Hobart sufficiently to cause him to withdraw, in the expectation that a new management, more to the liking of the rebels, would speedily re-incorporate them into the King's Theatre's programme. But this was a risky gamble, because Hobart clearly had the law on his side. The tactic adopted by his opponents was to test the range of the legal prohibition on unlicensed opera. Was it possible to perform one without full staging, or without costume, or in an abbreviated version, and still remain within the law? The title of the new venture 'harmoniac' and its location on premises run by Mrs Cornelys suggest that the intention was to present concert versions, with enough acting to satisfy opera lovers.

The anti-Hobart account of the dispute in the *London Magazine* is headed 'Musical Dissention', and the author takes the manager to task for the 'present deplorable state of the opera'. It had been the custom to treat performers with 'civility' at least, but now they were being regarded as so many 'miserable menials'. Having rendered himself 'obnoxious' to the public, Hobart had now been rejected by the principal musicians who had declared they would never again 'exhibit' under his direction.[23] The very illegality of the rival opera attracted much interest.[24] It was soon the talk of the town, and there is no doubt that its popularity was beginning to damage the King's Theatre, as noted by Mrs Harris on 12 January.[25] Hobart, recognising how serious a threat this posed to the continued existence of Italian opera at the Haymarket, at first tried to bargain:

27 January 1771   Horace Walpole to Lady Mary Coke

Oh! I had forgotten: there are desperate wars between the opera in the Haymarket and that of Mrs Cornelys's. There was a negotiation yesterday for a union, but I do not know what answer the definitive courier has brought. All I know is that Guadagni is much more haughty than the

King of Castille, Arragon, Leon, Granada etc. In the mean time King
Hobart is starving, and if the junction takes place his children must
starve, for he must pay the expenses of both theatres.[26]

Society gossip was all of 'the charms of the Harmoniac meeting'; the
'Anti-Harmoniacs' would allow no merit to the new operatic venue,
but they were clearly on the defensive.[27] Compromise was obviously
out of the question, and Hobart took decisive action by informing
the authorities, the effect of which was dramatic. The next Soho performance scheduled for 13 February was unexpectedly cancelled with
the illness of the singers given as the reason. This fooled nobody. Mrs
Harris was well aware of the situation and correctly predicted the
end of the venture: 'The truth is Mr. Hobart has informed against
them . . . The Harmoniac is over.'[28] Walpole reported to Sir Horace
Mann with ill-concealed glee that Guadagni 'is not only fined, but
was threatened to be sent to Bridewell'.[29] The report in the *London
Magazine* suggests that Hobart had acted with some cunning. Having
been informed that the first of the unlicensed 'operas' had taken
place, he covertly sent a servant to purchase a subscription ticket for
the remaining eleven, using the name of a friend so as not to cause
suspicion. He then turned up and witnessed a complete performance
of *Artaserse*, given 'upon a stage, and in the same manner as Operas
are usually performed'.[30] The court action was widely reported and
was the subject of a caricature in the *Oxford Magazine* (March 1771).
Guadagni was fined £50 for taking part, and Mrs Harris even suggested that the singer had been threatened with a whipping.[31] The
old cynic Walpole expressed himself 'delighted' at the quarrel and
correctly predicted that Guadagni's 'singing as well as loving days are
near over'.[32] There appears to have been a brief reconciliation when
the singer returned to the King's Theatre to appear in the title role of
Orfeo again, the first of these performances being given 'by command
of their Majesties' on 30 April 1771. In his preface to the programme
book, Guadagni expressed conciliatory sentiments: 'in performing
the part of Orpheus, I require no other bribe, or reward, than the
pleasure of shewing you a ready obedience'.[33] Although it failed, this

abortive attempt to set up a private opera did achieve significant support from both patrons and musicians. It is indicative that all was not well at the King's Theatre.

The debacle with Guadagni proved to be the central failure of Hobart's period of management. The singer's return came far too late in the season to prevent losses which were probably considerable. Worse still, *opera seria* did not quickly recover. For the next two seasons it remained at a low ebb, despite the rising reputation of Tenducci, the new *primo uomo*: 'Grass grows in the pit at the opera' was Walpole's tart comment.[34]

The financial consequences of Hobart's failure to make the best use of Guadagni (compounded by the losses incurred during the Cornelys venture) were serious, but success with comic opera might still have enabled him to save the situation. By the summer of 1770, Lovattini had completed four successful seasons in *La buona figliuola*, and the time was obviously right for a new work, even though a sequel, *La buona figliuola maritata*, had not lived up to expectations. Hobart thus attempted to recruit Piccinni. Burney, who agreed to act as his emissary, arrived in Naples in October 1770 and immediately presented the composer with a detailed proposal and a contract.[35] Piccinni firmly rejected the offer, despite Burney's warm advocacy of the financial benefits of a year in London. This was an imaginative move which might well have had the outcome desired by Hobart, since the composer's operas already in the repertoire, notably *La buona figliuola* and *La schiava*, continued to be popular with London audiences.

Towards the end of the 1770–1 season, audiences declined to an alarming extent. With no new castrato to offer to the public, Hobart took the only course of action open to him; he hired a star dancer from Paris – Heinel.[36] Mrs Harris reported that her fee was to be 1,200 guineas, but half of this sum was apparently to be raised by the 'Macaronis', a group of aristocratic supporters.[37] Burney confirms the unusual financial arrangements and hints that the very survival of the King's Theatre depended on the reception accorded to the dancer: 'At this time crowds assembled at the Opera-house more for the gratification of the eye than the ear; for neither the invention of a new composer, nor the talents of new singers, attracted the public to the theatre, which was almost abandoned till the arrival of Mademoiselle Heinel.'[38]

Some time during the last weeks of the season, Edward Pigott went to a performance of *Artaserse*. His brief account of a lively evening confirms the importance of dance:

> June 1772
>
> Went to the Opera, is a large and fine house, three Galleries one over an other, besides a number of boxes; the Opera was Artaxerxes, the Musick by To[s] Giordani a Neapolitan; the Actors are Savoi, Ristorini, Millico, Morigi, and Actrisses where [*sic*] Grassi, Giordani; I dont like the last; Millico, and Savoi charming Voices especially the first; the decorations extreemly fine; I saw Mad[lle] Heinel & Slingsby dance, la premiere a beaucoup de grases; le second dance avec Beaucoup gaitée et de legertée, il est estimé; the Orquester excellent lead by . . . two harpsichords no organs, delightfull musick, very well executed; they begin at seven and finish at half an hour after ten; people where [*sic*] not dresst so richly nor so well as at Paris; the common people throw peals of oranges on the stage before the play begins.[39]

Heinel was an unqualified success, and she inspired extraordinary emotions in some of her followers:

> 12 January 1773   George Bussy Villiers to Lady Spencer
>
> The operas go on as usual, & Mad[lle] Heinel continues to captivate from the highest to the lowest, but among all the conquests she has made, I do not know any that is more ridiculous than that of my former Friend James Bru[denel]: he can think or talk of nothing else, with all his uprightness and precise deportment, he is forever with her, & I suppose to ingratiate himself the more, is acquiring all the singular Gestures of the thinnest Macaroni.[40]

Burney noted that, following her arrival, dancing became a more important element in King's Theatre seasons generally.

By now, Hobart was in serious financial trouble. Failure to pay salaries was usually the first sign of a management in crisis, and hardly two months after the dancer's debut, there was gossip.[41] Despite his difficulties, Hobart held on for one more season, but once again, ill-fortune dogged his efforts. Millico had a moderately successful debut,[42] but both he and Sacchini fell victim to particularly nasty cabals, which used 'violent and virulent means' to poison their reception.[43] For a time, Millico seems to have been systematically hissed, for which Burney blamed admirers of Tenducci and Guadagni in particular. Sacchini's music was decried by the supporters of Cocchi, Guglielmi, Giardini, Vento and Bach. The 'manifest injustice and absurdity' of the campaign did not, unfortunately for Hobart, become evident until the triumphant première of *Il Cid*.[44] The final irony of his period as manager is that the financial and legal transactions necessary to transfer his share in the King's Theatre to new owners were underway within days of the opening of the opera that was to transform the theatre's prospects. It is hard to find fault with Hobart's artistic vision: Piccinni and Sacchini were his preferred composers, Guadagni and Millico his castrati, but success eluded him. When the new managers advertised their plans for the next season, they observed that receipts had 'generally been inadequate to the expenses' and pleaded for 'generous support and encouragement' for the future.[45] John Williams later noted: 'The Hon. Mr Hobart, now Earl of Buckinghamshire, then became sole Manager. He, after many years trial, and a tolerable taste for Italian music, it is generally supposed went out *minus* some thousand pounds.'[46]

Any change of management in the King's Theatre was a matter of considerable interest to the aristocratic opera-going classes, and when early in 1773 news began to circulate that Hobart had finally given up, rumours about the succession were rife. On 12 January, George Bussy Villiers reported that the opera house was now to be 'undertaken by several Gentlemen'. Changes were being made, and 'some new Boxes' were 'already added to the theatre'.[1] The leading figure in the financial take-over was James Brooke, who purchased from Hobart a half share of the company and then a further one-third share, giving him overall control.[2] The remaining one-sixth share was retained by Peter Crawford, who continued to work as treasurer.[3] Brooke was acting on behalf of his brother, the Reverend John Brooke and his wife Frances Brooke, and Richard and Mary Ann Yates. John Brooke seems to have had no active involvement in the King's Theatre at all. When the new managers took out a modest mortgage with the banker Henry Hoare, he was named as one of the three parties to the agreement who were: (1) James Brooke; (2) Richard and Mary Ann Yates; (3) John and Frances Brooke.[4] The mortgage, however, was for the 'joint and equal benefit' of the other four. James Brooke, acting on behalf of his brother's wife, is often described as one of the proprietors. On 10 November 1773, for example, the Lord Chamberlain's licence to perform Italian operas names him along with Richard and Mary Ann Yates.[5] There is no evidence, however, that he took part in the running of the King's Theatre, even though the opera account at Hoare & Co. was in his name and that of Richard Yates.

The new management team bought the opera house with a clear purpose in mind: in support of Frances Brooke's long-standing struggle to have her plays performed, they hoped to be able 'to obtain

permission to act plays with operas alternately', and in the expectation of this they paid, according to Michael Kelly, £7,400.[6] How performances of operas and plays could co-exist in one building, six
nights a week, was far from clear, and the prospect alarmed many
regular opera-goers. The first proposal to become public was that the
King's Theatre should be managed by Mary Ann Yates and the actor
William Smith. George Bussy Villiers, writing to Lady Spencer on 30
April, expressed a negative opinion, a view doubtless shared by
many: 'Hobart quits the management of the opera this season &
they now say that Smith and Mrs Yates are to undertake it; a playhouse administration will soon lower that spectacle.'[7] According to
Macklin, the two did apply for a licence: 'In the course of the said
spring [1773], *Mr Smith* associated with *Mrs Yates*, and they jointly used
[or rather attempted to use] their interest to obtain a Licence to Act
Theatrical Pieces, at the Opera-house in the Hay-Market four nights
in the week; but they were refused a Licence for that purpose.'[8]
Smith, in dispute with the manager of Covent Garden and negotiating to join Garrick at Drury Lane, saw this as an opportune prospect.
Having decided to throw his lot in with Mary Ann Yates, he wrote to
Garrick: 'I have been too ill-treated by Mr Colman ever to think of an
engagement with him without a certainty of better usage than I can
expect from so illiberal a mind; and have now no resource but with
the Yateses, with whom, as the license is now certain, I shall immediately close, and hope that I shall not by this step forfeit your esteem.'[9]
He had, however, been misinformed about the licence, or perhaps
deliberately misled. Formidable opposition was growing, both from
the owners of Drury Lane and Covent Garden who stood to lose
from the proposed change in the status of the King's Theatre, and
from opera-goers, contemptuous of the prospect of any 'playhouse'
involvement with their elite form of entertainment:

18 June 1773   George Bussy Villiers to Lady Spencer

Have you heard any thing of our opera here lately, I mean the Plan for
next year? perhaps not: Mr Hobart quits the management, & it is to be
undertaken by Mr and Mrs Yates, whose object is to get leave to act
Plays there the intermediate nights, but I hope & believe the King will

never give his consent to that – as to performers, I do not find they have engaged any: Mad^lle (alias Mad^me Fierville for she is married) has cruelly left us, & he [Fierville] is not yet engaged.[10]

By the summer, the application for the licence had been refused, leaving Smith little alternative but to attempt to re-establish relations with Garrick, who upbraided him for his flirtation with the new venture: 'the fact is, and you sh^d own it like a Man, as you are, the 3^d Company turn'd y^r head, & you had forgot what y^r heart had been wishing for'.[11] Garrick concluded by reassuring Smith that he was still his friend in spite of his 'folly'. Having failed to get their licence, the new owners of the King's Theatre had no alternative but to postpone their theatrical proposals and plan for the forthcoming opera season.

The three managers who now enjoyed sole responsibility for Italian opera in London had no previous experience of opera management, but they were formidable figures in their own worlds. A telling description of the Yates couple during their first year as opera managers is given by Fanny Burney. She had been invited by Brooke to go to the opera to hear Rauzzini. There, somewhat to her dismay, she was introduced to the actress:

> Her [Mrs Brooke's] House in Market Lane, by means of divers turnings & windings, has a passage to the Opera House. We intended to have sat in her Box, & have seen only her, but when we went, we found she was up stairs with Mrs Yates, & when she came down, she immediately asked us to go up stairs with her. This we declined, but she would not be refused, & we were obliged to follow her.
>
> It is very disagreeable that the Yates are half managers with the Brookes, nor can I understand how a woman of Character & reputation, such as Mrs Brooke, can have reconcil'd herself to becoming intimate with one whose fame will bear no scrutiny.
>
> We were led up a noble stair case, that brought us to a most magnificent Apartment, which is the same that belonged to the famous Heideger, & since his Time, has always been the property of the Head manager of the Opera. Here we saw Mrs Yates, seated like a stage Queen surrounded with gay Courtiers, & dressed with the utmost elegance & brilliancy'. . .
>
> Mrs Yates to a very fine Figure, joins a very handsome Face, though

not now in her *premiere Jeunnesse*; but the expression of her Face is infinitely haughty & hard.

With an *over done* civility, as soon as our Names were spoken, she rose from her seat hastily, & rather *rushed* towards us, than meerly advanced to meet us. But I doubt not it was meant as the very *pink of politeness*.

As to poor Mr Yates, he presumed not to take the liberty, in his own House, to act any other part than that of Waiter, in which capacity he arranged the Chairs.

We were not absolutely seated when the Door was opened by an Officer. Mrs Yates again started from her seat, & flew to receive him, Crying, 'General Cholmondely I am happy to see you!' Then turning to her *Jerry* [hen-pecked husband], 'Mr Yates, pray get the General a Chair'. Mr Yates obeyed, & then we rose, to go to the Opera.[12]

That Mary Ann Yates was the dominant partner in the marriage seems to have been widely agreed by contemporaries. Richard Yates ('Dicky') was a popular and genial comic actor in Shakespearean roles, but by the 1770s his reputation was overshadowed by that of his wife, the leading tragedienne of the London stage, who was celebrated both for the hauteur of her demeanour and the arrogance of her behaviour.

The third manager, Frances Brooke, is also described by Fanny Burney: 'Mrs Brooke is very short & fat, & squints, but has the art of shewing Agreeable Ugliness. She is very well bred, & expresses herself with much modesty, upon all subjects. – which in an *Authoress*, a Woman of *known* understanding, is extremely pleasing.'[13] Many years later she recalled further details of her physical appearance:

Mrs Brookes had much to combat in order to receive the justice due to her from the world; for nature had not been more kind in her mental, than hard in her corporeal gifts. She was short, broad, crooked, ill-featured, and ill-favoured; and she had a cast of eye that made it seem looking every way rather than that which she meant for its direction. Nevertheless, she always ultimately obtained the consideration that she merited. She was free from pretension, and extremely good-natured.[14]

Brooke was already known to the public as a successful novelist, author of *Lady Julia Mandeville*, but she had so far failed to have any of her plays accepted for performance on the London stage. The origins of her long struggle to achieve this ambition can be traced back to 1756, when she published a play entitled *Virginia*, which was rejected by Garrick, but only after the actor had retained it (so she thought) until Samuel Crisp's drama of the same title had been staged.[15] This perceived snub marked the start of the long-running quarrel, which, though intermittently pursued, later had a marked effect on her period as opera manager. Stung by his attitude to her play, she criticised him in an issue of her periodical.[16] Garrick was not amused and did not forget the insult:

> 13 June 1765   David Garrick to Marie Jeanne Riccoboni
>
> I am not acquainted with Mrs Brooke: she once wrote a play, which I did not like, & would not act, for which heinous offence, she vented her female Spite upon Me, in a paper she publish'd call'd y^e *Old Maid*, but I forgive her as thoroughly, as her Work is forgotten – I am told she has merit & is very capable of a good translation, tho not of an Original.[17]

The mutual antagonism engendered by this quarrel seems not to have diminished during the years the Brookes spent in Canada.

After her return to England, Brooke began work on an English opera entitled *Rosina*, in the hope that the piece could be staged at either Covent Garden or Drury Lane. First she tried to interest George Colman. In a letter to Richard Gifford dating from around this time, she intimated that influential friends were at work on her behalf:

> Colman has not yet sent an answer. I have a very bad opinion of all these gentry, & my greatest hope is that as neither of the installations [theatres] seem to please violently, one of them will have a vacancy & take it for their own sakes. I know neither will for mine. They will be pressed a good deal by some of my friends, & I don't despair.[18]

She explained the course of action that she would take if, as seemed likely, Colman refused:

> There is nothing to me so astonishing as that Colman should be another Garrick, which I am told he is: I scarce know how to believe it, & hope I shall not be *convinced*. My design is, if he refuses, to apply to G. & if he

refuses, to apply to the Ld. Chamberlain, for leave to act it at my own hazard, for twenty nights at Foote's, which if *thot* about, will probably pave the way for a third theatre, which is in agitation. I know the Lord Ch. is very angry at some instances of theatrical tyranny, & think I can refer my story up, & back it with friends that will carry my point, & the best female singer we have, Miss Catley, is in town, & not engaged at either house, & as ready to take such a revenge as I can be; but if I hint my design, they will engage her, and prevent it. I cannot do this till I have tried both houses, because till then I have no right to complain. There is no saying what hurt such a scheme would do them, & I have spirit enough, & friends enough, to carry it thro' if anybody could. Do you approve? If it should take, it might be more profitable than its being received at the other theatres. You see I ought to be secret as to this scheme.[19]

Her absolute determination not to be defeated by the theatre managers is very evident. The 'agitation' for a third theatre probably relates to a petition submitted to the Lord Chamberlain around 1770 (Appendix 2a). Entitled 'Considerations on the State of the Stage', it argues strongly for a relaxation of the exclusive right to stage plays enjoyed by Covent Garden and Drury Lane.[20] The author points out the great increase in London's population since the arrangement came into force and argues that the powers given to the Lord Chamberlain were to enable him to 'banish indelicacy' from plays, rather than to restrict unnecessarily the access of the London theatre-going public to playhouses.

Having failed with Colman, she wrote to Garrick, her long-time adversary, appealing, rather awkwardly, for an early answer:

Glanville Street 13 July [1772 ?]   Frances Brooke to David Garrick

SIR,

I SHOULD last year have asked your protection for an opera begun in the autumn, had I not been told YOU had engagements which rendered your receiving any thing more impossible. As it is now earlier in the season, you will exceedingly oblige me by favouring it with a perusal, after I have made a few alterations, which will be finished in a week or ten days.

If this little piece appears to you fit for the stage, I will flatter myself you will give it a trial; if otherwise, that you return me as early an answer as is consistent with your avocations. I am influenced to expect this by my firm belief, that unless when obliged to a different behaviour by the too general duplicity of mankind, plainness of conduct in business is inseparable from great superiority of understanding and talents. Of that superiority and those talents, I had rather speak to any person than Mr. Garrick, and to him on any occasion rather than this. Even modest praise appears flattery at the moment of soliciting a favour, and the variety of applications made to you by writers of the first merit makes this a very unimportant one.

> I am, Sir,
> with the greatest esteem,
> Your most obedient Servant.[21]

To appeal for openness in business dealings while plotting her next move with the singer Catley, shows Brooke capable of calculated deception, a characteristic which she was to use to good effect in her later Birmingham licence application. Garrick's reply, once again, was negative, and Samuel Foote persuaded her against performing her opera during his own short summer season, advising her instead to write to the Lord Chamberlain for permission to play it 'for a few nights in winter'.[22] This was a decisive moment in Brooke's career. Her failure to have *Rosina* accepted rekindled all her earlier resentment, and the radical idea of taking over the opera house and applying for permission to stage plays herself was thus conceived. It was indeed a fateful decision. By campaigning so vigorously for the King's Theatre to be granted permission to operate as London's third theatre, Brooke ensnared the opera house in the wider world of theatre politics. When in 1778 the two theatre managers (Sheridan and Harris) defeated a rival impresario with a more traditional background in the world of opera (Gallini) in the battle to assume control, it was in some ways the logical conclusion of the new direction initiated in 1773.

In making her move, Brooke was joined by Mary Ann Yates, who certainly shared her antipathy towards Colman, manager of Covent

Garden, as she had recently quit that theatre after a heated dispute with him.[23] Contemporary opinion recognised that the driving force behind the new opera management was the partnership between the two women, Fanny Burney amusingly depicting Richard Yates as a mere factotum. Once it had become clear that their bid to stage plays at the King's Theatre had failed, Yates had to consider her own acting career, and she therefore signed up with Garrick. A review of her performance as Clytemnestra in *Electra* on 15 October 1774 noted: 'After the play Mrs Yates entertained her friends with a very excellent Epilogue, also written by Mr Garrick, in which she informed them she had quitted the elegant scene of the Opera House, and all the Signiors and Signioras for Drury-lane; that she had conferred that drudgery upon her husband, and crowned him "Richard, King of Quavers".'[24]

In taking on the capricious tragedienne, Garrick was uninfluenced by his low opinion of her friend Brooke. He recognised hers as a major talent which it would be foolish to ignore. His invention of the amusing title 'King of Quavers' for the epilogue is significant. This was the first appearance of the satirical characterisation of the Yates couple as the 'King and Queen of Quavers' that came into greater prominence in the later stages of his quarrel with Brooke.

How the three managers divided up the duties of running the opera house is clear enough, at least in general terms. Richard Yates took on the responsibilities of house manager, placating angry subscribers when necessary, and keeping tight control over running expenses. Mary Ann Yates filled to perfection the part of glamorous society hostess, holding court like a queen. In addition to their extensive theatrical expertise, the Yates couple brought to the King's Theatre considerable financial resources. When in 1783 (five years after they had given up their interest in the opera house) it was suggested that the two had retired from the stage with a considerable fortune, Richard Yates sought to refute both his retirement and his fortune. With nice irony, however, he agreed that 'though not worth *quite* 40,000*l*' he could still eat his mutton without an engagement.[25]

So far as is known, neither Richard nor Mary Ann Yates had any previous experience of Italian opera. The all-important responsibility for artistic policy – the hiring of singers and the choice of repertory – was thus assumed by Brooke. A determined and in many ways admirable woman, she emerges as a figure of some importance in the history of Italian opera in London.

Soon after taking over from Hobart early in 1773, the new managers were in the fortunate position of seeing their investment begin to prosper. Although the opera house had a meagre recent record of success and abundant potential for continuing loss, the opening of *Il Cid* on 19 January 1773 marked a turning point. During the season as a whole, the work received twenty-two performances, more than any other *opera seria* in late eighteenth-century London. Its success demonstrated clearly that both Sacchini and Millico had prevailed against the activities of hostile cabals. Fanny Burney's journal gives a vivid impression of the crowds which attended on Saturday nights early in the run. On 22 January the opera house was 'so violently crowded, & the stage so filled with gentlemen' that the excessive heat and the encores fatigued Millico 'almost to illness'.[26] Of the performance on 6 February she wrote:

> Last Saturday Evening, Mama suddenly proposed going to the Opera, Il Cid, the fame of which had excited her curiosity. Susy & myself joyfully skipt at the proposal, & the Coach was instantly ordered. It was very late, & the Overture & 5 songs were over when we got there. The Opera is the sweetest I ever heard, & Millico sung like an Angel. The House was amazingly crowded & we had very back seats, but were glad of any, &, indeed, to hear such music & such singing, I would be content to sit in a Barn.[27]

Few operatic events were so widely noticed. General Cunningham observed the transformation in the fortunes of the opera house. On 23 November 1772, he reported that Vento's *Sofonisba* was attended by 'but a thin audience'[28], whereas by 23 January it was 'impossible to get a seat after six o clock'.[29] Mrs Howe wrote in similar vein[30], and Mrs

Delaney reported 'an opera that enchants the *degenerated* taste of the musical world'.[31] The dancers also won approval:

> Duke Street 26 February 1773   William Jones to Lady Spencer
>
> We have a new serious Opera called the *Cid*, and set to musik by *Sacchini*, which is greatly admired. I am not very fond of the piece, though the Musick is, certainly fine; but the dancing by Fierville, and Mad[lle] Heinel is far superiour to anything of the kind that I ever saw.[32]

Walpole was typically grudging in a letter to Lady Ossory dated 25 January: 'There is a new opera that pretends to be liked and consequently is crouded to excess.'[33] On 3 April he wrote again: 'I shall give up the opera (indeed it is very bad).'[34]

It was not unusual for audiences to build up early in the New Year after a quiet start, but this was no ordinary success and it had far-reaching consequences for the King's Theatre, even though Sacchini's next opera *Tamerlano* (which opened on 6 May) was less successful. Fanny Burney, who attended the second performance, noted that it 'went off extremely well, & with great applause'. This greatly pleased her as she had heard 'so bad an account of its success on the first Night of Representation'.[35] The probable explanation for its poor initial reception is that the cabals which had so diminished Millico's debut the previous year were still intermittently active. The successful composer and the star singer were feted by the Burneys. Sacchini, described by Fanny Burney as 'a very elegant man, & extremely handsome', was startled by how well the Burneys knew the music of *Il Cid* which had not yet been published:

> Hetty [Esther Burney], on first sitting Down, while Celestini tuned his Violin, began a Rondeau in the Overture to Sacchini's new Opera, which has been performed but twice; but she had been to 3 Rehearsals, & has gotten almost half the Opera by ear.
>   Sacchini almost started – he looked at first in the utmost perplexity, as if doubting his own Ears, as the music of *il Cid* has never been published. Millico clapt his Hands, & laughed, – 'ah! Brava, Brava! –' Sacchini then Bowed – and my father explained the manner of her having got this Rondeau! at which he seemed much pleased.[36]

Millico, with whom Fanny Burney seems to have been somewhat infatuated, is described as 'an immense Figure, and not handsome *at all*, *at all*, but his countenance is strongly expressive of Sweetness of Disposition, & his Conversation is exceedingly sensible'. Of his singing she wrote:

> I have no Words to express the delight which his singing gave me. More, far away, than I have ever received – even at the opera – for his Voice is so sweet, that it wants no Instruments to cover it. – He was not, however, satisfied with himself – he complained again of his Cold, – but seeing us all charmed, – with a sweetness that enchanted me in so great a Performer, he said 'Eh bien, Encore une fois; – la Voix commence a venir.' – & sung it again – & O! how divinely! . . . For my own part, the mere recollection fills me with *rapture* – my terms are strong, & yet they but weakly express my meaning.

The violinist who accompanied Sacchini and Millico to this musical evening was Eligio Celestino, the 'very neat and expressive performer' whom Charles Burney had first heard in Rome.[37] In the summer of 1772 Celestino seems to have been recruited to lead the orchestra at the King's Theatre for the coming season, and this may explain his close association with Sacchini and Millico in the early months of 1773. Fanny Burney records her father as saying 'that there are hardly in Italy 3 such modest men as Millico, Sacchini, & Celestino'.[38]

The success of Sacchini and Millico revitalised the *opera seria* tradition in London, which had been at a rather low ebb over the past six years. With ardent support from the influential Burneys, there was now every chance that the pair would be re-engaged for the following season.

Sacchini's brilliant debut marked a turning point, not only in the financial fortunes of the King's Theatre, but also in the revitalisation of *opera seria* as a genre in London. The extraordinary impact of *Il Cid* and *Tamerlano* struck Charles Burney so forcibly that he later singled them out for special commendation, describing the two operas as 'so *entire*, so masterly, yet so new and natural, that there was nothing left for criticism to censure, though [they had] innumerable beauties to point out and admire'. He also felt it worthy of note that Sacchini had been 'totally occupied with the ideas of the poet, and the propriety, consistency, and effect of the whole drama'.[1] In the light of this last comment, the remarkable reception accorded to *Il Cid* is best interpreted against the background of the pasticcio culture that had come to dominate *opera seria* at the King's Theatre. The decline of serious opera had in fact been so marked that the employment of a good composer (as distinct from an arranger) was coming to seem almost superfluous. The total number of performances of original works in the three years before Sacchini's arrival had dwindled to a mere thirteen, eight of Guglielmi's *Ezio*, two of the same composer's *Demetrio* and three of Cocchi's *Semiramide riconosciuto*.[2] London seemed in danger of forgetting the theatrical impact that a drama under the creative control of a single musician could have.

A move away from the pasticcio culture implied an improvement in the status of the composer, and it is perhaps significant that there was a calculated attempt to 'sell' Sacchini in the libretto of *Il Cid*. In the dedication, the composer is commended as a lover of 'beautiful simplicity', as a man contemptuous of 'decorations', sparing with his passage work, willing to silence the ornaments when the passions must speak, above all, as a musician whose music enters and remains in the heart.[3] This statement is manifestly influenced by the ideals of the reform movement, and it amounts in effect to an indirect acknowledgement of Gluck's famous preface of 1769, in which the same words ('una bella semplicità') are used to sum up the ideal of operatic writing, after the removal of the 'useless superfluity of ornaments'. Sacchini would not have attempted to institute any radical change of direction in London without the consent of the manager, and it is thus reasonable to surmise that Hobart, who had travelled extensively on the Continent in the late 1760s, had some sympathy with reform ideals. Sacchini's early London operas incorporate a range of musical elements advocated by reformers: much greater use of the chorus; some attempt to integrate ballet into opera; rich orchestration; and the development of the dramatic role of the accompanied recitative. For a time, there was also a trend away from plots on subjects from Greek and Roman history in favour of those with a more exotic flavour, notably *Tamerlano* and *Motezuma*, and those deriving from mythology, such as *Perseo*.

Quite apart from any desire to emulate Parisian opera, the incorporation of dances within *Il Cid* represented a pragmatic recognition of the growing importance of ballet at the King's Theatre. It was generally recognised that Heinel's triumph had saved Hobart's management from total collapse. *Il Cid* features a ballet sequence within the plot of Act II: 'The scene is opened with a chearful dance of youths and damsels crowned with flowers: two of the principals, carry two garlands, with which they adorn the hair of the brides.' This potentially significant development did not in fact mark the beginning of a new era for opera with integral dance in London, and the traditional separation between the two genres remained largely intact. One exception was Sacchini's own *Enea e Lavinia* of 1779, which included a full-scale ballet sequence by Stamitz.[4]

Of much greater significance for the immediate future of Italian opera in London was the decision to expand the role of the chorus. The nature and extent of choral writing in opera had recently been a matter of some controversy. A letter from one 'Arcangelo Bimolle' published in 1763 had revealed the extent of the antipathy of the Italian opera establishment to J. C. Bach, after his success with

Orione. His argument was predicated upon the belief that 'the pon-
derous harmony of Handel' carried much greater weight with the
English than 'the elegant taste of Italian melody'. Bach stood accused
of pandering to this regrettable preference: 'This [taste], *Bach*, at first
did not suspect; but finding it, by experience, has prudently changed
his style; and now his chorusses roar, his basses thunder, and his airs
float in an ocean of symphony. In a word he has Handelized; and
acquired a reputation here, by the very thing which would have
ruined him in Italy.' 'Bimolle' further criticised Bach's rich orchestration of flutes, oboes, bassoons and clarinets, but it is clear that his
over-use of the chorus was the main point of contention. There
were, however, at least a few discerning individuals in the enthusiastic audience who 'perceived with pain our Italian *Cantilena* toiling to
animate a dull German *Contrappunteur*'.[5] The two factions were still
in dispute in 1764, when the Italian establishment rejoiced at the cool
reception accorded to Bach's *Adriano in Siria*.[6] Bach refused to
concede the point, and in 1767 he included choruses in *Carattaco*. A
sympathetic reviewer spoke of the 'masterly stile' of the music and in
particular of the 'grandeur of the chorusses'. The composer was
deemed to be in a good position to reform the present 'corrupted
taste of our modern music' and 'like a second Handel' once again
restore 'that elegance and perfection we have for some time been
strangers to'. The critique in fact reads more like a contribution to
the debate between supporters of 'ancient' and modern music than a
review of Italian opera. In comparing J. C. Bach with Handel, the
reviewer specifically refers to the quality of the writing for chorus:
'His chorusses elevate the soul and put us in mind of those of the
immortal Handel, and of his own favourite *Orione*.'[7] At the King's
Theatre, however, Bach was an isolated exception. For the most part,
the place of the chorus in London opera productions remained a per-
functory one.

The decision to encourage Sacchini to make full use of the chorus
in his early London operas provided a neat closure to the national
aspect of the debate between the Italian faction and Bach, but it left
unresolved the question of the potential stylistic incongruity of

counterpoint in Italian opera. In retrospect, Burney felt that this incongruity fatally flawed the entire experiment:

> The late exquisite composer Sacchini, finding how fond the English were of Handel's oratorio choruses, introduced solemn and elaborate choruses into some of his operas; but though excellent in their kind, they never had a good effect; the mixture of English singers with the Italian, as well as the aukward figure they cut, as actors, joined to the difficulty of getting their parts by heart, rendered those compositions ridiculous, which in still life would have been admirable.[8]

This account suggests that the enhanced role of the chorus was a change of policy, agreed between Sacchini and the management, and it clearly demonstrates that the context of the composer's espousal of choral writing in opera for London was not that of Gluck and opera in Paris, but that of Handel and oratorio in England.

In his discussion of Handel operas, Burney outlined the features that a good opera chorus ought to possess:

> After this we have a *chorus* of Athenians; but not like his oratorio choruses, for an evident reason: in these the subject being generally, solemn, and in the church style, should partake of choral complication; and the performers having the Music before them, are not obliged to get it by heart; whereas an opera chorus, being in action, and committed to memory, must necessarily be short, easy, and dramatic.[9]

A single chorus only survives in Bremner's published selection of music from *Il Cid*. Towards the climax of Act III, Rodrigo, accompanied by a group of friends, appears in 'a subterranean place'. In the sombre chorus 'Tacite ombre', his supporters express the wish that his torment over Cimene be stilled. In a flash, there appear 'messaggieri di gioia'; Rodrigo is to be re-united with Cimene with honour, and the opera ends with a triumphant chorus (now lost) 'Viva il Cid'. Sacchini's piece is well suited to its dramatic context. It is richly scored for flutes, clarinets, bassoons and horns, and the writing is mainly chordal, although some passages are contrapuntally more elaborate (see example 1), while others use plangent harmonies with suspensions (see example 2). The combination of the gloomy

Ex. 1 Sacchini, *Il Cid* (London, 1773): excerpt from the chorus 'Tacite ombre'

Ex. 1 (cont.)

Ex. 2 Sacchini, *Il Cid* (London, 1773): excerpt from the chorus 'Tacite ombre'

Ex. 2 (cont.)

setting, anguished emotions, choral counterpoint and rich harmony was intended to impress, and it did so. Twining wrote to Jenner: 'Well, but as to Music: how do you like Sacchini? If you don't think Se pietà, with the recit before it, enchanting, I give you up. But I know you do. And what say you to the chorus, "Tacite ombre"? Say, if Music can go beyond that.'[10] While newspaper critics were dismissive of the libretto, they warmly approved the choruses, focusing on their grandeur, a characteristic term of Handel reception. One reviewer thought them 'grand and adapted with nice judgment to the subject'.[11] Another concurred, describing them as 'grand throughout'.[12]

The practical problems to which the pragmatic Burney ascribed the ultimate failure of Sacchini's opera choruses had not yet become public, but they were evidently being discussed in private. Fanny Burney could see that Millico was critical, and she noted down a little skit on the subject of one of the pieces in *Tamerlano*:

> My father then told Sacchini how much he had been charmed with Tamerlano, which he had heard the night before. Signor Sacchini receives compliments with the graceful modesty of a man by nature diffident, yet by custom inured to them. Millico pursued the conversation concerning the opera, and very drolly going over to the harpsichord, played a passage in one of the chorusses, and mimicked a most terrible man, who in spite of all the instruction he has had, always ruins it. This chorus is exceeding spirited, and though very indifferently performed, has a very fine effect, and is very much admired.[13]

Little is known about who sang in the opera chorus at the King's Theatre in the 1770s, but occasional disparaging references to boys suggest choir singers. Few discriminating commentators thought their (acting) performances adequate.

Two months after the triumphant première of Sacchini's *Il Cid*, the London audience had its only chance in the eighteenth century to hear a true reform opera, a production of Gluck's masterpiece *Orfeo*, in a version reasonably close to the composer's own score. The decision to replace the pasticcio version previously given in London was in part a pragmatic one, so that the London audience could hear Millico in one of his most celebrated roles, but it is also possible that the King's Theatre management wished to test out the reaction of the audience to a reform opera. Had the production been a real success, the future history of Italian opera at the King's Theatre might have been radically different. The version previously sung by Guadagni in London bore little resemblance to Gluck's opera. As Burney aptly put it, 'the unity, simplicity, and dramatic excellence' of the work had been ruined by the 'heterogeneous mixture of music, of other composers, in a quite different style'.[14] The published collection of songs from this pasticcio version includes additions by Bach (the principal reviser) and Guglielmi.[15] As Patricia Howard has shown, the version that Millico performed in 1773, both in its dramatic structure and orchestration, was closely based on Gluck's Parma version of 1769.[16]

The first performance of the new production was scheduled for 4 March 1773, but Millico was indisposed, and it was postponed until 9 March, when it was given as part of a double bill, repeated on 13 March. The advertisement in the *Public Advertiser* of 9 March stresses the dances and the choruses:

> At the King's Theatre in the Haymarket, / This Day will be performed a New Pastoral Piece, call'd / IL TRIOMFO D'AMORE / In ONE ACT, / After which will be performed the favourite Serious / Opera, called / ORFEO. / (Altered as it originally was performed at Vienna.) / The Music composed by Signor GLUCH. / With new Dances adapted to the Opera, intermixed / with grand Chorusses. / New Cloaths and Decorations.[17]

The published libretto confirms that this London production was based on the Parma, one-act version, although divided by Bottarelli into four rather than seven scenes.[18]

The King's Theatre audience had the rare opportunity to compare the two castrati who had sung *Orfeo* for Gluck himself – Guadagni (Vienna, 1762 and London, 1771) and Millico (Parma, 1769 and London 1773). Not surprisingly, the relative merits of the two performances attracted some comment. The *Morning Chronicle* on 10 March thought that Millico had 'exceeded Guadagni in the favourite air of *che farò senza Euridice*, etc., although he did not play the character altogether so well'. Another reviewer reported that Millico had 'sung the famous air *che farò*' in a taste different from Guadagni, but with equal success. Guadagni, however, was adjudged superior 'in the infernal part'.[19] A particularly fascinating glimpse of this debate is provided by an aristocratic opera-goer:

> London 16 March 1773   George Bussy Villiers to Lady Spencer
>
> In the Line of Spectacle, great disputes subsist at present about the Superiority of Millico & Guadagni in 'che faro' in the Orfeo: But it seems rather to be given in favor of the former [it is unfortunate that the word 'former' here is slightly ambiguous; it could signify Guadagni, the first of the two to appear in London, or, less likely, Millico, as the first of the aforementioned singers], without any just reason I think, because the whole comes to this Point whether a Man should be affected by a sudden Event of distress, passionately & hastily, or with despondency & dejection. These are their two ways of Singing it, & that must depend upon the constitution & temper of each person, both may be equally just.[20]

Brief though it is, this comparison is of great interest. One singer (probably Guadagni) reacted to the loss of Euridice with great passion, while the other (probably Millico) stressed bleak resignation. What is so interesting is that these two singers should have differed so markedly in their interpretation of the most dramatic moment in this seminal eighteenth-century opera. All too little is known, even at this basic level, about how such moments were actually presented on stage.

The early failure of this production of *Orfeo* – there were only two performances – marked the end of authentic Gluck productions in eighteenth-century England. Only two months later, the pasticcio version was resurrected. Although advertised with 'new Dances, cloaths, and scenes, Intermixed with grand chorusses' this was the version 'as it originally was performed at this Theatre by Sig.

Guadagni'.[21] As Howard points out, this implies the possibility that Millico might even have performed the substitute air written by Guadagni. Not much is known about how this end-of-season revival was received. Fanny Burney was admitted to a rehearsal of the opera and was of the opinion that 'all the part of Orfeo' was charming.[22] Later performances of *Orfeo* in England included an 'abridged' version at the Salisbury music week in September 1782[23], and Tenducci's version sung in Dublin in 1784 and at the King's Theatre in 1785.[24]

Summing up the reception of *Orfeo* in England, Burney observed that the work had 'the fate of all other Italian dramas, which are pronounced good or bad in proportion to the talents and favour of the singers'.[25] This was surely the underlying reason why the 'unity' of an opera like *Il Cid* made such an impression.

4 | Recruitment procedures and artistic policy

Having assumed control of the King's Theatre in early 1773, Brooke
soon found that she had inherited a theatre in better shape than must
have seemed likely when negotiations with Hobart began. The
obvious course of action was to retain Sacchini in order to build upon
the success of *Il Cid*. Her main problem as she assumed responsibility
for the longer-term direction of the King's Theatre as an opera house
was the formulation of an artistic policy. Even for a manager with a
background in opera, this was a complex task with several strands:
the recruitment of 'first' singers of sufficient quality who could work
together; the maintenance of a satisfactory balance of *opera seria*,
comic opera and ballet; and the choice of individual works. Brooke
had no background in opera, but she enjoyed one stroke of good
fortune, because among her acquaintances was Charles Burney, who
in the summer of 1770 had undertaken a 'musical' tour of Italy to
collect materials for his history of music. During his time abroad, he
had visited the major centres of Italian opera in Turin, Milan,
Bologna, Venice, Florence, Rome and Naples.[1] In 1772 he set off
again, this time for the Low Countries, Germany and Austria,
whence he returned in November 1772.[2] The presence in London of a
man who was an enthusiastic supporter of the King's Theatre and an
exceptionally knowledgeable informant about the current state of
Italian opera in Europe, made January 1773 an auspicious month
indeed for an inexperienced manager to start making plans. Brooke
lost no time in seeking his assistance. As Fanny Burney later recalled:
'Mrs Brookes . . . having become a joint proprietor of the Opera
House with Mr and Mrs Yates, earnestly coveted the acquaintance of
Dr Burney; in which, of course, was included the benefit of his
musical opinions, his skill, and his counsel.'[3] Their shared interest in
the future prosperity of the King's Theatre would have been enough

to establish a working relationship between Burney and the new manager, but Fanny Burney (who already had ambitions to become a novelist) was also keen to become acquainted with Brooke as a literary figure of some renown.[4]

In view of Millico's success, it obviously made sense to retain him for a second year, but Brooke's first new signing constituted an imaginative break with tradition. She hired the English soprano Cecilia Davies, who was the only Englishwoman yet to have received acclaim in Italy as a 'first' singer.[5] Known there as 'inglesina', her reputation was growing rapidly. The recruitment was not without some risk. It was suggested privately by one opera-goer that English audiences might fail to support their own countrywoman singing in Italian:

Middleton Park 28 July 1773   George Bussy Villiers to Lady Spencer

I shall only then add a word or two upon the opera for next winter. Fierville, Millico, Sacchini as composer, are engaged, the rest are all new ones, among them is a Miss Davis of whom I own I have little hopes as the first singer, for I never yet heard an English woman pronounce well Italian airs or words. Galli is to be second man.[6]

Others felt the hiring of an English soprano long overdue. Joel Collier with irony congratulated the opera managers 'for having at last condescended to permit an Englishwoman to be called Signora, and by virtue of that title to share some of the princely incomes which have hitherto been lavished on Italians'.[7] Given the sense of injustice felt by Brooke at her treatment by Garrick, it is tempting to see in her recruitment of Davies support for a woman artist attempting to break into a closed shop, in this case for Italian singers. A piece of opera criticism published by her two decades earlier had expressed some antipathy to Italian opera singers, on the grounds that the patronage bestowed on them was unacceptably lavish.[8] She had also stated that although she was 'no enemy to the Opera', she found it difficult to account for the praises lavished on Mingotti, because the listeners 'not understanding the language . . . can be but indifferent judges'.[9] Ironically enough, she was now herself about to increase the rates paid to Italian singers. Any suggestion that Davies did not merit her recruitment would be unfair. Her growing reputation in Italy was well known in England, and an additional point in her favour was the success she had enjoyed with the English community in Florence.[10] A London engagement was becoming more and more likely.

Despite the astonishing success of the *opera seria* programme in 1773, Brooke was well aware of the need to re-establish *opera buffa* at the King's Theatre. Her choice of singer to lead the re-formed comic troupe was Carabaldi, hailed in the *Public Advertiser* on 6 May 1773 as 'the most celebrated buffo in Europe'. Not hitherto known in England, the singer might have been suggested by Burney in person, but even if the new opera manager had only browsed through the published record of the Italian tour, she might well have come up with the same name. The most casual reader of this work could hardly miss the fact that Burney was unimpressed with the state of comic opera in Italy. There was little to recommend the burlettas at Turin;[11] at Florence there was a good tenor, but Burney considered 'neither his voice or taste equal to those of Signor Lovattini';[12] at Naples the vocal performance of the burletta singers was 'wretched', although there was an excellent comic actor.[13] Nowhere in his travels did he find three performers on a single stage to match Lovattini, Morigi and Guadagni, the comic trio who had performed in London during the 1769–70 season.[14] There was only one choice left: Carabaldi, whom Burney heard at Milan. After his first visit to the comic opera there, the English historian was cool: the seven characters were 'all pretty well done', but 'no one *very* well, as to singing'.[15] But at the next performance Carabaldi shone:

> The second opera which I heard here was *La Lavandara Astuta*, a *Pasticcio*, with a large portion of Piccini's airs in it. Garibaldi [Carabaldi], the first man, had a better part in this burletta than in the first, and sung very well. He has a pleasing voice, and much taste and expression; was encored, *alla Italiana*, two or three times.[16]

Burney returned for another performance only to discover that 'the first tenor, and only good singer' was ill.[17]

When full details of the forthcoming season were announced on 18 October, it was evident that the recruitment of Carabaldi had fallen through, and Brooke found herself having to issue a rather lame apology: 'The ill health of Sg Carabaldi having prevented his setting out in time, making it impossible for him to be here at the opening of the theatre, Sg Scheroli, the tenor who has played the first buffo with the greatest reputation in Italy, has kindly undertaken to play the part until his arrival.' Carabaldi did not come, and Scheroli was no substitute. As a result there was still a notable imbalance (six to one) between performances of serious and comic opera.

To recruit supporting casts of singers and dancers for the following year's programme of opera and ballet, Brooke sensibly opted to use methods that had become well established during the 1760s and the early 1770s. Hiring traditionally took place during the late spring and summer. Later in the century recruitment by post was usual, but in the mid century it was thought better to send a recruiter on a trip to the Continent. The story of Leone's trip for Giardini in the summer of 1763 has been told in detail;[18] lack of communication and lack of trust made the venture a notable fiasco. In the three seasons following this débâcle, only *opera seria* was staged at the King's Theatre, but in 1766 the decision was taken to reintroduce comic opera, which greatly increased the complexity of the task faced by recruiters. As Burney noted:

> During the summer of this year [1766] a new plan was formed by the opera managers for the ensuing season, which involved future *impresarii* in great difficulties and expence. The lyric theatre having been much neglected on Tuesdays, even when it was crouded on Saturdays, it was thought expedient, in order to excite curiosity by a different species of entertainment to engage two distinct companies of singers for the performance of serious operas on Saturdays, and comic on Tuesdays; and for this purpose Mr Gordon, one of the managers, went to Italy, during the recess, in order to engage performers.[19]

One result of John Gordon's trip was an important coup – the recruitment of Lovattini to perform in Piccinni's *La buona figliuola*. There is good evidence to suggest that Gordon also sought out opera scores.

In the correspondence of Sir William Hamilton there is a request for payment, submitted to the bankers Hart & Wilkins on 30 July 1766, for an opera score for Gordon: 'Sirs, Please to pay Emanuel Barbella . . . including eight ducats for an opera wrote out for Mr Gordon.'[20] The following year Gordon again went abroad. Lady Mary Coke reported on 7 August 1767: 'I was sorry to hear . . . that Gordon has not been successful in Italy. All the fine Women singers are ingaged; 'tis bad news for our Opera.'[21]

When Hobart took over the King's Theatre in 1769, he seems to have retained Gordon as a recruiter – there are several references to the cellist visiting the Continent at this period, though the reason is not made explicit.[22] Early in 1773, Brooke lost no time in sending him abroad. Her brother-in-law instructed Henry Hoare to supply the him with letters of credit:

> Fortingham 2 January 1773   James Brooke to Henry Hoare
>
> Sirs,
>
> Be pleased to pay John Gordon Esqr or order Fifty pounds and place it to my acco – And be pleased also to furnish him with letters of credit on your banker at Paris for Two hundred and fifty pounds more, placing the Dra^t to that amount when they become payable to my Acco^t.
>
>   I am,
>   Sirs,
>   Your most Obed^t Servt Jam[es] Brooke

This letter also demonstrates that Brooke had started to take control of artistic affairs at the opera house, even before the financial transactions were complete, and well before details of the sale to the new proprietors had become public. In another hand are listed the dates when Gordon was paid – 8 and 27 January and 2 and 24 March.[23] From France, Gordon went on to Italy. In the 6 May advertisement in the *Public Advertiser*, it was reported that: 'Mr Gordon is still in Italy, with full power to engage the best singers, both serious and comic, that can be procured.' When details of the season were announced, it was claimed that he had spent seven months in Italy and had recently made two trips to Paris to recruit dancers.[24] The length of the recruiter's stay in Italy suggests that the new manager wanted a full appraisal of the current market for opera singers in Italy.

One structural problem with the spring recruitment trip was that back in London decisions had to be made about which of the current singers and composers were to be retained for the following season. In June 1773 Sacchini was still uncertain of his future and was waiting with some annoyance for news of Gordon's progress in Italy. Fanny Burney broached what was obviously a sensitive subject: 'I asked him [Sacchini] if he was yet certain of staying another year? He said no, for a Mr. Gordon is sent over to Italy, by the stupid managers with unlimited powers to engage what singers or composers they will, & Signor Sacchini cannot be either engaged or at liberty, till they hear what this man has done.'[25] Brooke could not afford to risk losing Sacchini, and by 28 July the composer had been re-engaged.[26] To complete the cast, Brooke took the sensible decision to build upon the vogue for dancing started by Heinel. For the new season she recruited 'stars' from Paris – Nina and Mimi Favière – described unkindly by Walpole as 'a fat old woman and her lean daughter'.[27]

Nothing was more certain at the King's Theatre in the 1770s than the fact that a season's success or failure would depend on the reception accorded to the leading singers. It was thus imperative to be in the market for the top stars as early as possible. Negotiations with Manzuoli, the big sensation of the 1764–5 season, took place well before May 1764.[28] Throughout her years at the King's Theatre, Brooke made a practice of approaching her principal singers very early. In the opera accounts at Hoare & Co. there are payments to Gordon on 19 November and 31 December 1773, suggesting that he was already at work signing up the following season's star singers.[29] Her choice as *primo uomo* for the season after next was Rauzzini, almost certainly a suggestion of Burney's. At his first meeting with the singer in Munich in August 1772, he had been impressed by him as an all-round musician:

> The first singer in the serious opera here is Signor Rauzzini, a young Roman performer, of singular merit, who has been six years in the service of this court; but is engaged to sing in an opera composed by

young Mozart, at the next Carnival at Milan; he is not only a charming singer, a pleasing figure, and a good actor; but a more excellent contrapuntist, and performer on the harpsichord, than a singer is usually allowed to be, as all kind of application to the harpsichord, or composition, is supposed, by the Italians, to be prejudicial to the voice. Signor Rauzzini has set two or three comic operas here which have been very much approved; and shewed and sung to me several airs of a serious cast, that were well written, and in an exquisite taste.[30]

Burney no doubt ascertained whether the singer would be willing to come to London if asked. The sequence of events was then as follows: Burney was back in London by November 1772; in January 1773 Brooke took over at the King's Theatre; in April 1773 the account of the German tour was published; and by the end of 1773, Rauzzini's recruitment had been accomplished. In her journal for February 1774, Fanny Burney recorded a conversation between herself, Brooke and Dr Shebbeare in which Burney's influence in the recruitment of Rauzzini is openly acknowledged:

> DR SHEBBEARE: Who are you to have for a singer next year?
> MRS BROOKE: Rauzini, a most excellent performer.
> DR SHEBBEARE: Ay, it's in your Interest to say so.
> MRS BROOKE: Well, I sha'n't Talk to *you*, but I know Dr Burney's opinion of him.[31]

As usual, the engagement of a new *primo uomo* was soon common knowledge.[32] The following year Fanny Burney noted that she had been in correspondence with Brooke but that the opera manager 'had only wrote [in reply] queries concerning my Father's absence, return, & so forth'.[33]

It is reasonable to suppose that Burney exerted a considerable influence on the recruitment policy adopted by Brooke and thus on the future direction of the King's Theatre. It would in fact hardly be an exaggeration to describe him as an 'artistic adviser'. The relationship explains how, despite her lack of experience, Brooke was able to develop a clear recruitment strategy. Its early focus was primarily on singers, and it is clear that the breadth of her adviser's personal experience of performers in most of the leading opera houses of Europe enabled informed judgements to be made. With Sacchini still in London, there was no immediate need to look for another major composer, but in due course Burney was able to provide advice about this as well. His reward was what he craved: access to singers and composers and invitations to rehearsals.[34] In fact the family seems to have enjoyed complete and uninhibited access. Fanny Burney, recalling the sensational debut of Gabrielli, wrote that her family, who were to enter at a private door 'per favour of Mrs Brookes', rushed in so quickly that they missed the handbills announcing the cancellation.[35]

All in all, it seemed as though most of the ingredients of a successful opera programme were being put in place, but Brooke was about to experience a dramatic reversal in her fortunes.

Probably no quality was more necessary for an opera impresario than the ability to cope with a crisis. Between 1774 and 1776, Brooke had to contend with a whole series of interlocking problems involving the irreconcilable demands of her leading singers, litigation over a broken contract and competition from a rival promoter of Italian opera stars. These were just the kinds of difficulties that had engulfed Hobart in 1771. The forceful and clear-sighted manner with which she surmounted the problems amounts to an impressive example of crisis management.

The new season began with Sacchini's *Lucio vero*, and on 29 January *Perseo* received its première. Both were successful, receiving sixteen and seventeen performances respectively. A reviewer in the *Public Advertiser* thought the music of *Perseo* up to Sacchini's usual standard, having 'all the fire, all the elegance, all the pathos of that celebrated composer'.[1] The choruses were still attracting favourable comment, being deemed 'pleasing' and one in particular 'beautifully pathetic'. High-profile theatrical spectacle, prominent in Sacchini's first London operas, is still much in evidence. A lavish production meant lavish expenditure, and whatever his own inclinations, the composer could not have taken this course without the support of the opera management. Reviewers had remarked on the studied magnificence of the costumes and the elegance of the scenery in *Il Cid*,[2] and Burney later praised the 'knowledge of stage effects' shown in this opera and in *Tamerlano*.[3] Brooke obviously approved of this new emphasis, and Sacchini was thus permitted to continue to exploit the major set-piece spectacles of conventional *opera seria* plots. *Perseo* begins with a storm scene, Andromeda having been condemned to be devoured by a sea monster. The libretto ('compiled and curtailed' from Gamerra by Bottarelli) sets the scene in a temple. A 'gay symphony' is interrupted by a thunderclap and flashes of lightning. A loud symphony is accompanied by the screams of the chorus, who sing 'Qual fiero caso'. While bearing no comparison with Mozart's sustained storm depiction in *Idomeneo*, Sacchini's is at least briefly dramatic, with exaggerated dynamics, a rapid move to the subdominant minor and (two) rushing string scales (see example 3). This was the kind of writing which led London critics to balance praise of Sacchini's lyrical simplicity with his 'fire'. Fanny Burney reported her father as praising one chorus in *Tamerlano* thus: 'notwithstanding his mildness and sweetness, he breaks out, now and then, with all the Neapolitan fire: he is a *Vesuvius* at times!'[4]

An impresario might provide splendid costumes and sets and a composer vivid music for a spectacular storm scene, but in performance the effect could be ruined by a feeble acting performance on the part of the chorus. There is much evidence to suggest that the singers employed by the King's Theatre were woefully inadequate actors. Burney thought they cut 'aukward figures' on stage, and Le Texier was regularly scandalised by the behaviour of the boys. The Italian opera establishment in London seemed to wish to ignore the relatively high standards of acting on view in Paris, but English opera lovers travelling to France were less coy about making comparisons. In the scale and magnificence of the spectacle it provided, the Paris opera house easily outshone the King's Theatre. Robert Clive was struck by the sheer brilliance of the sight:

Versailles 5 December 1773 Robert Clive to Margaret Clive

We have been to the Opera, the Italian Commedy and the Boulevards . . . You remember seeing the Opera House when we were last at Paris, only imagine what must be the effect when that House was well lighted up and filld by the Royal Family and all the great Personages of France. Indeed in magnificence and Grandeur it exceeds all Description and I am persuaded I shall never see such a sight again. The Stage was filled with at least 300 Personages all as fine as Gold, Silver Brocade and Tissue could make them. There were at least 60 Dancers not one bad one among them. The best was Mad^elle Heinil and Guimar. You may remember the last who danced with such Grace and Elegance at Paris. There were at least 100 who sang in Chorus, the rest were actors, actresses and Military. The Scenery was Grand beyond all conception.[5]

Ex. 3 Sacchini, *Perseo* (London, 1774): excerpt from the chorus 'Qual fiero caso'

Ex. 3 (cont.)

Ex. 3 (*cont.*)

Ex. 3 (cont.)

Yet it was not merely the visual spectacle that so astonished English travellers. Francis Fowke, writing from Paris in 1788, was impressed by the dramatic power of a well-directed chorus:

Paris 4 May 1788   Francis Fowke to Margaret Benn

In point of music I see no advantage the French have over us but fine choruses, the fullness of which I think very fine, and they act them with great spirit, sometimes walking and running in confusion about the stage, where the subject requires it, and continuing to sing the whole time. I was very much struck with this in the opera of Armida. Before Armida quits the Pagan camp an old Pagan hero is brought in desperately wounded (I forget his name); the whole assembly breaks out into the most passionate expression of revenge and run about in the agitated manner I have described.[6]

Fowke was probably referring to the end of Act I in Gluck's *Armida*, where news of the escape of the Christian prisoners is brought to the camp. It is quite clear that the London chorus was no match for this.

The partnership between Millico and Davies in Sacchini's two operas *Lucio vero* and *Perseo* provided a good start to the season, but early in 1774 Brooke began to experience difficulties with her *prima donna*. Well merited though the recruitment of Davies had been, the entry of an English singer into the closed world of the London Italian opera establishment always had the potential to cause problems. Walpole noticed growing evidence of a rift with Millico.[7] One opera-goer even hinted that a row had erupted during a public performance, 'a kind of riot at the opera'.[8] Fanny Burney expressed amazement that Davies should be 'engaged in perpetual Quarrels at the Opera', and she could only assume that the singer was being ill advised by her sister.[9] The probable source of her anger is hinted at in the Hoare & Co. opera accounts, which suggest that she was paid less than her partner. Yet Millico also had cause for dissatisfaction. It seems that he was learning the harsh lesson that no matter how enthusiastic the early reception, London audiences tended to tire quickly of singers. Considered judgements of the 1773–4 season stress the dominance of Davies. Even Walpole had to concede that 'Miss

Davies, the Inglesina, is more admired than anything I remember of late years in operas.'[10] Her success was reported to Sir William Hamilton in Italy.[11] The real scale of her triumph, however, is most apparent from an extended appraisal of the current state of Italian opera at the King's Theatre in the *Hibernian Magazine*. This begins like a puff, noting that Richard Yates, the comedian, has spared no pains or assiduity to render the operas 'as agreeable as possible', by engaging the best performers and by dressing all the characters 'to the greatest advantage'. The orchestra consists of 'upwards of thirty instrumental performers, some of the most capital hands that can be found'. Millico has great judgement and execution, 'though there is something whining in his manner that takes off great part of his merit'. Davies, however, has been the real star: 'When I speak of this lady, I must tell you I have been particularly charmed with an Englishwoman, who surpasses in compass of voice and judgement all the Italians, at least in England, even in their own opera. The plaudits she receives are scarce to be paralleled, and the *encores* constantly echo through the house after every air she sings.'[12] Burney had only minor reservations. Her voice was 'clear and perfectly in tune', her shake (trill) 'excellent, open, distinct' and she had great agility. Only in the cantabile style was it felt that her performance wanted 'that colouring, passion, and variety of expression, which render *adagios* truly touching'.[13]

With such a public following, Davies must now have felt in a strong position to negotiate for the following season, but Brooke faced an insoluble dilemma; Rauzzini, her chosen *primo uomo* for the new season, was insisting on his pupil Schindlerin as his leading woman. Specifically in relation to the hiring of the leading stars that year, Burney commented on how 'injudicious' it was for managers to defer to a principal singer about who his or her partner should be. In his view it was not unusual for a 'first' singer to suggest or even insist on a pupil or other lesser candidate in order not to be outshone. Schindlerin, he reported, had been engaged at Rauzzini's recommendation, and the singer had subsequently made several 'ingenious manoeuvres' to have her for his partner a second season.[14] Having pacified Rauzzini by hiring Schindlerin, Brooke apparently found herself having to pull out of an agreement already made with Davies, whose response was to file a suit for breach of contract. The defence offered by the King's Theatre lawyers was that the singer herself had broken her contract, specifically the clause preventing her from performing elsewhere without prior consent. After her successful debut at the opera house, Davies, like most opera stars, accepted engagements at private soirées.[15] By the early months of 1775, however, when her action was under consideration, she was taking exceptional precautions not to be caught out on this legal point. Fanny Burney tried in vain to persuade her to sing at a soirée:

> *Cecilia* was as engaging as ever, but would not be prevailed upon to sing, to the great disappointment of Mr Twining; but she said that she *dared* not, for that her Law suit was not yet decided, & her articles with the Opera managers tied her down to never singing to any Company: she invited our Family, however, to visit *her*, & said that *at Home* she supposed she might be allowed to *practice*, & therefore if it would be any Amusement to us, she would be happy to do whatever was in her power.

She went on to express sympathy with the young singer:

> The Law suit is a very singular one. If the managers lose it, they will [have] the Costs to pay, & a whole season's salary to Miss Davies, though she has never sung a Note for them, & though the singer who has succeeded her, & who must also be paid, has never been a favourite with the Public, which is always a most cruel circumstance to the managers. And if Miss Davies fails, she will have lost a whole year's singing & have the Damages to pay. Where the *Right* lays I know not, but it is impossible to be in Company with Miss Davies & not wish her success.[16]

In a letter to Samuel Crisp, Fanny Burney reported a few more details of her conversation with Davies. The reason for the law suit being not yet decided, according to the singer herself, was that 'the managers did every thing in their power to delay & procrastinate'. She also claimed of being 'very ill used & much abused in the news papers'.[17]

The action was decided on 30 May in a sitting which lasted from 10 in the morning to 6 o'clock at night. The case attracted intense interest among those concerned with Italian opera in London:

2 June 1775   Mrs Harris to her son

You see by the papers that Miss Davis has been triumphant over Yates, and got 1,500 *l.*, with costs. I should have been sorry if Miss Davis had lost it, and now I cannot help being sorry for Yates. He is a civil, good-humoured man. All the Italians and fine opera men attended the trial. Sacchini was summoned, but he could not tell for which party, so stayed in Westminster Hall from nine in the morning till six in the evening, was never called in, nor did he understand anything that was going on.[18]

Sacchini, it seems, adopted an air of neutrality, probably wishing to offend neither the managers nor the singer. The newspapers reported the case, but with conspicuous lack of agreement about the details. It is worth citing three reports, simply as a demonstration of the general level of inaccuracy that is to be expected:

London Post   31 May 1775

The same day [30 May] came on in the Court of Common Pleas, before Lord Chief Justice de Grey, and a special jury, a cause wherein Miss Caecelia Davies was plaintiff, and Mr. Yates, as manager of the Opera-house, defendant. The action was brought by the plaintiff for the recovery of the first of four instalments, due to her upon an engagement for her singing this season at the Opera-house, but which was prevented by a misunderstanding between the parties, respecting a clear benefit to the former, though she repeatedly tendered her services during the season. The trial lasted from ten in the morning till six in the evening, when the jury, as soon as the evidence was summed up, gave a verdict for the plaintiff, with 375 *l.* and costs.

Morning Chronicle   31 May 1775

Yesterday a cause was tried in the court of Common Pleas, in which Miss Davies, formerly a singer at the Opera House, was plaintiff, and Richard Yates, Esq: Manager of that House defendant. The trial lasted from ten in the morning, till six in the evening, when the Jury found a verdict for the plaintiff for 1500 *l.* and costs. The action was brought to recover 1000 *l.* (the terms of her engagement for a season) and 500 *l.* for her benefit, at which she valued it. Mr Yates and his wife were in court during the trial.

Morning Gazette   31 May 1775

On Monday last came on in the Court of King's Bench, before Lord
Chief Justice Mansfield, a cause wherein Miss Davis, late singer at the
Opera-house, was plaintiff, and Mr Yates, manager of the same defendant. The action was laid for non-performance of an agreement
whereby Miss Davis was engaged, the season before last, to sing at the
Opera-house, at a stipulated salary, the payment of which was con-
tested. The Jury without going out of Court gave a verdict for the
plaintiff, and 1500 *l.* damages.

Manifestly inaccurate though the standard of reporting is, the basis
of the action seems clear enough. The *London Post* was surely correct
to state that the case concerned the contract for the current season.
The £1,000 basic salary reported by the *Morning Chronicle* seems in
line with what was being paid to 'first' singers of top quality. The
information that the dispute also embraced a 'misunderstanding'
over a benefit (valued by the singer at £500) seems plausible. The use
of the term 'clear benefit' in the *London Post* report suggests that she
was anticipating a performance for which the managers would bear
the costs. For her part, Brooke probably wanted a 'benefit' of the
kind in which there was a reversion of all the benefit income in return
for a good basic salary. Although the potential for a genuine misunderstanding is obvious, the manager perhaps provoked the
dispute, specifically in order to let Schindlerin in as a partner for
Rauzzini. The procrastination of the King's Theatre management
prior to the judgement certainly suggests that defeat was expected. In
the event, the court found decisively in favour of the singer. As usual
with legal actions of this kind, both parties emerged damaged. The
payment of £1,500 with costs would certainly have reduced drasti-
cally any profit that might have been made on the season as a whole.
Fanny Burney reported that the management was going to lose 'near
£2,000'.[19] For her part, Davies had been prevented from exploiting
her notably successful first year at the opera house in London, having
been obliged to withdraw from all public performance.

The opera accounts at Hoare & Co. record three payments to

Davies: the first on 27 June 1775 for £333. 6s. 8d., which suggests that the intention was to pay the £1,000 salary at the three regular payment times. But the remaining two come close together: on 23 January for £450 (probably the recompense for the lost benefit) and on 5 February for £333. 6s. 8d., the second instalment of her salary.[20] What seems to be missing from the Hoare accounts is the third instalment of the salary. It is not impossible that the singer reached an out-of-court agreement at this point – for example, by winning a commitment to rehire her in return for the waiving of the final payment. A curious comment by Walpole perhaps relates to this settlement: 'Miss Davies has carried her cause against Mrs Yates, and is to sing again at the opera.'[21] According to the editors of the Yale edition of his correspondence, the letter is dated 31 January 1775, but this is puzzling. The court action did not take place until 30 May that year. If, however, the letter has been misdated and was actually written on 31 January 1776, the comment could be seen as confirmation that some such final settlement was reached early in the new year. Davies did in fact return to the King's Theatre the next season.

In the summer of 1774, Brooke was confronted with a new problem that had the potential to inflict much more lasting damage than the one-off dispute with Davies. The Pantheon, a recently built and very fashionable concert venue, announced plans to feature Agujari, a major star of Italian opera.[22] Although opera could not be *staged* in the Pantheon, Brooke recognised that popular concert performances of Italian opera airs by a singer of this calibre might well have an adverse impact on attendance levels at the King's Theatre, and her actions over the next two seasons were determined by the need to respond effectively to this new competitor. There is one piece of evidence to suggest that the King's Theatre management tried to outbid the Pantheon by negotiating directly with Agujari. On 27 November 1774, Walpole, usually well informed on such matters, reported: 'I am just going to Lady Bingham's to hear the Bastardella [Agujari], whom, though the first singer in Italy, Mrs Yates *could not* or *would not* [my italics] agree with; and she is to have twelve hundred pounds for singing twelve times at the Pantheon.'[23] It is likely that Brooke was unable to hire Agujari because of her prior agreement with Rauzzini to take Schindlerin. The £1,200 offered to Agujari by the Pantheon was not an unusually high fee for a woman opera singer of her status; what was so shocking about it was what it represented as value for money – £50 per song. When entertaining the singer, Fanny Burney was only too well aware of her fee, observing wryly: 'We were all of us excessively eager to hear her sing, but as it was not convenient to offer her her Pantheon-price of 50 Guineas a song, we were rather fearful of asking that favour.'[24]

The emergence of the Pantheon as a promoter of major Italian opera stars can be seen as part of a broader trend in London concert life. There was an increasing polarisation between two sharply divergent ways of presenting large-scale musical events. On the one hand, there were occasions like the Handel Commemorations where the musical performance itself, undiluted by extraneous attractions, was the focus of attention. Any socialising would be done on the periphery of the event, during intervals or afterwards. The more informal alternative was to present music as part of a social package, in which the performance occupied a less central position. On such occasions, music might have to compete with numerous other activities, such as walking, taking tea, playing cards, dancing and conversation. The pleasure gardens and private concert series thrived on this kind of informality. The Pantheon rose to prominence in the 1770s as a leading provider of this style of informal musical entertainment. Its strategy was to exploit the pulling power of major Italian opera stars, who could sing the most popular songs from any Italian opera in vogue, and to compensate for the lack of opera itself by the quality and variety of its other activities. Where the King's Theatre was cramped and uncomfortable, the Pantheon was a fashionable building of acknowledged splendour and elegance, and it certainly offered far superior facilities for all the above-mentioned ancillary activities. It is easy to see why this was such an alarming prospect for the King's Theatre, especially given that the audience for Italian opera was a limited one. It must have seemed to Brooke that the forthcoming confrontation was about to test the extent to which staged drama itself was the essential attraction for the aristocratic audience, upon which the opera house depended year after year for its survival. The finances of the King's Theatre were still very precarious, and if a significant number of opera patrons were to be seduced away to the new auditorium, even for a relatively small number of performances, the prospects for the King's Theatre would indeed have been poor.

A fine impression of the Pantheon around this period is given by Edward Piggott in his account of a visit there:

Monday 29 April 1776

Monday the 29th of April went with Miss Fairfax, Markham, my Father and Mother to the Pantheon, it being a Concert Night [they] pay but half a Guinea each; found this place very fine and Elegant, the Dome very handsome, but too large for music; number of Elegant pillars the composition of which resembles so much to marble that I took them for such; very well lighted, number of fine lusters which have a very pretty effect, on the Masquerade nights it is much better lighted, and charmingly decorated; four chimneys which heats the room very much; I found the structure of the room very fine tho too much like a church & rather naked where the musicians are; upstairs is a Gallery which conducts all round from whence the sight of the company and music seen down is very prety there is several small rooms joining this Gallery, some for tea, others for dancing & all elegant; below the Great room there is another large one, where at about eleven every body runs down to get seats for to drink tea & coffee bread and butter, this room has some what the appearance of a cellar, when every body has finished their tea, was done in a sociable and gay manner, they returned to the fine room, where country dances is play'd and any body may dance this night there was only one cotillon and two minuets danced; there was but few people this night in all about 500, the room seemed very Empty; masks were let in but there was but five or six; the musicians were Mr Saville, Mrs Barthelemon, Mr Florio, Sig^r Massimino & Sig^{ra} Schindlerin, this last has a very preety voice but not strong; La Motte & others play'd solo's and exceedingly well as generally those capital performers does, every body are seated on benchs oposit the music which is hardely heared, the concert was over at 10 or 11; we stay'd walking till about one, at which hour every body began to retire; in short I found this place charming tho not so well as I expected; if you take but *one ticket* it cost you a Guinea, but take two or more they cost but half each; on the Masquerade night three Guineas per person; a *very good regulation for the coaches.*[25]

The Pantheon was undoubtedly a very impressive structure, and it proved fashionable, and yet, as comes across clearly in this account, it ultimately failed to satisfy as a musical auditorium, being perceived as too large and impersonal for satisfactory concert performance.

As problems mounted up for the King's Theatre in the summer of 1774, another challenge to its position was gaining momentum. Brooke's first attempt to win a theatrical licence for the King's Theatre had been unsuccessful, but far from abandoning the idea, she had opened the 1773–4 season with a very public declaration of intent, in front of the audience at the opening night of the new season. Burney witnessed this speech: 'In November 1773, Mrs Yates, who was now joint manager with Mrs Brooke, spoke a *poetical exordium* at the opening of the King's Theatre; by which it appeared that she intended mixing plays with operas, and entertaining the public with singing and declamation, alternately.'[26] The vigour with which Brooke was now waging her campaign for a theatrical license spurred Garrick into action. It seems to have occurred to him that if his opponent's position at the opera house could be weakened, then Drury Lane and Covent Garden would stand a better chance of retaining their valuable monopoly. In general, the London theatres attracted audiences from a much wider social spectrum than the opera house, and, despite some overlap, the casts of performers for English opera productions were usually distinct. In one area, however, that of dance, the theatres and the opera house could come into direct competition. It seems a little too much of a coincidence that some time in the summer or autumn of 1773, Garrick opened negotiations with the leading ballet master of the day, Jean-Georges Noverre, with a view to bringing him over to London for a season at Drury Lane. The initial failure of these negotiations was reported to Richard Cox early in the new year:

1 February 1774   David Garrick to Richard Cox

You must take what I have to say to you about Noverre, in plain, dull prose. That most fantastick toe, & great Genius & I have been in treaty for some time – I left the business to be settled by his Brother, & I imagin'd that he, & his dancing crew, would have *caper'd* Tragedy at Drury Lane, as we are not at present in the highest repute to *Act* it. If he has preferr'd Milan to London, we must be contented, the distance between us & the Brother's inexperience of Treaty-making may have Occasion'd some blunder.[27]

Garrick's troubled dealings with the ballet master earlier in his career are very well known. Noverre's first season in London in 1755 had been terminated abruptly by anti-French riots, and his second season was marred by sharp disputes over contracts, which resulted in the exchange of some heated correspondence.[28] In the intervening years, however, tempers had cooled, and when Garrick approached Noverre in the mid 1770s, it was in the friendliest of terms. No documentation survives from the continuing discussions in 1774, but in a letter to Sir William Parsons, written on 5 June 1775, he alludes to an approach the previous year. Parsons, acting on behalf of Drury Lane, was first asked to contact the dancer Paccini, and then details of a message he was to pass on to Noverre are given:

I must likewise desire you if you go to Milan, where I hear the Famous Noverre is, will you tell him that I have the greatest regard for him as a Man, & ye highest Esteem as a Man of Genius that I should be glad to make an Engagement with him directly & that I fear as I had agreed last year to all his conditions that some art had been us'd to prevent our coming together – that if he is disengag'd Either for ye next Winter, or Winter after – I will article with him for as long a time as he pleases as for 2 or 3 winters, as he shall determine – that if he pleases to write me a letter & open his mind to me, I will answer it in bad French but very clearly, with my own hand, & will not let even *his Brother* know of our Correspondence – I fear that I have trusted too much to other People, & have been deceiv'd.[29]

Garrick's wish for a full reconciliation is obvious, as is his anxiety to agree a contract. An undated letter from Charles Greville, who was entrusted with the negotiations after Sheridan took over in 1776, shows that a huge fee was under discussion: 'I called on you that I might give you the earliest intelligence about Noverre. It happens that he will come for one Year Certain, and according to the demand he makes the establishment will amount to full £3,000.'[30] News of the proposed recruitment of Noverre was made public in the *London Packet* of 17–19 July 1776, in which readers were informed that 'a chevalier dancer' had been procured 'at an enormous salary'. In the event, Noverre chose to go to Paris instead.

The context of this relatively little-known episode of Garrick's last active years as a manager is clearly the dispute with Brooke. Both legally and morally he was at liberty to hire any dancer he wished, and there were doubtless many positive reasons (including his desire to compete effectively with Covent Garden) for his attempts to secure Noverre's services. Even so, the idea that at this critical juncture in London theatre politics he might have sought to hire the celebrated ballet master specifically in order to inflict some damage on the King's Theatre, in response to Brooke's campaign for a theatrical licence, seems probable.

Successive managers at the King's Theatre were well aware of the critical importance of ballet in maintaining audience attendance at an economically viable level. In view of the secrecy of Garrick's message to Noverre, however, it seems likely that Brooke was as yet unaware of the threat from this quarter. Her most immediate concern was thus the Pantheon, and it was to bolster the position of the opera house in the forthcoming struggle with this competitor that she took every available measure. No episode in her managerial career at the King's Theatre so clearly demonstrates her qualities of persistence and determination.

Faced with the prospect of having to compete with Agujari at the Pantheon, and knowing that her own *seria* stars were not of the first rank, Brooke decided as a matter of urgency to revitalise the programme of comic opera. *Opera buffa* had been more or less defunct at the King's Theatre for two years as a result of failures in the recruitment programme. If, as she perhaps already suspected might be the outcome, her untried castrato and his undistinguished partner were to fail to measure up to the Pantheon star, the fortunes of the King's Theatre might end up largely dependant on a successful season of *opera buffa*.

The extent to which comic opera had been dominant during the six seasons at the King's Theatre prior to Brooke's management can be demonstrated by figures compiled by Petty.[1] This was the era of Lovattini, and during the period of his ascendancy *opera seria* accounted for only one quarter of all performances. But for the brief revival in the 1769–70 season featuring Guadagni, the disparity would have been even greater. (See table 1.)

Shortly after Lovattini's debut, Walpole observed the negative effect that Piccinni's hit was having on serious opera:

8 December 1766   Horace Walpole to Horace Mann

Our burlettas will make the fortunes of the managers. The *Buona figliuola* which has more charming music than ever I heard in a single piece, is crouded every time; the King and Queen scarce ever miss it. Lovattini is incomparable both for voice and action. But the serious opera, which is alternate, suffers for it. Guarducci's voice is universally admired, but he is lifeless, and the rest of the company not to be borne.[2]

The diary of Lady Mary Coke in early 1767 gives a good impression of the impact of the piece. She was a regular attender at the King's Theatre, and on several occasions (20 and 27 January, 10 February, 24

Table 1 *Opera buffa and opera seria performances in London 1766–72*

	Opera buffa	Opera seria
1766–7	57	16
1767–8	52	16
1768–9	72	0
1769–70	27	38
1770–1	47	16
1771–2	46	15

and 31 March) she commented on how full the house was. At the height of this exceptional success, Lovattini had his benefit, a performance on 12 March of *Il signor dottore* of which Lady Mary reported: 'Twas the fullest House I ever saw.'[3] The sequel *La buona figliuola maritata*, with which it was hoped to build on the triumph, failed to please, yet Lovattini emerged from his triumph early in 1767 as the one comic performer who could rival the most fêted *opera seria* stars in the affections of the London public. No one has left a better impression of Lovattini's qualities than Thomas Twining, who noted among the singer's most remarkable excellencies: 'the most perfect intonation I think I ever heard'; 'the most accurate, distinct, articulate execution'; 'no cursed *bravura*, no tricks, nothing disagreeable (unless on purpose as a buffoon)'; 'all his graces in admirable taste, and in *time*, never breaking in upon the measure, or making the ear wait for them'; 'a fine, sturdy, sostenuto tone of voice, beyond expression tender and delicate in the piano, or mezzo-forte, & when flung out of most amazing power & strength'.[4]

Lovattini was not only a powerful performer with personal magnetism, he was also regarded with affection, and his stage mannerisms became the subject of friendly caricature. Lady Mary Coke witnessed one such impromptu performance on 3 April 1767: 'A natural daughter of Lord Pigot's, a Girl of nine or ten years of Age, sung several songs out of the Comic Operas, & imitated so exactly the action & manner of two of the principal performers, that it was

impossible to mistake who She intended taking off.'[5] Two years after
the singer's final departure from England, Fanny Burney described
Richard Burney's take-off of his manner of performance.[6] In his considered judgement, Charles Burney admitted Lovattini's admirable
qualities, but attributed his success partly to Piccinni: 'the Music of
this drama was so admirable, from its originality, fire, and instrumental effects, that a worse singer than Lovattini, would have been sure of
a favourable reception'.[7] The singer had to cope with the failure of *La
buona figliuola maritata*, but Burney goes on to record many more successes, admirable performances in Piccinni's *La schiava* and other
comic operas by Galuppi and Guglielmi.

The departure of Lovattini in the summer of 1772 and the failure to
recruit a comic singer of sufficient stature to replace him left *opera
seria* in a dominant position. Of the sixty-two performances in the
1772–3 season, only three (all benefits) were comic operas. Such an
imbalance was obviously unwise, and Brooke's first action as
manager was to attempt to restore a better balance. With the help of
Burney, she identified Carabaldi as a star worth recruiting, but his
failure to arrive meant that for a second year there were few comic
operas, nine out of a total of sixty-four.[8] In an over-gloomy assessment of the future of the opera house written in January before
Davies had made her full impact, Walpole singled out the failure of
comic opera.[9] As the summer recruiting period approached, the most
urgent task was thus the recruitment of a male singer to lead the
comic troupe. Perhaps suspecting that her first choice Carabaldi
would again be unfit or unwilling to travel, Brooke prepared an alternative: a relaunch of *La buona figliuola* with its well-liked star. In a
world in which novelty was a key consideration in the choice both of
singers and repertoire, Brooke's decision to feature an older opera
ran counter to received wisdom, yet it was a logical move. Owing to
its lasting popularity, Piccinni's opera was starting to acquire the
status of a classic, a repertoire work performed year after year. After
its initial success, it did not in fact fall out of the repertoire. It received
the following numbers of performances during Lovattini's first six
seasons at the King's Theatre: twenty-eight; twelve; nine; four; nine;
two. In each of the two years that he was away it was given once, on

both occasions as a benefit.[10] As a result of Brooke's decision to relaunch it, *La buona figliuola* remained in the King's Theatre repertoire until the mid 1780s, and it was still receiving sporadic performances into the 1790s. The decision to bring back Lovattini was also astute. London audiences tended to tire quickly of Italian opera stars, but when they did not (as later was the case with Pacchierotti) a loyal following was the result. Even after his return to Italy, Lovattini's performances were still being admired by English visitors.[11]

To expedite the all-important recruitment of her next *opera buffa* star, Brooke made good use of her connections in the artistic community. She sent urgent letters to James Butler, who was travelling to Italy with his son. Butler had left England in mid July, but because his ship was becalmed in the Mediterranean, he did not arrive at Salerno until early September. He was given his mail in which he discovered urgent letters from London asking for his assistance in recruiting a leading comic singer and giving him detailed instructions and letters of credit to enable the usual retainer to be paid. Almost immediately, though, there was a hitch. His ship was detained under the quarantine regulations in the Bay of Salerno. This was a common occurrence. When Michael Kelly arrived in the Bay of Naples in 1779, the officers of health came on board to give him the unwelcome information that 'as there was a report that the plague was raging on the African coast', they must 'perform quarantine' before being allowed to land.[12] Butler's period of quarantine was set at twenty-one days, a delay that could have posed a serious threat to his mission. He turned for assistance to his friend and fellow artist, then resident in Rome, Ozias Humphry:

James Butler to Ozias Humphry

On Board the Devonshire in the Bay of Salerno Tuesday the 6th of Sep[t] 1774

Dear Sir,

    After a long Passage of near Seven Weeks I am arrived with my son at Salerno in my way to Naples. Am obliged to stay some days for the usual quarantine which is always kept in the Ports of Italy, but having found here letters from England of some importance take the liberty to beg your assistance in a commission I am charged with at Rome. We arrived here last Saturday Morning.

The managers of the Opera have desired me to make Enquiry concerning the health of Carabaldi. Shou'd be obliged to you to inform me immediately whether he realy is in a state capable of taking the journey to England or Not. I dare say as you love Musick you know him and if you do, it will be of use to me, if you will take occasion to say we are acquainted, that I am coming to Rome, and shall be charmed to hear him sing; it will also be of great Service that I shall be spoke of as a fair dealing Man, as it will be a great step towards the success of my Commission to have him prejudiced in my favour, which I am sure you wou'd do tho' I did not ask it; but for Gods Sake dont drop a hint as yet that I have any commission to him.

I am also desired to bring with me a compleat Score of a Comic Opera Anfossi composed last year at Rome. They have not sent me the title of it, you had better apply for this to Mr Wiseman who knows how to get it, and also if it is properly copied; you will be so good not to mention to him my having any further Commission relating to the Opera; you cant conceive how necessary this caution is.

I reckon too much on your Friendship to make an Apology for giving you this trouble, on the contrary shall desire further of you to take care of any letters that come directed to me at the English Coffee house at Rome, having settled with my Friends that towards the End of this Month I shou'd be wrote to there. This Opera Business may perhaps bring me immediately and oblige me to return again to Naples.

[His wife would have come but she was ill.]

Tho' our passage has been long it has not been fatiguing, we have not had either wind, rain, or thunder & lightning the whole passage. Our greatest misfortune has been too fine weather, which has produced such continued calms since we pass'd Gibraltar that we were three and twenty [days] coming the last three hundred leagues. My son was very sick for a fortnight, but except about two days coming out of the Channel I myself have been perfectly well.

It is quite useless for me to say how glad I shall be to meet you in Rome, because I am persuaded you believe I should be glad to see you any where. Pray give my best Compliments to Mr Romney & M^r and Mrs Paine. I call'd at Mr Crow's before I left England to know if they had any commands for Rome but they were in the Country and not expected for some time.

Please to direct for me to the care of Mr Leigh Banker at Naples, and do me the favour to answer this as soon as possible. My Son joins in Comp^{ts} to you and our abovemention'd Friends.

I am, Dear Sir,
Y^r Sincere Friend and Humble Ser^t,
Ja^s Butler.[13]

Following directions from the managers in London, Butler first had the task of establishing whether Carabaldi was fit to travel, which suggests that illness had indeed been a factor in the previous year's cancellation, then of approaching the singer with a proposal. In the new situation caused by his quarantine, he now had to make contact with him through the good offices of Humphry, who was given the delicate task of trying to establish the emissary's reputation as a 'fair dealing' man, without giving any hint that a firm proposal was under active consideration. As there must have been negotiations of some kind with the singer the previous year, this was surely an unrealistic suggestion. Butler, however, knew only as much of the background as Brooke had revealed in her letters and was probably improvising as best he could. Another indication that the emissary's quarantine was causing the abandonment of the secrecy evidently insisted upon by Brooke in her first letter is the reference to Wiseman. In his first letter to Humphry, Butler, bound by an emphatic prohibition from the London management, insisted that knowledge of their recruitment intentions should be kept from this man, and that he should be asked only to find and check the Anfossi score they wished to purchase, yet the very next letter in the correspondence shows that Butler (on direct instructions from Brooke) had revealed his entire negotiating hand to Wiseman with a view to employing his services. As a long-term resident in Italy – he later claimed to have served the King's Theatre for forty years – Wiseman was beginning to lose his English. The following letter in his own hand and with his own spelling peculiarities is a copy for Humphry of the letter he received from Butler:

James Butler to Charles Wiseman [copy in Wiseman's hand for Ozias Humphry]

Sʳ Sepᵗ: 17ᵗʰ 1774

I arrived here the 3ᵈ. Inst. after a passage of more than six weeks but having had the ill fortune to meet an algerine Galley in the Mediteraneo, and our Captain being forced to go on board him to show his passport we became Subject to a quarantine of twenty one Days from our arrival. This wood have been mitigated but to compleat our ill luck, a worthless fellow of a Cabin Boy took it into his head to breake quarantine and run away; which has made such a Bustle that in all Probability we shall Lay our hole time.

It was some days before I recd my Letters from Naples. In on[e] from Mrs Brookes was Informed that she had wrote to you that I was employd in the affaire of the Manegers of the Opera; and by onother Letters I recivid yesterday, that you was Desire to let me know the state of Caribaldis Health. Circumstances as I am it is Impossible for me to do any thing, and no time most be lost, must therefore take Leave to acquaint you with my Instructions which I here by promise to stand to.

I ham Directed first, to angage Carabaldi on his own terms if he is able to undertake the journey and to perform. If not in the second place to engage L'Ovattini if I can get him on reasonable terms. And Lastly if that fails to git the best Comic Man I can. As to the first, it must Depend Intirely on the State of his Health, you are to judge of that, and if you sincerely thinke him Caple, pray engage him for me on his own terms which are eight hundred pounds sterling and a Benefit.

I am Desird to accompany him to England which I fear will be Impossible; My Errand here is to fix my Son, but this Confinement will not per[mit] me to finish that Business time enough. Caribaldi shoud be informed that there is a Man in England who has a powder which is a certain specifico for Bleeding both External and internal if that is his complaint, he may probably be cured.

As to L'Ovattini; by the Post that brought me Mrs Brookes' Letter, I recivd another from one Sigʳ Carmanini at Bolognia to let me know he has Commission from the Manegers to treat with me on Lovattini account. He had Demanded à thousand pounds and the Manegers to have the profit of his Benefit which Last article he was to promise to keepe Secret; But he now offers him self for nine hundred pounds, and the same conditions tò the Benefit, and expects two Hundred Zechins andwance [advance].

Sig^r Carmanini in case I have not pover to give Lovattini that price, mentions one Agostino Lipparini as à good succedaneum [a person who replaces another] he haskes five Hundred pounds and à Benefit, and one hundred & fifty Zechins advance.

Now Sir if Caribaldi his not well enough to go, tho it exceeds my Commission, Yet I will give L'Ovattini the nine hundred pound (reserving the profit of the Benefit as above said to the maneggers) for the ensuing Season, and will transmit the two hundred Zequin on reciving advice of his signing the Contract. By that time I shall be at Liberty, before which I cant make the remittance which must be done at Naples.

I returnid an imediately answer to Sig^{nr} Carmanini Informing him of my Situation, and assuring him that when I was at Liberty I woude either write again or go to Bolognia to treate with him. Coud give no other answer as I was to treate with Caribaldi first and have heard nothing from you about him. Whoever is engaged it is expected they shoud set out Immediately on reciving there remittance. Caribaldi had better go by easy Journeys. If you are obliged to go to Bologna to treat with L'Ovattini I shall take care when I come to Rome to Defray the expence. It is to no purpose to luse time in writing to me till the Contract is signd, which you will get properly Drawn. Thay have I belive each of them Contracts from England which shew the usual form, if not you most employe some able Man to Dra so [Draft] them, for I ham not capable, of Doing it. By rights a Copy of the proper Contract should have been sent to me from England – the oddress of Sig^{nr} Carmanini is in Casa Del Sig: Conte Senatore Zambeccari: Ministro di Spagna &. It is strange he is not mencion nor spoke of in Mrs Brooke's letters. One thing I had like forgot, which is that there is a Report that L'Ovattinis voice [is] Impair'd, so many Musical peaple in Rome must have Lately heard him that you will easily ascertain that fact. If it shoud be so, at Rome also you will have certain intelligence what Lupperin his, if you dont know him, and must use your Discretion as to engaging him there is nothing else to be done pressd as we are.

Before you receive this I shall have a letter from you I belive about Carabaldis health. If I find is not capable of going will immediately write to Sig^{nr} Carmanini that I accept Lovattini is offer and have given you full pover to to [*sic*] conclude with him, my confinement making it Impossible for me to be at Bolognia time enough.

I beg you will immediately write to England to the Manegers to Imform what you do. I sincerely pity the uncertain state they are in.

Mr Humphry has before this arrives, Desird you to get a Compleat Copy in Score of a Comic Opera of Anfossi which had greate success Last year at Rome, pray send it to England Directly and be so good to procure any Comic Musick that Either you or the singer you engage thinke will be usefull. Please to direct for me to the care of Mr Leigh Banker at Naples.

The Contract must I thinke be Drawn in the names of Mr Richard Yates and Mr James Brooke, and I most sign the counterpart or you for me as their Agent, but the Lowyer you employ will settle all this. Observe that the mony advanced must be in part payment of the Salary. I make nò apology for giving you so much trouble; we are serving our Friends and promoting the Science we profess.

I ham very truly,
Your most Humble Servt Ja^s Butler
[pasted slip] To Mr Humphry[14]

With permission to act for Butler and if necessary to sign a contract on the managers' behalf, Wiseman now had to consider the question of Carabaldi's health. An approach had already been made by Signor Carmanini, Lovattini's representative in Bologna, with a slightly reduced offer for his client's services. This man claimed to have been contacted directly by the managers in London, and he was thus able to pitch his demands accordingly. The choice in financial terms was now between £800 plus benefit for Carabaldi or £900 (with the proceeds of a benefit reverting to the managers) for Lovattini. This seems to have been Lovattini's normal fee for the King's Theatre. The secrecy clause concerning the sale of his benefit to the managers for a flat fee had very likely been adopted during one of his earlier seasons in England. Such an arrangement might have been deemed beneficial by both parties, allowing the singer to maintain his reputation as a high earner and the managers to reap the rewards of his popularity at the customary benefit. Carmanini was obviously aware that a cheaper singer might be required and so slipped in a suggestion, the name of Agostino Lipparini, for whose services £500 was requested.[15]

In due course Butler was released from quarantine and set about executing his commission. He travelled from Salerno to Naples to settle his son, who was to study music with Piccinni. His next destination was Rome, where he hoped to see Wiseman. Carabaldi had by now been ruled out on health grounds, and Butler therefore put in hand the financial arrangements for securing a contract with Lovattini by presenting his credit from the bankers Messrs Hart and Wilkins of Naples to Francesco Barazzi, the banker in Rome who was to provide the money. At this point, Butler's sudden death in Rome placed the deal in serious jeopardy. The money now held by Barazzi to enable Butler to pay Lovattini's advance would for the foreseeable future be unavailable. Time was very short indeed, and Humphry found himself attempting to sort out Butler's affairs. An immediate task was to convey news of his father's death to the young Butler in Naples. Humphry wrote to Sir William Hamilton on the subject and was careful to include a brief résumé of the state of the opera negotiations:

Ozias Humphry to Sir William Hamilton

[n.d., *c*. October 1774]

> I am very sorry to be under a necessity of acquainting you with the melancholy news that poor Mr Butler who lately left you in good health at Naples, arrived here exceedingly Ill.
>
> [details of the unsuccessful attempts to treat him]
>
> I don't know where to address a Letter to his son young Mr Butler. If I did I shou'd prefer this method of acquainting him with the melancholy truth. You may be assur'd that he had every kind of assistance but his constitution was too weak to resist any attack above a slow fever that he was subject to in England. I am sorry from my soul for the loss & young Mr Butler and his family. You will be so kind to let him know it in the most gentle and gradual manner and acquaint that if he wishes to know further particulars I will answer any Letter he may chuse to send & shall be happy if I can do him service or pleasure. I shall write to Mrs Butler by tomorrows post. I must not omit to add that the Business poor

Mr Butler was entrusted with for the proprietors of the opera will now entirely [be] put a stop to unless Messrs Hart & Wilkins will empower Mr Barazzi to fulfill the Contract with Lovatini or whatever singer is engag'd at Bologna by Mr Wiseman to go to England. It is of the [unclear] importance [?] to the proprietors & to the subscribers to the Opera. I have written to them by this post a long letter upon the subject but in the hurry of ordering Mr Butlers Burial I scarcely know what I write.[16]

Next he contacted the English bankers in the hope of persuading them to allow the deal to proceed. From this letter it becomes clear that he had already incurred some small expense in the matter:

Ozias Humphry to Hart & Wilkins [draft letter]

[n.d., *c*. October 1774]

But the chief reason of my troubling you with this letter is to acquaint you that during Mr Butlers confinement at Salerno he wrote to me ^{at some} ^{time} to desire that I w^d assist him in engaging Caribaldi wth all the Expedition I cou'd, to go to sing in the Comic Opera in London. If his health wou'd not permit him to take the Journey [*I was to order* deleted] Sig. Carlo Wiseman was ordered by another letter to send Lovatini at Bologna or the best Comic Singer that coud be got. Caribaldi is too Ill to think of going & accordingly I sent Wiseman to Bologna and expect to hear every hour that he has engaged Lovatini upon the terms agreed to by the proprietors of the Opera [*poor Mr Butler death* deleted] one of wch is that the Sig Lovatini is to receive a 150 or 200 Sequins advance. Mr Butler had produced his credit to Mr Barazzi, but unfortunately his illness & finally his Death prevented his making any use of it. I understand the proprietors of the Opera had given him credit upon you for 200 pds sterl for the purpose above mentioned etc. etc. Now if Mr Barazzi is not empower'd by you to execute the contract wth Lovatini & to pay the Money the Opera in England will be without a first comic singer. Of Course the proprietors will sustain an infinite loss & London be deprived of that part of its amusement for a year. I do not even know who are the proprietors & nothing can be more foreign than there concerns from mine. Of course I will not act any further in the affair. I have already advanced 40 Sequins out of respect to Mr Butler for the proprietors wch I hope you will empower Mr Barazzi to repay me, at the same time that he is commission'd to conclude wth Lovatini, or whatever singer is engag'd.

The object of this Letter once more is to signify that without you empowering Mr Barazzi to act & to pay the money wch he has in his hands the proprietors will suffer infinitely and the people of Quality in London be deprived of their comic opera for the winter. Because I have already paid not knowing even who are the proprietors I will not take any further step in the Business.

> I have the Honor to be,
> Gentlemen,
> Y^r most obn^t humble Sev^t.[17]

Notwithstanding his intention not to take matters any further, Humphry, apparently after learning the identity of the opera managers in London, did continue to act for them. He contacted John Udney, consul at Venice (1773–4), who had long been involved in assisting the financial transactions of the King's Theatre in Italy.[18] Udney immediately forwarded the necessary advance to Lovattini, while Humphry, not yet knowing whether the payment had been made, wrote to Brooke in London offering to lend the sum himself, but asking that the managers wait for a second letter, which would either confirm his offer of the loan or cancel it, if Udney had already advanced the money. A letter of thanks from Brooke makes clear the position:

11 November 1774   Frances Brooke to Ozias Humphry

A Mon^r Humphrey au Caffe Anglois a Rome (By way of France)

Sir,

I receiv'd both your obliging letters, & have to thank you for your great kindness in offering to advance the money for Lovattini: Mr & Mrs Yates & my brother join me in thanking you, & Mr and Mrs Yates take it particularly kind, as you advanc'd it after finding they were concern'd in the opera, my brother & I being strangers to you. Your draft came yesterday, & as Mr Udny had advanc'd the money for Lovattini, we follow'd your directions in desiring to wait another letter from you before we accepted the bill: to prevent any inconvenience to Mr Jenkins, we explained the affair to Mr Child's clerk, & show'd him that part of your letter where you desire us to wait till we hear whether you advance the money, & also Mr Udny's & Lovattini's, which show that he is already paid, & therefore that you did not advance the money; he was very well satisfied, but wou'd it not have been more regular if Mr Jenkins had delay'd drawing the bill till he knew whether Lovattini took the money. He will however, I make no doubt, take care to set it right in a post or two. The bill you draw on us for the money advanc'd to Mr Wiseman, we will pay, with thanks, I hope for an opportunity of showing our sense of your very genteel Behaviour.

Our poor friend's death will, I am afraid, cause some embarrasment to us in respect to our £200 left in Sig. Barazzi's hands: We cannot at present speak to poor Mrs Butler about it, but will as soon as it is proper: in the mean time, you will be so good, both for her sake & ours, to take care of the receipt given by Barazzi for the money; & either send it by a careful hand to young Butler, or keep it sending him an acknowledge-ment that you have it. If it was not too much trouble, you wou'd serve both Mrs Butler & us by receiving this money, when a proper power is sent for that purpose. Messrs Hoare have wrote to Sig. Barazzi to pay you, if not already paid, but I suppose you will have drawn first.

You will be so good to send the opera Sir William Hamilton was so good to give us by the first English gentleman who will be so obliging to take the care of it, but not by the post.

Allow me again to thank you in the name of Mr & Mrs Yates, & my brother, as well as myself, for your very friendly offer in respect to Lovattini, & to assure you of our gratitude

> I am, Sir,
> With great Regard
> Your most Obed[t] Servt Fr Brooke

Mr & Mrs Yates & my brother desire their compliments.[19]

Before she received Humphry's second letter, Brooke had confirmation from both Udney and Lovattini that the singer had been paid his advance. The draft arranged by Humphry through Jenkins, the leading English banker in Rome, was therefore unneces-sary, and Brooke took steps to have it cancelled. She reimbursed Humphry for the money he had already advanced to Wiseman for the purchase of the Anfossi score and for his expenses in helping to recruit Lovattini. Not so easy to resolve was the matter of the £200 being held by Barazzi. In London, Hoare & Co. paid the £200 'To Ja[s] Butler's bill to Hart & Co' on 26 November, but the money had already passed from Hart to Barazzi. Brooke clearly felt it improper to approach Mrs Butler so soon after her husband's death for the necessary document releasing the money. She thus asked Humphry to secure the receipt and then in due course to take care of the money. On 17 December, Humphry finally delivered to Barazzi the original letter of credit (dated 1 October) from the English bankers in Naples, without which he was refusing to release the money. The banker confirmed in a written note that he had received the money and given Butler a receipt.[20] Another document in the Humphry papers, dated 19 October shortly after Butler's death, confirms that Barazzi still held the money.[21]

Brooke's final request to Humphry concerned the opera score which Sir William Hamilton had obtained for the King's Theatre. She probably knew of this from James Harris, who had been in communication with Sir William on another opera-related matter. J. C. Bach had apparently been engaged to compose operas for the Naples opera house, but had been prevented by his royal duties in England from taking up the post. There was some anxiety that Bach should not be blamed for this. James Harris was requested to write to Sir William to explain the circumstances:

> Salisbury 15 September 1774   James Harris to Sir William Hamilton
>
> You will excuse the liberty I take in troubling you with this letter . . .
> Mr Bach (our able and well known composer) was engaged this Summer to compose two Operas for the Theatre at Naples and was to have gone thither for that purpose. But by her Majesty's Command (whose Servant he is) he has remained in England, and is still here, attending at Kew, as often as her Majesty pleases to command him. I am commanded to write to you on this occasion, with a desire, that, should any doubts arise with regard to Mr Bach's Conduct, and his disappointment of the Managers, you would be so good to offer this very just apology on his behalf.

I am directed to write this letter without delay, so can send you little news, had I any to send.[22]

In reply Sir William Hamilton confirmed that Bach was in the clear as far as the Naples opera management was concerned, and he went on to mention the opera that he had given to Butler:

Naples 11 October 1774   Sir William Hamilton to James Harris

Dear Sir,

In consequence of your obliging Letter of the 15th of Sept[r] which I received last Post I spoke to the Marquis Tanucci (for here the first Minister is likewise the principal Director of the Opera) relative to Bach's engagement in Her Majestys Service preventing his coming to Naples this Season. The Marquis Tanucci was perfectly satisfied that he cou'd not have acted otherwise; I shall acquaint the other Managers like-wise with the same and you may assure Bach from me that no blame will fall on him. He is in the right however to wish to have this matter cleared up, as he was expected at Naples with great impatience, having had great success in his former compositions for this Theatre.

Jomelli died here lately. Picini was engaged by Mad[me] du Barré but the death of Louis 15th prevented our losing him which I shou'd have greatly regretted as he certainly is the greatest Composer for the Bullettas [sic] that ever existed. He has not succeeded of late so well in the Serious way – I gave Butler the Score of an Opera of his called the *Furbi burlati* which I realy think as good if not better than his *buona figliola* . . .

> I am Dear Sir ever
> Y[r] most obedient & obliged humble Serv[t]
> W[m] Hamilton[23]

Sir William's role in the affair of J. C. Bach is an interesting example of the use of formal diplomatic channels to resolve a potentially awkward clash of interests over the hiring of a composer with an international reputation. Equally noteworthy is his more informal role as a provider of up-to-date assessments of operatic reputations. In due course, Brooke acted on Sir William's recommendation, commissioning an original opera from Piccinni.

The story of the rehiring of Lovattini illustrates well the problems faced by London opera impresarios. Unforeseen delays in communication could make it difficult to settle matters satisfactorily, even if a recruiter had been sent to Italy with specific instructions to hire an agreed cast of singers. But if the recruitments were being made by post, it would almost always be necessary to seek the assistance of English residents in Italy. Support would be provided upon request by diplomatic establishments. During the 1770s, the King's Theatre could call upon the services not only of Sir William Hamilton in Naples, but also of John Udney in Venice and Sir Horace Mann in Florence. But the documentation of Lovattini's recruitment shows that the English artistic community, as represented in this instance by James Butler and Ozias Humphry, was equally supportive. Self-interest, as much as a personal love of opera, probably motivated some artists to respond to requests for assistance, despite the potential inconvenience. Support for the King's Theatre was especially strong among the aristocracy. An English artist working in Italy might thus have had good reason to expect that his relationship with this wealthy clientele would be enhanced, if news got about that he had offered material assistance to the King's Theatre management in hiring opera stars for the forthcoming season.

The prosperity and high reputation of the English community in Rome would have been hard to predict when diplomatic relations between London and the Vatican were severed after the defeat of James II by William of Orange. For many decades, the Pope's support for the Jacobite cause made Rome an uncomfortable place for aristocratic English visitors. But the influence of the Jacobites began to wane, and by the mid century Rome had become one of the most important destinations on the Grand Tour.[1] Thomas Jones reported that Romans arranged their English visitors in three classes: 'Artisti', who came for 'Study and Improvement'; 'Mezzi Cavalieri', 'who lived genteely, independent of any profession'; and 'Cavalieri' or 'Milordi Inglesi', who moved in a 'Circle of Superior Splendour surrounded by a group of Satellites under the denomination of Travelling Tutors, Antiquarians, Dealers in Virtu, English Grooms, French Valets and Italian running footmen'.[2] 'To be a native of Great Britain', Kelly wrote of his experiences in Italy in the late 1770s, 'was a *passe*-partout' all over the country.'[3] With no formal representation as yet at the Vatican, the large English community relied on a leading banker, Thomas Jenkins, who functioned in effect as an unofficial ambassador. As James Northcote pointed out in 1778, Jenkins was 'of vast use to all the English, who fly to him as they would an Ambassador, for the King sends none to the Pope'.[4] At the height of his influence (which was very considerable indeed), Jenkins could readily gain admission to the Vatican for English artists who wished to study or make copies. Burney's entrance to the Vatican library in 1770 was arranged by this man with a minimum of formalities.[5] But purchasing works of art from Jenkins could be a risky business. Not to mince matters, he had a reputation as a con man and was reported to have sold Lord Clive a painting for £1,500 that would have been overpriced at £50.[6]

The Humphry correspondence is well known as a valuable source of evidence concerning the large community of English artists in Rome during the 1770s; the letters relating to the recruitment of Lovattini for the King's Theatre shed much light on the network of emissaries, agents, artists, bankers and ambassadors, upon whose services opera impresarios in London had to rely.

THE EMISSARY

For what was evidently a mission of considerable importance to the success of the forthcoming season, Brooke relied on an artist, travelling to Italy on musical business of his own. The exact identity of James Butler cannot be established with certainty, the name being a common one, but the evidence of his letters strongly suggests that he was indeed a painter, who moved in artistic circles. His acquaintances included Humphry, Romney and Paine. It is possible that he was the James Butler who had works exhibited at the Free Society of Artists in 1763.[7] His musical business in Naples was to settle his son Thomas as a pupil of Piccinni.[8] After his father's death, Thomas Hamly Butler remained in Naples under the protection of Sir William Hamilton, until in November 1776 Piccinni left for Paris.[9]

THE AGENT

The most interesting character to emerge from the shadows as a result of the Lovattini affair is Charles Wiseman, the long-standing agent of the King's Theatre. He had lived so long in Rome that he was rapidly losing his English and indeed was sometimes referred to as Signor Carlo Wiseman. In much the same way that antiquarians, art-dealers and bankers made a good living by providing services for wealthy English visitors, Wiseman acted as a musical broker. When Sir Watkin Williams Wynn visited Rome in 1768, he provided him with music and arranged concerts for him.[10] Burney lost no time in visiting Wiseman, shortly after his arrival in Rome:

> To the Villa Rafaele without the gates of Rome I had a long, hot, and dusty walk. It is now occupied by a Mr Wiseman, a worthy Music-Master and Copyist, a native of England, who has resided at Rome 19 years and is esteemed by all the English in Rome. He now speaks broken English like an Italian . . . During the first winter months, till the operas begin, Mr Wiseman has a weekly Concert here for our noblemen and gentlemen.[11]

These concerts are known to have included opera singers.[12] Burney quickly realised that Wiseman would make an excellent guide, and a few days after his arrival the two set off 'to seek old music'. Even more useful to the English historian, however, was Wiseman's memory, and on one occasion Burney records 'a long musical conversation' with him.[13] The results are to be found in *A General History of Music*. Wiseman proved a particularly useful source on Italian violinists of an earlier generation. His information on Corelli, gathered from people who had known the composer, establish that he (Wiseman) had been in Rome since *c*.1733, far longer than the nineteen years first mentioned by Burney:

> Corelli's *Solos*, as a classical book for forming the hand of a young practitioner on the violin, has ever been regarded as a most useful and valuable work, by the greatest masters of that instrument. I was told by Mr. Wiseman at Rome, that when he first arrived in that city, about twenty years after Corelli's decease, he was informed by several persons who had been acquainted with him, that his *opera quinta*, on which all good schools for the violin have since been founded, cost him three years to revise and correct.[14]

Wiseman was himself a violinist. A manuscript of his *Sei sonate a violino solo e basso, con dodici divertimenti*, Rome, 1738–1741 has a dedication to Lord Sandwich, who visited Italy in 1738.[15] He was also able to provide Burney with first-hand recollections of Tartini and his pupil Pasqualino Bini.[16] The only hint in Burney's writings of Wiseman's role as agent for the London opera comes in his report of Hobart's attempt to recruit Piccinni. As the emissary, Burney had details of the proposal, a contract and 'Mr Wyseman, his agent's letter', but what the purpose of this letter was is far from clear. The demarcation of responsibilities between a visiting emissary and a resident agent was evidently an area of some uncertainty.[17]

After Brooke took over in London, Wiseman's position seems to have become less secure. As we have seen, there was some initial hesitation in using his services in the 1774 recruitment of Lovattini, although the crisis caused by Butler's quarantine forced her hand. But the relationship seems subsequently to have broken down completely. Shortly before the end of his life, Wiseman wrote an extraordinary letter to Ozias Humphry, by now back in London, pleading with the artist to intercede with the opera managers on his behalf. It is written in broken English, with a strongly Italianate use of vowels, accents and the letter 'h'. The sense of betrayal is overwhelming. In the following transcription, punctuation and capital letters have been added, but the spelling has been left unaltered to give the document its full impact:

Rome 26 November 1777   Charles Wiseman to Ozias Humphry

Dear Sir,
You must Excuse me if I trouble you with this Letter as I cood not Implore batter Friend then you Dr Mr Humphry in the case I am at present with Mr Yats. You must know that they was very well contended of my Conduct, as I took all the care to sarve them in the best onest way as any Man cood dò, tó save there money to git the best subjects. For that I went to Bologna several times to inquire and to hear this peaples Merit; as I dont want nó body raccomended to me in this case I know annof as any other man and about Musick inparticolar. In short I never lost nò time tò do my Duty and Obey there Orders.

You must know D^r S^r that some body as wrote against me and this his one Sig^{nr} Vergani Broker of Exchange at Bologna which he Desired mè tò raccomand him to Mr Yats as I Did, but this Man advance him selfe tu much; at least not to make a Long Discourse he as procure to over set me with false rapports, and as Manegge some affairs aut of my Conduct with great Disadvantage for the Interest of Mr Yats, and this Depends that they are to good and belive peaple that they dont mind but there on interest.

By this reason they dont write to me any more they dont let me know what reason they have. I have sent them some musick by different way they dont give any answer to my letters. Besides I see that onest men dos very little other peaple with roguery as more luck. I that have procure to assist them with the least interest I find my honour in other peaple hands, which I can not persuade my selfe.

So you must be sò good for my honour to speake to Mr Yats and give my caracter to him, as they may know very well, besides it his not there intention but Destroyed as I can give thousond prove of haverything of what I may be impose.

You may say that I trouble you for my Vantigge. Nò D^r S^r first place for my honour as after 40 Years that I have the pleseur to assist the Royall Opera House, with greate merit never was use so as att present, besides I have over set all my affairs. Particolar I have lost my place in the Opera di alibert as I was obbligc that year to assiste the orders from Mr Yats, so I wanted to go abaut to all the play House and when one his engaged to one place as no rights of Liberty as you know.

I have fatigue for the year 1778 and 1779 and my hopes was to continue, whence they have nò reason to discharge mè after I have don sò much for them; indeede they are very Happy after my fatigue to Engage singers but not with the same Vantigge; nò they wont find any other man like me. And they will want me, as them peaple they belive there frinds time will let them know.

Anything that they can say against me to you, I can any scure prove of my very onest way, and if there was to save one shiling I tooke all the Care to dò that. The same I was use with his Royall Hynes but I was innocent only Immpos'd and false rapports, after that my honour was in more credit.

Excuse my Liberty, but you are sò good that will make me have some hopes, for my honour; dont forgit me Dr Mr Humphry to persuade Mr Yats or Miss Brooke, as they know my right conduct.

D^r S^r

Your most humble and Ob^t Servant,
Charles Wiseman[18]

If Wiseman's claim that he had assisted the London opera for forty years is to be believed, and it is consistent with the known date of his arrival in Rome, he could have had dealings with management teams as far back as the days of Handel. Of particular interest is his statement that he had occupied some kind of formal position at the Opera di Alibert in Rome but had been obliged to relinquish it because of the conflict of loyalties. The cause of his present anger was the emergence of a rival. He had probably gone to Bologna as a talent scout, only to find himself superseded by the broker Vergani.[19] The Hoare & Co. accounts show payments to Donat Vergani in the summer of 1776. Other transactions by a man of this name in Bologna can be seen in an exchange of letters between Padre Martini (13 January 1778) and Burney (22 June 1778). Vergani had undertaken to send two volumes of Martini's collection of contrapuntal models to the English historian which had not arrived.[20] Whatever his rival may or may not have said about him, one thing is quite clear: the Englishman was no longer receiving payment for work that he felt that he had already put in for the 1778 and 1779 seasons. A small payment of £40 to Wiseman on 17 July 1776 suggests reinbursement for music supplied, but the Hoare & Co. accounts begin to dwindle in the spring of 1777 and there is no way of checking whether he received any further payments. The failure of the managers to answer his letters in the latter part of 1777 is likely to have been because they were moving towards the decision to sell the opera house. In the event the question of his continuing employment as an agent for the King's Theatre proved an academic one, as early in 1778 he died.[21] It is hard to know whether to put the agent's suspicions down to sheer paranoia – an unsurprising state of mind in an eighteenth-century opera agent, given what is known of the ethics of the profession – or to give credence to his view that his professional ability to get good deals for the King's Theatre had been undermined. Trust was certainly an essential prerequisite of the whole process of recruitment, and when it broke down the results could be disastrous. As a long-term agent of the King's Theatre in Rome, Wiseman's position was in some respects comparable to that of Earl Cowper in Florence.[22] Both were actively

involved in music over a long period and were obviously knowledgeable about Italian musicians. What Wiseman lacked, however, was
Cowper's social status, and in the end this left him vulnerable.

THE ARTIST

English artists studying or working in Italy were well placed to assist
in the recruitment of opera singers because they tended to stay in the
country for longer periods than mere tourists. Like many artists of
the period, Humphry had a fashionable interest in music. As a young
man he boarded with the Linleys in Bath, where, according to his
autobiographical memoir, he experienced a wide range of music and
became acquainted with many leading musicians. This passage is
worth citing in full, because it gives details of Thomas Linley's early
musical education and his mother's musical abilities:

> In 1762 when Mr H first engaged their Apartments, Eliz: Mrs Sheridan
> was in her ninth year & Thomas nearly seven. Mr Linley's avocation's
> angaged him almost continualy either at the Pump Room, the Theatre,
> or in teaching the numerous Scholars. He had also a certain number of
> Benefit Concerts each Season, at which Miss Linley assisted with her
> vocal powers, and Thomas, by his early and extraordinary Performances
> on the Violin. To prepare and urge forward their respective Talents, for
> such early exhibitions, was the Father's task, for which his Habits and
> Education [were assisted] by the solid knowledge and professional
> powers of Mr David Richards on the Violin, since so eminent as a leader
> at Ranelegh, Drury Lane, and in other public Concerts of the
> Metropolis. To these must be superadded the occasional and superior
> aids of Sig^n Giardini, Abel, Bach and various other performers of the
> first class from time to time, who were induced every season to visit
> Bath. Mr Gainsborough lived in great Intimacy with the Family, who was
> passionately fond of music as well as Painting, and never fail'd to com-
> municate useful Hints, or good general Instruction. The Elegies of Mr
> Jackson of Exeter were then newly compos'd and had never been pub-
> lickly performed, who was therefore frequently with them, for the
> purpose of assisting at the Rehearsals, and explaining his Ideas, and gen-
> erally conduced to regulate their studies. The Habits of these were often

accidental depending upon the prevailing Sentiments, or Circumstances of the Parties, but always Musical.

Elizabeth, then a rising Bud of matchless Beauty, wou'd sometimes be required by her father, to rehearse & complete her Songs or duetts for public Exhibition: and it often occur'd that Mr Richards came, and assisted (as a vocal performer) in performing duetts and Trio's from Handel & other Masters.

The Elegies of Jackson were then new, and had never been publickly perform'd, therefore to comprehend their chracter, and to execute them perfectly, occupied much of their attention; and to this must be imputed their impressive effect upon the publick, wch established their high character.

Catches and Glees were occasionally sung by this party round their table after dinner, in the most joyous and convivial manner.

It frequently happened, that our artist wou'd hear Mrs Linley, whilst painting in his own appartment, singing to herself below stairs in the parlour, when he seldom fail'd to hasten down and request her to come and sit wth him. She generally comply'd and if not interrupted wou'd sing to him the whole of the Airs of Thomas and Sally, the Chaplet, the Beggars Opera, & Love in a Village etc for she was never weary.

To these she occasionally added the most admir'd Songs of Handel, Giardini, Jackson, Doctor Arne & others. Mrs Linley's feeling was of the first degree, and she acquired by attention so much stile expression and manner wth a voce di camera that her singing was in the best English taste: wch afterwards shone, with perhaps superiour Lustre in the daughters Elizabeth, Maria, and Mary, at the Oratorios in London, and excited universal wonder.[23]

During his years in Italy, Humphry became part of the large community of aspiring artists whose activities lay at the very centre of English life in Rome. Their regular meeting place was the English Coffee House. When Thomas Jones first visited it in November 1776, he was introduced to an impressive array of artistic talent, which included Humphry:

We were Usher'd into the English coffee-house, where I found my Old London Acquaintance Messrs Pars, Humphrey, Durno, Day, Jeffreys, J. More & Cousins painters, Banks the Sculptor & Nat. Marchant the Seal

Engraver – by them I was introduced to Messrs Tresham, Fuzeli, Rouby, Miller, Hume, Nevy, & Hurlestone, painters – Huetson & Foy, Sculptors & old Nulty the Antiquarian.[24]

Jones gives a memorable description of the room itself:

> For relief [from the poor Roman houses] – there was no other Alternative but flying to the English Coffee House, a filthy vaulted room, the walls of which were painted with sphinxes, Obelisks and Pyramids, from capricious designs of *Piranesi*, and fitter to adorn the inside of an Egyptian-Sepulchre, than a room of social conversation – Here – seated round a brazier of hot embers placed in the Center, we endeavoured to amuse ourselves for an hour or two over a Cup of Coffee or glass of Punch and then grope out our way home darkling in Solitude and Silence.[25]

This was the place which James Butler intended to use as his base until negotiations over the opera contract had been concluded. It was in fact the recognised clearing house for correspondence addressed to English artists and their friends.[26]

When he first contacted Humphry to help him out, Butler thought it likely from his love of music that the artist already knew Carabaldi. The connection proved a useful one to the London management. Having been put in touch with him via her emissary, Brooke continued to make use of his services, and through him of information provided by other artists such as Maria Cosway (née Hadfield). Other letters from the period of Humphry's residence in Italy provide evidence of his interest in opera. There are hints in Humphry's later correspondence of a continuing interest in Italian opera in London.[27]

THE BANKER

The provision of financial services to English visitors to Rome was a very lucrative business. Bankers used by this conspicuously wealthy clientele were expected to provide a far wider range of assistance than merely financial. The services on offer included hospitality, help with practical matters, notably with regard to the prompt dispatch and receipt of letters, and advice in the case of sudden emergencies. Such men were of great value in facilitating the difficult business of long-distance opera recruitment. Apart from the general assistance they could offer, bankers were needed to undertake the two financial transactions that were usually required to finalise a contract in Italy: the payment of an advance and the provision of insurance against non-payment of the salary. When Butler was first detained under the quarantine regulations, he turned for assistance to Mr Leigh, a well-known banker in Naples, probably a member of the partnership of Wills & Leigh who in 1763 had guaranteed Mazziotti's contract.[28] Leigh in the usual way offered both hospitality and postal services for the English. In September 1778 Thomas Jones commended his 'true old English hospitality keeping an Open table for all his friends & Countrymen every day in the week, except the Post days'.[29] The firm acted for the opera managers in the autumn of 1776.

In Rome, where it was hoped a contract would be signed with Carabaldi, the opera managers turned to a man who was very well known indeed to the English community, Francesco Barazzi, who is sometimes described as a merchant, more commonly as a banker.[30] Any Englishman in trouble would be sent to Barazzi. The rather pathetic story of James Northcote's arrival in Rome on 23 May 1777 relates how the young artist ended up sitting on his portmanteau outside the post office, unable, with his one word of Italian ('hotel') to communicate. As soon as he took out a letter of introduction to Barazzi from his bank in Genoa, everything fell into place, and he was taken to the banker, who immediately directed him to an English landscape painter at the English Coffee House.[31]

In 1774 Barazzi was approaching the end of his long period of supremacy. At the beginning of 1777 Jones reported that he 'had been for some Years the chief Banker imploy'd by the English, and, as he spoke the language, his house was found Convenient – but Mr J [Jenkins] – having opened a Bank in Opposition, had almost superseded him in this line'.[32] Evidence of Barazzi's money-lending activities goes back at least to the 1750s. He was apparently so confident of the wealth of visiting Englishmen that he was sometimes willing to lend in advance of receiving notification of credit.[33] Opera was a significant interest of Barazzi's fashionable clients, and anything that was close to their hearts was of understandable concern to him. His letter to Leone in 1764 shows that he had been trying to arrange credit for him as well as overseeing the delivery of a package. References to Vento and Baini underline his contacts with the musical world.[34] In the 1774 recruitment of Lovattini, his role was to provide the finance to enable the contract to be secured upon receipt of the letter of credit from Hart and Wilkins.[35] Barazzi was still acting for the opera managers in June 1776 when he submitted for payment bills for £59 and £71.

THE AMBASSADOR

A small number of highly influential English ambassadors in Italy played a part in the recruitment of Italian opera stars for the London stage. There was diplomatic representation in Rome and so Sir William Hamilton the Neapolitan envoy, celebrated for his passion for music and for his musical first wife, was the obvious person for Humphry to contact.[36] The knowledge that he was sympathetic to musicians led to many requests for assistance. An exchange of letters in the Althorpe Correspondence shows one instance of this. Vincenzo Orgitano, a Neapolitan composer, had requested Sir William's assistance in getting his compositions published in London. Lady Spencer, to whom the ambassador had turned, was not very encouraging:

Hot Wells, Bristol 26 November 1782   Lady Spencer to
                                         Sir William Hamilton

Tell me what I shall do with poor Orgitano's Musick, I have sent it to the musick shops and they will not print it under 18 or 20 £ and if I do pay that for it, they assure me unless some of the great Masters undertook to recommend it, they would not expect to sell many Copies. His letter like himself does not abound in Words, he refers me to you, and I shall therefore wait till you tell me how to proceed.[37]

Sir William did his best to advise:

Caserta 28 January 1783   Sir William Hamilton to Lady Spencer

> Orgitano, except upon the Harpsichord coud never explain himself very
> clearly – all I know is that he is very desirous of having his musick
> printed and at as little expense as possible. He thinks it woud be of
> service to him at this Court when he is teaching the young Princesses. I
> am sensible of what the Musick Printers say – all depends upon the
> Musick Masters in London – if as many books cou'd be sold in London
> as woud pay half the Expence, and the remainder of the books were to
> be sent to him he woud not I am sure grudge being at the expence of
> £10.[38]

In the case of the crisis over the recruitment of Lovattini, Sir William
acted as the focal point for the exchange of information. Alone of all
the participants in the unfolding drama, he was in touch with all the
parties: the manager in London (Brooke); the widow of the emissary
(Butler); the artist (Humphry). If necessary, he could also have sorted
out any financial problems with Barazzi or made recommendations
for alternative singers or singers' agents. To be in a position to offer
effective help, it was necessary for him to be well informed about the
doings of Italian opera stars. There is some evidence that other
English ambassadors knew of his interests and sought to pass on
information. Two letters sent in 1767 by Sir Horace Mann, ambassador in Florence, concern the singer De Amicis. On 20 October he
wrote to Sir William: 'I told the de Amicis yesterday of the interest
you take in what relates to her and of my desire to be usefull to her.
We were already acquainted; she had dined here and knows that I
wish to do her any service.'[39] This was followed on 10 November by a
long account of the rage of the mother of De Amicis at finding her
daughter had married without her consent.[40] Gossip of this kind was
of interest to opera managers in London. The general health, well-
being and personal stability of an opera star in whom a large financial
investment was being contemplated, were matters of relevance, as
well as the more obvious questions of reputation, ability and star
quality.

The long delay in the recruitment of Lovattini meant that the 1774–5 *opera buffa* season began with something of a rush. It was just as well that the first work was to be *La buona figliuola*, for which little rehearsal with the singer would have been needed. The advertisements for the opening night suggest that he arrived at the very last moment. In a notice published on 13 December, the managers included his name in a list of singers for that day's performance, but the next day an apology appeared, which blamed the indisposition of the singer for the cancellation of the opening night: 'The managers of the opera are extremely concerned for the Disappointment of the house last night at Sg Lovatini's illness. As soon as they were apprised of it they took every precaution by posting bills etc. and sent word to as many subscribers as time would permit.'[1] One has visions of Lovattini hurrying off the cross-Channel boat, rushing up to London for a last-minute dress rehearsal, and then collapsing with exhaustion. In the event *La buona figliuola* opened a week later on 20 December. A postponed opening night was becoming something of a habit with the Brooke–Yates management. The previous year's opening night had suffered a similar fate. There was first a postponement because the dancers Mimi and Nina Faviere 'are not yet arrived from Florence', and then on the opening night: 'Mesdames Favier having arrived from Florence, but being indisposed from the great fatigue of the journey are incapable of dancing this day.'[2]

The revival of *La buona figliuola* was a notable success. In a comment indicative of the work's growing status as a classic, a reviewer ventured the prediction that the music of this favourite opera 'will for ever remain the standard of true harmonical taste'.[3] A revival, even one of a work as popular as this, would not by itself suffice for a successful comic season, and so an additional part of

Butler's commission had been to purchase the score of a comic opera by Anfossi, whose sudden and unexpected eclipse of Piccinni in 1773 had obviously been reported to Brooke. By not informing her emissary of the title of the opera she was interested in, she perhaps received the wrong work. Anfossi's big success in 1773 had been *L'incognita perseguitata*, but Wiseman sent a more recent work, *La finta giardiniera*, first performed in Rome in the early months of 1774. The score was doubtless sent on ahead of Lovattini, but it can hardly have arrived in England much before the end of November. In the new year, the company moved with some speed to get the piece into production under its new title *La marchesa giardiniera*. By 28 February, final rehearsals were underway.[4] Fanny Burney heard the work and was favourably impressed with the 'excellent Lovattini' and the 'excessively pretty' Sestini.[5] Charles Burney thought Sestini's face beautiful, her figure elegant and her action graceful; her voice, 'though by nature not perfectly clear and sweet toned, had been well directed in her studies, and she sang with considerable agility, as well as taste and expression'.[6] Hers was one of those minor triumphs upon which the opera house relied in the intervals between the appearances of singers of superstar charisma. Anfossi's opera, however, met with critical indifference, being described by one writer as 'no more than Piccini at second hand'.[7] In following Italian opera fashions with too much haste, there was always the danger of over-rating a temporary success in a particular city. Even in Italy, Anfossi's popularity was uneven.[8] As the season progressed, it became more and more apparent that Brooke's recruitment of Lovattini had been a very astute move. The two comic operas *La buona figliuola* and *La marchesa giardiniera* both proved reasonably popular with audiences, each receiving eleven performances. In the view of one seasoned observer, the star singer of the comic troupe had lost none of his powers. Mrs Harris wrote to her son on 6 February: 'Lovatini is as good as ever. This Buona Figliola will carry it all to nothing against our friend Sacchini's new serious opera which comes out to-morrow.'[9]

The success of the comic troupe led by Lovattini was very welcome, but it masked an alarming state of affairs in the *opera seria* programme. The opening night at the King's Theatre, a performance of the pasticcio *Armida*, was well attended, but this was no guide to the likely success of the season as a whole. The opera itself inspired little enthusiasm. Mrs Howe wrote to Lady Spencer the day after the opening night: 'I did not think the opera or dancing very enchanting last night, the first man is vastly liked by every body, Rauzzini I believe is his name.'[10] By 12 November, Walpole had already heard a 'deplorable account' of the opera.[11] One critic savaged the work, writing that 'a more tedious, heavy performance' had not been seen or heard upon any stage. It would be better termed a 'sleeping opera' than a serious opera.[12] In the light of all these comments, the eulogy published by 'a member of the audience' in the *Public Advertiser* on 22 November reads suspiciously like a public relations puff inserted by the managers. Rauzzini is commended as 'the Italian Roscius' and Schindlerin as the best actress to have appeared on 'our Italian stage'. The reality was rather different, although first reactions to Rauzzini were favourable.[13] Schindlerin's relative failure was obvious, and just as Brooke had feared, invidious comparisons with Agujari at the Pantheon were not long in following:

Privy Gardens 17 December 1774   Hans Stanley MP to Lady Spencer

I beg my respects to Lord Spencer of whom I had just a Glimpse at the Opera, of which I wish I could give you a better Character; we have however at the Pantheon a Signora Ajuzari who will surprise and please you when you hear her.[14]

Brooke herself apparently did not think much of Schindlerin. In her novel *The Excursion* she describes her heroine's reaction to the second performance of *Motezuma* on 11 February 1775:

They went early, and seated themselves between the two centre pillars in the pit.

Lady Hardy amused her young friend till the Opera began, with telling her the names of all the Company as they came in.

The overture was played, and the curtain drew up; the opera advanced; Rauzzini appeared; he sung an air; our heroine was enchanted.

Maria adored music; the first passion of her heart was the theatre: she had never heard Italian music but at her own harpsichord; she had never seen any theatrical representation but in a country town.

My reader will therefore imagine her transport: she gave attention still as night to the whole.

The music (worthy of Sacchini); the voice, the taste, the blooming youth, the animated action, of Rauzzini; the beauty of the theatre; the splendour of the decorations; the force, the execution, of the brilliant Bacelli; the grace of Vallouy; and let me add, what is not the least ornament of an opera, the striking *coup d'oeil* of the assembled audience; an audience which the world cannot parallel, composed of all that is great and lovely in the kingdom; struck her young mind with an extasy almost too great for words.[15]

In what was effectively a review of her own production, Brooke failed even to mention Schindlerin. By the time that more considered critical judgements were formed, it quickly became apparent that the singer was no match at all for Agujari. Burney considered that Rauzzini's unfortunate pupil had an elegant figure and that she was a good actress, but that off stage she was 'coquettish, silly, and insipid'. Her voice was 'a mere thread, for the weakness of which there was neither taste nor knowledge to compensate'.[16]

The season had got off to a very poor start, and it is evident that a great deal depended on the reception of Sacchini's new opera *Motezuma*, which received its première on 7 February. The libretto taken from *Antonio de Solis* by Bottarelli tells the story of the landing of the Spaniards in Mexico, their entry into the capital, and ends with the arrest, release, betrayal and death of Motezuma. Full use is made of the chorus to represent the Spaniards and the Mexicans. At the start of Act II, both nations sing 'Viva il Messico, e l'Iberia', but it is the arrest of Motezuma towards the end of the act which sets up the climax of the opera, a scene that was undoubtedly intended as a show-piece for the singing and acting talents of Rauzzini. Act II opens with Motezuma in prison, 'seated in the utmost affliction'. Cortes enters to unbind his chains, and there is premature rejoicing among the chorus of Mexican nobles. But Motezuma has been betrayed, and shortly after leaving he returns fatally wounded. In his preface, Bottarelli felt it necessary to justify this death on stage: 'I do not see what objections can arise against *Motezuma*'s dying upon the *Opera-Stage*, breathing the language of *harmony* when *actors* die on other stages in *tragedy*, speaking the language of the *muses*.'[17] Dennis Libby aptly characterises the libretti of Sacchini's early London operas as containing 'a succession of situations, relatively concise and easily grasped but highly charged'. This was deemed the formula 'likely to engage the attention of the London audience'.[18] All that needs to be added to this admirably concise summary is that it was conventional to focus the overall plot on one emotive moment of especially high drama or pathos. The dying Motezuma's accompanied recitative and aria was to provide Rauzzini with his chance to star (see example 4). It begins in G major, but moves rapidly and symbolically to the remote key of B flat minor, accompanied by tremolando strings marked 'con l'arco sciolte'. As his strength ebbs away, Motezuma gasps out the name of his wife, Guacazinga. In the final largo in B flat major, his dying breaths are vividly depicted by Sacchini with fragmented phrases, sudden brief outbursts and a return to B flat minor.

There is no doubt that Rauzzini made a considerable impression in this title role. There was widespread gossip to the effect that Garrick, a known critic of acting standards at the King's Theatre, had approved the singer's affecting expiry.[19] The following year, Edward Pigott reported that Garrick considered Rauzzini's performance as Aeneas in *Didone* to be 'the best he had ever seen'.[20] In her own description of *Motezuma*, however, Brooke debunks the singer's success with a nice touch of irony. Just at the moment when the expiring Rauzzini 'shews himself not less an actor than he is an accomplished singer', she arranges for her young heroine's eye to be caught by an aristocratic admirer.[21] This, after all, was what a visit to the opera was really all about! A visiting German was even harsher: 'Instead of Virgil's Aeneas, and gallant Montezuma, who had two hundred wives pregnant at the same time, I see here a fat eunuch with calves right down to his heels, putting his hand on his sluggish

Ex. 4 Sacchini, *Motezuma* (London, 1775): the recitative/aria 'Fernando fortunato'/'Manco Fernando addio'

Ex. 4 (cont.)

Ex. 4 (*cont.*)

Ex. 4 (*cont.*)

Ex. 4 (*cont.*)

heart and warbling of love, till a stone would have compassion on him.'[22] This, however, is clearly an anti-castrato diatribe.

Motezuma was an immediate success, receiving eleven performances:

21 February 1775   Mrs Harris to her son

> The operas are much in fashion, both for serious and comic. 'Tis well for Yates: such crowds every night that you must go by six or have no place in the pit; you cannot even get your coach to the door.[23]

The appearance of prosperity, however, was deceptive. An overall analysis of the opera accounts for the 1774–5 season suggests that there was a large drop in income by comparison with the previous year. Brief periods of full attendance, such as the one that Mrs Harris witnessed, were no substitute for a good season-long occupancy rate. The obvious conclusion is that Agujari at the Pantheon was indeed inflicting some damage on attendance at the King's Theatre.

The reception accorded to the Pantheon star, a 'truly wonderful' performer in Burney's view, was enthusiastic. Fanny Burney was rapturous in her appreciation:

> I could compare her to nothing *I* ever *heard* but only to what I have heard of – Your Carestino – Farinelli – Senesino – alone are worthy to be ranked with the Bastardini. Such a powerful voice! – so astonishing a Compass – reaching from C in the middle of the Harpsichord, to 2 notes *above* the Harpsichord! Every tone so clear, so full – so charming! Then her *shake* – so *plump* – so true, so open! – it is [as] strong & distinct as Mr Burney's upon the Harpsichord –
> Besides it's [*sic*] great power, her voice is all sweetness, – &, when she pleases, all softness & delicacy. She sings in the highest style of Taste, & with an *Expression* so pathetic, it is impossible to hear it unmoved.[24]

The contest with Brooke's star was over before it had begun. Despite her lucrative engagement at the Pantheon, Agujari resented that she had not been hired as the *prima donna* at the King's Theatre. Fanny Burney stated bluntly: 'she professes great contempt for the managers'.[25] When she put to the singer her regret that she was appearing at the Pantheon as she was 'so much formed for the *theatre*', she received the sarcastic retort: 'oui – *comme une* statue! – *comme une petite Ecoliere!*'[26] In general Agujari was dismissive of Schindlerin, and made a point of letting everyone know that she had not been near the King's Theatre and had no intention of hearing her rival. Mrs Harris's report of Agujari strongly suggests she had been talking to the Burneys:

21 March 1775   Mrs Harris to her son

I . . . went on to the Pantheon with Miss Wyndham. Nothing worth going there for but the Agujari. She is a most surprising singer, and in my opinion a pleasing one; She goes two notes higher in her voice than the notes of the harpsichord. The *ton* is to say 'she is more surprising than pleasing', but I do not subscribe to that, for she has a very good method . . . This woman always fills the Pantheon with a great mixture of company. The best company goes off soon after the concert is over. We stayed an hour longer, and then it is beyond all things deplorable.[27]

The verdict 'more surprising than pleasing' (or, as the case might be, 'more pleasing than surprising') is a characteristic piece of Burney phraseology at this period.[28]

Of the factors affecting a singer's reception in London, power and, in the case of women singers, altitude were major talking points. Agujari's huge range was much discussed. Burney described her as having a 'fair natural voice' of two octaves from a to a''', and reported that in her youth she was able to go up at least a further octave. Sacchini had heard her reach a high b flat.[29] Such an exceptional range was bound to attract comment, and Agujari's voice remained the standard by which other singers with a comparable range (such as Danzi) were measured.

The repertoire sung by Agujari, both at her Pantheon concerts and in private performances, consisted largely of music by her companion, the composer Giuseppe Colla, a fact of which Burney disapproved. Arias from his opera *Didone* proved especially popular. Fanny thought that the singer's best performance, during the five hours that she spent with the Burneys, was in the song 'Son Regina & son[o] amante' from this work: 'Good God! what a song! & how sung!' She also approved an '*Arria* Parlante' from the same opera which Agujari 'acted . . . through out, with great spirit & feeling'.[30] Brooke knew that her own star had been utterly outclassed, but she took careful note of the manner of Agujari's triumph and made preparations for her reply. Next season at the King's Theatre, she would present her own superstar, Caterina Gabrielli, in a production of the same libretto *Didone*, featuring 'Son Regina' as set by her own house composer Sacchini.

In the spring of 1775, Brooke was under considerable pressure, and there were renewed skirmishes with Garrick, on this occasion over a clash of benefit nights. Difficulties arose when he was requested to change the night of a benefit at Drury Lane so as not to clash with Maria Macklin's benefit at Covent Garden. The new date coincided with a performance of Anfossi's *La marchesa giardiniera* at the King's Theatre for the benefit of the dancers, and Brooke wrote to complain about the clash. In his reply, Garrick cuttingly pointed out that Macklin, although engaged at Covent Garden, had helped him carry on business when 'Ladies [i.e. Mary Ann Yates] belonging to us would not'.[31] Having signed on at Drury Lane with Garrick, Mary-Ann Yates was in an awkward position, with loyalties to both the opera house and theatre. If Garrick had been expecting her to devote her whole attention to Drury Lane, he was soon to be disappointed. Inevitably it was not long before the question arose of how she intended to combine her acting career with her continuing interests at the King's Theatre. The answer seemed to be that she would fail to honour her obligations at Drury Lane whenever it suited her. After a series of late cancellations Garrick expressed extreme exasperation at her behaviour in the well-known note to her husband:

29 October 1775   David Garrick to Richard Yates

You left word with M[r] Hopkins *that we are to think no more of M[rs] Yates, 'till She will let us know her pleasure*, or words to that Effect. Do You, & M[rs] Yates imagine that the Proprietors will submit to this manner of going on, or that they will pay such a large Sum of Money for having

their Busines[s] so destroy'd as it was in great part of the last Season and
has been wholly this, by waiting for Mrs Yates's pleasure to perform? –
She play'd but Thirty times last Season, and as She goes on, in the proportion of four times in Six weeks she will play Twenty times in this
Season. – Indeed Mr Yates this will not do, and I give you fair Notice. We
lost greatly by her not playing the first Night she was advertis'd, & to
this day no reason could be given for the disappointment, nor did you
offer any to my Brother, but *that you could not help it, and you did all in
your power to oblige her to Act.*[32]

Obviously the demands of the opera house were resulting in the
actress cutting back progressively on Drury Lane appearances. Her
missed debut in the new season on 5 October 1775 may be explained
by the fact that the King's Theatre was then gearing up for the sensational first appearance of Gabrielli, whose talent and temperament
were easily a match for those of her own.

The cumulative effect of all these problems was an impending
financial crisis. Confirmation that the opera house was in serious
financial trouble comes from a petition Brooke now sent to the Lord
Chamberlain, the full text of which is reprinted in Appendix 2b. The
document is undated, but a clear reference to Agujari's salary suggests that it was written in 1775. The complaint is that Italian opera at
the King's Theatre is not financially viable, and the proposed solution
is a renewal of the request for permission to stage English plays. It
was earlier suggested that Garrick's attempt to hire Noverre in 1774
and 1775 was a spoiling tactic, intended to do damage to the opera
house. It is abundantly clear from her 1775 petition that, whether or
not she knew about the negotiations with Noverre, Brooke did
indeed feel her interests in the King's Theatre to be under direct
attack from the managers of Drury Lane and Covent Garden. Having
briefly recounted the history of relations between the theatres and
the opera house, she directly accuses Garrick and Colman of having
deliberately 'given the strongest pieces they possibly cou'd at both
houses, on Opera Nights', including both comic and serious English
operas with Italian music, 'to the great detriment of the Managers of
the Opera'. But Brooke was now fighting on two fronts. She states:

the Pantheon a new undertaking, establish'd since the present Managers came to the King's Theatre in the manner it is now carry'd on, is to the utmost degree ruinous to the Opera, as they not only divide the Musical audiences, but by offering the most exorbitant terms to Italian Singers make it almost impossible for the Managers of the Opera to engage any Performers, except at prices which even the utmost success can never enable them to pay.

As a rival promoter of major Italian opera stars, the Pantheon thus stood accused of splitting the audience and thereby diminishing the King's Theatre's receipts, while at the same time driving up salary levels for the top stars. The reference here is clearly to Agujari's salary of £1,200, and probably by then Gabrielli's forthcoming salary of £1,500 would already have been negotiated. Much of the remainder of the petition is taken up with rehearsing the arguments for a third theatre made in the 1770 submission – the indisputable increase in London's population, and the fact that the Act of Limitation was intended, so Brooke argued, as a curb on the 'licentiousness' of the theatres rather than as a limit on their number. Claiming the support of the 'Nobility and Gentry', she thus requested that 'the licence for the Opera House, now confin'd to Italian performances, may be extended on the intermediate Nights to theatrical entertainments in the English language also'. Failing that, she once again sought permission to stage 'English operas', doubtless to begin with *Rosina*, on intermediate nights, or for a short summer licence 'in the nature of Mr Foote's patent but on different nights'. As Brooke pointed out, the essential inequality between the opera house and the theatres lay in the disparity between the number of nights that each could open. With only twenty-five profitable nights (the Saturdays of the season) the King's Theatre operated at a considerable disadvantage. As thus stated, the case for some reform appeared a strong one, and it is easy to see why the theatre managers became steadily more alarmed, as Brooke persisted in arguing it.

Once again, the Lord Chamberlain rejected the petition, which left Brooke and her partners with the choice of selling up or of continuing the struggle to make Italian opera at the King's Theatre break even. Characteristically stubborn, she did not give up. One factor in her favour was that the combined efforts of Lovattini and Sacchini had resulted in a disappointing season, rather than a financial catastrophe. Lovattini in particular had done all that could have been expected of him. His final benefit, a performance of *I viaggiatori ridicoli*, was on 30 April 1775, while *La buona figliuola* ran until June. With seven substantial English fees now to his credit, he was able to retire with 'very ample means'.[33] But of more significance was the fact that Brooke by now had lined up a formidable weapon of her own, with which to strike back at her rivals: the superstar Caterina Gabrielli.

Brooke's growing experience as an opera manager is shown by the fact that her preparations were much further advanced in the summer of 1775 than they had been the previous year. The major stars, Gabrielli, Rauzzini and the new *buffo* Trebbi, were all under contract. One important matter remained to be resolved – the programme. Well aware of the lack of good *opera buffa* repertoire in London, Brooke took active steps to seek out new works from the best composers in this genre. The continuing popularity of Piccinni's operas in London made a new work from this source a very attractive proposition, but she would have known, as a result of Burney's earlier approach on behalf of Hobart, that it was unlikely the composer would agree to make the journey to London. Paisiello's works were not yet known to London audiences, but his music had greatly impressed Burney during his Italian journey. After first hearing *Le trame per amore* in Naples in 1770, he wrote: 'it was full of fire and fancy, the ritornels abounding in new passages, and the vocal parts in elegant and simple melodies, such as might be remembered and carried away after the first hearing, or be performed in private by a small band'.[1] The strength of this recommendation from her knowledgeable adviser was enough to persuade Brooke to open negotiations with the composer, with a view to bringing him to the King's Theatre the season after next.

In the interim, it was necessary to find works for immediate production, and Brooke wrote to her new contact in Italy:

8 September 1775   Frances Brooke to Ozias Humphry

Dear Sir
I had the pleasure of your letter from Florence a few days ago, & we are all extremely oblig'd to you for your polite remembrance of us, & your very kind offer of doing any thing for us in Italy.

We cannot show a sense of your kindness so strongly as by accepting it, & therefore I make no scruple to say, that if there is any very good comic opera play'd this autumn at Florence set by a capital master, you will greatly oblige us by sending us the whole score & the book; I shou'd particularly wish it Piccini's or Paesiello's, & if we cou'd have it directly I mean *instantly* it wou'd be of great service to us. If you can do this for us, & will be so obliging to draw on Mr. Yates or my brother for the amount, you will lay us under a great Obligation. I am not sure there is a comic opera at Florence, but I write on that supposition.

I was in hopes you were coming to England when I heard of your leaving Rome, but find I am mistaken. I hope you have not quite forsaken us: I wish very much to have the pleasure of seeing you here, & very much also to have a picture of my friend Mrs. Yates by your hand . . .

The Gabrielli is here; she is a charming woman looks about six & twenty. She is perfectly welbred, with the air & deportment of a woman of the first rank.

We have Trebbi instead of Lovattini, & he promises to replace him very well; he is, or I am mistaken, a much better actor. They say he is a good singer.

If you cou'd add to the opera, supposing you find one worth sending with the music, two or three good comic books: not the music, but meerly the books, you wou'd much oblige us.

At all events I will trouble you for a line as soon as you receive this, to know whether there is any new opera play'd worth sending, & if there is, when we may expect it, & which way: I shou'd suppose it easy to send it from Leghorn by sea.

Is there anything we can do here for you to show our gratitude? At present the balance is terribly against us, & we have nothing to plead but having a very lively sense of your obliging attention to us, & a strong desire to know how we can acknowledge it. Mr & Mrs Yates & my brother are all in the country at present, but I expect them in town soon.

> I am, Sir,
> > With great esteem,
> > > Your most Oblig'd & Obedient Servant, F[r] Brooke.[2]

Over the years, the King's Theatre had derived much of its repertoire from operas deemed to have been a success in Italy. It is interesting that Brooke was also looking for libretti, which perhaps suggests that, as a writer herself, she did not have a very high opinion of Bottarelli, who did most of the adaptations for the London opera house.

The value of an artistic contact like Ozias Humphry lay not simply in the practical help that he himself could offer, but in the access that he offered to the wider English community in Italy. It is very evident that he took Brooke's request for assistance seriously, and that he was soon in touch with friends and patrons to ask about currently successful operas in different cities. One of his musical correspondents was the young artist Maria Cosway (née Hadfield). In a letter to Humphry written before Brooke's missive could have arrived, she gives one of the last known glimpses of two major opera stars of the previous generation, both well known to English audiences: 'I have been to an oratorio where Manzuoli, Guarducci and the tenor from the opera sang. The music was most beautiful and gained further from being sung by such skilful masters.'[3] Cosway continued to supply Humphry with up-to-date information. Towards the end of the year, she reported that an opera of Zannetti's had opened on 26 December 1775, but that it had been indifferently received. The castrato Rubinelli, however, was of considerable merit:

20 January 1776   Maria Cosway to Ozias Humphry

> The first man is called Rubinelli and is a contralto. His appearance cannot be praised enough, being the most beautiful I have ever seen. If the first lady [Carara] is beautiful, the first man is more so. His voice is the most beautiful that it is possible to hear. He has not the roughness of voice that Millico had, but a certain dolorousness and uniformity [of tone colour?] which gives pleasure to all. His manner of singing is very good and in good taste. He sings very much in the manner of Mr Parson[s]. I am not able to rate his cantabile singing above that of Millico, or his performance of embellishments above that of Aprile, but he has something of the both of them. What with his beautiful appearance, his good voice, and his very beautiful manner of singing, it is impossible to find better.[4]

Cosway went on to mention an opera by Traetta, which the composer himself said was 'the best he had ever composed'.[5] The first lady Carara, she continued, 'cuts a good figure in the recitatives which she sings with great expression and is greatly applauded, but in the arias she loses all the applause'.[6] The following month, she wrote again, on this occasion praising a tenor aria with the newly popular wind instrumentation of clarinets and horns:

c. February 1776   Maria Cosway to Ozias Humphry

The music is very beautiful, especially the overture, the duo, the trio and an aria of the tenor's accompanied by clarinets and hunting horns, that is the best music I have heard. Millico does not cut a better figure in this than in the other one, because his part in the other opera, at least the first aria, it seems to me was better than any in this . . . If you would like to have the libretto I will send it to you on the first opportunity . . . Millico is a rough figure throughout.[7]

Humphry was proving a very effective channel of communication for up-to-date intelligence about opera in Italy. Brooke had asked him for libretti, he had in turn asked Cosway, who now offered him one. It was not always possible to make use of information immediately. Rubinelli's success was noted, but he did not make his debut in London until May 1786. Interestingly, one of his first private appearances in England was at the home of Maria Cosway herself.[8]

Another emissary who was perhaps acting on Brooke's behalf was Charles Greville, a life-long supporter of Italian opera in London.[9] During a brief visit to Naples, he sought out Piccinni and commissioned three songs from him. Sir William Hamilton wrote to inform him when the commission had been completed, and in his letter, the ambassador gives intriguing details of how the music was to be forwarded to England:

Naples 14 November 1775   Sir William Hamilton to Charles Greville

Picini's 3 Songs are in the hands of Mr. Hodges, who proposes to deliver them to you in London next month. Picini & his wife came here, & we had a rehersal of them; they are delightfull, and will, I am sure, perfectly answer your purpose. By Astier's advice I gave him 10 Ounces each – in all, 60 Ducats – which will go to your account; to be sure, it was paying *en Milord Anglais*. They are sealed up, and Hodges has promised that if it is necessary to open them at any Custom he will seal them up directly. They are the originals in Picini's own hand & your *divinity* may be assured that no one is in possession of another copy.[10]

The songs could of course have been a purely private commission, but the unusual level of security insisted upon by the ambassador perhaps points to Greville having acted for the opera house. If the curious reference to 'your divinity' is an allusion to the temperamental Gabrielli, the three songs might have been intended for use in a pasticcio. Alternatively, they could have been substitutions for numbers in Piccinni's own *Caio Mario*, an opera given its London première on 20 April 1776, many years after its original production.[11] In subsequent seasons, small payments to Piccinni were made out of the opera accounts, presumably for small packets of airs to use as substitutions.

Brooke's attempt to purchase a high-quality comic opera by Piccinni or Paisiello for the 1775–6 season came to nothing, and lesser works were featured, a new *opera buffa* by Vento, revivals of works by Rauzzini and Sacchini, and the still popular *La buona figliuola*. Trebbi, the comic tenor who replaced Lovattini, met with a mixed critical response. Burney was at first impressed. He told Twining that he was 'a good singer of the kind, & an excellent actor',[12] but his considered verdict was harsher: 'his voice was not so sweet, his taste so good, or his humour so risible, as those of his predecessor [Lovattini]'.[13] Susan Burney was later even more scathing, describing him 'as usual, a Buffoon without humour'.[14] Sestini, though outclassed by the *prima donna seria*, continued to please. Pigott wrote: 'Sestini sung, her voice is much inferior to Gabrielli's tho very pleasing, the name of the opera was *Dale Damore* [Rauzzini's *L'ali d'amore*].'[15]

Although Brooke put much effort into the development of a popular programme of comic opera, it was certain that the season as a whole would stand or fall by the reception accorded to Gabrielli. The recruitment of the one singer who was likely to be a match for Agujari was an important *coup*. It had been known for some time that she was interested in visiting London. An English gentleman visiting St Petersburg in 1774 published 'A Character of the fair Gabrielli, the celebrated Italian singer'. He reported his conversation with the *prima donna* thus:

> She had no reason to be dissatisfied with her present situation; but that notwithstanding, she had a passionate desire to see England. I assured her, that the English would be very happy to see among them a woman of such pre-eminent merit, and that they were the most generous patrons to all performers in the fine arts.

Her fee was discussed:

> She was at Milan when the Empress engaged her to sing in her Court. The price she demanded was about 1500 L sterling per annum, besides a house and carriage, nor would she relax the least article of this sum. They remonstrated on the unreasonableness of so enormous a salary; and to induce her to make some abatement, they assured her that a Field Marshal had no more – 'If that be the case (said she) I would advize her Majesty to make one of the Marschals sing.'[16]

Gabrielli was under contract by early 1775. An anonymous correspondent of Sir William Hamilton assumed that by 28 March he would already have heard that 'the Gabrielli is engaged for the Opera in London next winter, & the Schindlerin our prima Donna at present is to go to Petersburg'.[17] Her fee, as the Hoare & Co. accounts show, was indeed £1,500, and she was also provided with a house and carriage. Her celebrated 'temperament' was soon on display, causing one observer to doubt whether the managers could cope with her:

> Grosvenor Square 31 October 1775 George Bussy Villiers to Lady Spencer
>
> I believe we are not upon very sure grounds as to the opera, for the Gabrieli was actually in her chaise to go away the other day & her Caprices are such they will never manage her.[18]

This sort of behaviour, however, only added to the general sense of anticipation. Fanny Burney captured the atmosphere of excitement in the following well-known passage.

> As to the Gabriellé – she has taken a House in Golden Square, & has has a Brass plate put on the Door, with *M*ʳˢ Gabrielle on it. She & Rauzzini seem admirably suited for each other, for let her Live ever so much *en*

princesse, he will always keep her in Countenance by living *en prince*. He has had his Drawing room painted after the manner of the Card Rooms at the Pantheon, with Pink & Green, & finely ornamented. The first opera is to be next Saturday, when if you do not come to Town I shall think & Conclude that you are lost to all the St Cecelian powers of attraction. Indeed if niether Agujari or Gabrielli have charms to allure you to the Opera or Pantheon, one may imagine that you are become as indifferent to music, as to Dancing or Horse-Racing. The opera is to be Metastasio's *Didone*, which is the very opera that Agujari sung to us 12 songs from, composed by her maestro Sig^r Colla. It is to be a *half* pastic-cio, but all the Recitatives by Sacchini, as well as a Cantabile for Rauzzini, & *All the part* of la Gabrielli. This I very much rejoice at, as I had rather hear her first in the music of his [Sacchini's] Composition, than of any other maestro whose Works I am acquainted with.

I am extremely glad, also, that the squalling Galli is dismissed, & Savoi once more taken as second man. A sister of Gabrielli is to be 2^d Woman, & I hear she is very pretty but no further has yet transpired.

The Rehearsals are begun, & the managers are very busy. My father, at the earnest invitation of M^r & Mrs Yates & Mrs Brooke, Dined at their House last week, with the following delicious party; – Rauzzini, Sacchini, the sister, & the Gabriclli herself! He tells us that she is still very pretty, & extremely elegant, very well bred, & has the air & manner of a woman of Rank. She did not sing, niether did any presume to ask her: but she has invited my Father to her House, & desired to cultivate his acquaintance. There's for you! He intends, notwithstanding the value of his Time, to shortly avail himself of this graciousness.

Nothing could ever exceed the expectations of people of all Ranks & all ways of thinking, concerning this so Celebrated singer. For my part, should any thing unfortunately prevent my hearing her first perfor-mance, I shall regard it ever after as a very great misfortune.[19]

For the London audience, this was one of the most eagerly antici-pated operatic events of the century. The season began with two 'warm-up' performances of a pasticcio, but the public was waiting for Gabrielli's debut in *Didone*, which, as everyone knew, was intended to place the singer in direct competition with Agujari, who had sung songs from Colla's *Didone* the previous year. A firm announcement of the date of the singer's debut was daily expected. William Parsons

reported to Ozias Humphry: 'we are in great expectation of hearing
Gabrielli next Tuesday; but we are not at all certain as she has disappointed us twice already', presumably by not appearing in the pasticcio.[20] On the night fixed for Gabrielli's debut, a huge crowd thronged
to the King's Theatre, but at the very last moment the performance
had to be cancelled because of her illness.[21] This was the third season
in a row in which an opening night had been postponed, but on this
occasion the cancellation led to what all managers dreaded – a major
public relations fiasco. Fanny Burney describes vividly the scene as
the disappointed subscribers vented their anger, leaving the hapless
Richard Yates to attempt to limit the damage:

> The Crowd was prodigious. They [the managers] gave us Hand Bills on
> which were written *There can be no Opera this Evening on account of the
> Indisposition of the 2 Capital Serious Singers*. People were in horrid pas-
> sions. Some said it was scandalous – others that it was a shame; – others
> called for the managers; one gentleman blustered furiously, Vowing he
> had come 20 miles since Dinner on purpose to hear her.
>
> Poor Yates the manager, was obliged to stand at the Door from 5 till
> past 7 o' Clock, to appease the rage of the disappointed Public: though
> every person he sent away caused him a pang, as he could not but say –
> 'There goes 3 shillings! there 5! – there half a Guinea!' Yet if he had not
> been there, the House would have been probably pulled down.
>
> We all came Home horribly out of humour, & as to Hetty she deter-
> mined from that moment not to like her; & prayed most devoutly that
> she might be Hissed whenever she should honour England with the
> sound of her Voice.[22]

In the ensuing furore, Burney ascertained that the managers, doubt-
ing whether the singer's illness was genuine, had had the temerity to
broach the subject with her and been dismissed with the suggestion
that she would 'Dress herself & make her Appearance, – that the
Opera might be performed, – but that for herself, she would make a
Curtsie, & *point to her Throat*, to excuse her singing'.

The postponed debut inevitably attracted an even greater crowd.
Anticipating the crush, the Burneys arrived before 5 o'clock. Gabrielli
made the most of the situation, and at her first entry she 'took a *sweep*

from the full length of the stage, amidst peels of Applause, which seemed as if they would shake the foundation of the Theatre'.[23] It was some considerable time before the clapping subsided sufficiently to enable the singer to hear the orchestra. Once the opera began, Gabrielli was the sole focus of attention. The impression given in some accounts is that the rest of the cast need hardly have bothered to turn up. Early in the new year, Piggot attended a performance, and he recorded his impressions of Gabrielli:

London 1776

January the 20th went to the Opera of Didone abandonata, the piece is I think but indifferent, the Decorations very well especially the Trees at the end their was a preety view of Cartage in flames; but did not find them very supprising, the house which is handsom, is tho not to be compared to that at Paris, the benches are incommode to get out; Gabrielli who acted Didone has a finer voice than ever I have heared, she draws a note for an imasing long time and with Great softness, She acts as bad as she sings well, is exceedingly saucey, talking to people behind the Scenes while her lover is a singing, and Curtches [curtsies] to people in the boxes; her salary is 1500 pounds and a benefit, and Mr Pierce who kecps her gives her 2000 pounds as it is said; Venazi Rauzzini acted the part of Eneas, he is young, has an exceeding handsome face, he acts better than has yet been seen, Garrick says he never saw better, his Voice answers his figure and talents, being very strong, soft and sonorous, and sing with supprising tast; the next good singer was Savoi; that Dancing good, but I think well enough for an opera, are very inferior to the French Dancers. The Opera ended at half after ten, on one side of the house is a large room where the people of fashion stay till their coaches are called up; here you may stay for near an hour, the Crouds being so great and the regulation of the coaches so *bad* each driving which way they chuse, that you cannot get away without runing great risk of breaking your carrage.[24]

This is a truly remarkable picture of eighteenth-century stage behaviour. While poor Rauzzini endeavoured to thrill the King's Theatre audience with his own singing, Gabrielli was mounting a 'performance' of her own, flirting and chatting with the audience offstage.

It seems very likely that Gabrielli's stage and public persona was to some extent an assumed one. After an extended conversation with the singer, Burney found her 'the most intelligent and best bred virtuosa' with whom he had ever conversed. Yet, neither audience nor opera management had any real interest in seeing a modest, well-conceived musical and acting performance. What they wanted (and got) was a star with the personal magnetism to cause a sensation. It is little wonder that Gabrielli was not highly regarded as an actress. The part that she was playing on stage was essentially herself. Many years later, Richard Mount-Edgcumbe caustically observed that all he could remember of the singer was 'the care with which she tucked up her great hoop as she sidled into the flames of Carthage' at the climax of the opera.[25] It is not likely that this dramatic infelicity would have much concerned the packed audience on the memorable opening night. The drama in the King's Theatre was certainly electric, but it had little to do with the plot of the libretto.

After this sensational debut, the debate over Gabrielli's merits as a performer was extraordinarily intense. As Fanny Burney put it: 'She is the universal subject of Conversation, & no 2 people think alike of her.'[26] She describes a scene in the Burney household, as acquaintances enter one by one, each in turn being pressed for an opinion of Gabrielli.[27] In a letter to Twining, Burney conveys a clear sense of the first reaction: disappointment at expectations unfulfilled:

> I was carried out of a sick-bed to the Opera on Saturday. The public was
> in general disappointed. They expected a Giant in Gabrielli, & behold! a
> pigmy. I was more pleased than surprised or disappointed. A little,
> dapper, short-armed, elegant, appetissante figure, was not likely to have
> the voice of a Stentor. She had a cold, & was put out of humour by the
> brutality of John in the Gallery hissing her Sister. But through all the
> clouds & storms I discovered a voice more like Mrs Sheridan's in the
> clear places, than any one I know of: an execution rapid & neat to a very
> superior degree.[28]

The difficulty in living up to extreme publicity hype was a problem faced by any major star making a debut in London. Such was the focus on the voice, that in the period of intense speculation that preceded a major debut, unrealistic expectations, especially concerning vocal power, could easily take hold. If a star could survive this rush to judgement, a calmer appreciation of true merit would usually prevail. Gabrielli, however, had to contend not only with exaggerated expectations, but also the comparison with her rival Agujari, who had a very powerful voice. As the King's Theatre had recruited her specifically to compete with the Pantheon star, it is hardly surprising that the opera-going public avidly compared their voices.

Gabrielli's reception makes an especially interesting case study in London's attitude towards the vocal qualities of star singers, because the debate focused on the issue of sheer volume versus musicality. It soon became apparent that Gabrielli did indeed have a smaller voice than her rival Agujari, and for some this lack of volume alone was enough to justify an adverse verdict. Lady Edgecumbe is reported as saying: 'By *Gabrielli*, Rauzzini seemed to have a great Voice; by *Agujari* he appeared a Child.'[29] In Fanny's account of her sister's reaction, she seems to be gently satirising the extremity with which adverse opinions were often given:

> Hetty [Esther Burney], because she was not an Agujari, would allow her *Nothing*; declared that she would not quit her *Room* to hear her, that she did not care whether she went to another Opera the whole season, & that every shilling of the money ought to be returned – But Hetty is abominably provoked if she does not meet with every thing she expects. & will not allow *any* thing where there is the least defficiency.[30]

Walpole was characteristically colder and more cutting in his observations:

8 December 1775   Horace Walpole to Horace Mann

> Tell me truly; is or has the Gabrielli been a great singer? She has, at least, not honoured us but with a most slender, low voice. Her action is just, but colder than a vestal's. However, as you know, she carries the resemblance no further.[31]

In equating a disappointing absence of power with a lack of warmth or commitment, Walpole was for once making a judgement which many made. Others, however, discerned a magical quality in

Gabrielli's soft singing. In a rare comment on music, Burney's second wife, Elizabeth Allen Burney, came down firmly in favour of the King's Theatre star:

St Martin's Street July 11 [1776]   Elizabeth Allen Burney to
                                                                                        Charles Burney

I've just been having a disputation with Madam Sukey – I can't for the life of me persuade her that Aguara's voice is not superior to Gabbrielli's – to be sure I'm no judge, I know what pleases me – I only say – *I* dont [like] that violent furious style of singing – it goes thro' my head! but Gabbrielli's is so round & so soft & so sweet, it runs quite warm down the mallow of my back![32]

This issue was debated vigorously in Burney circles. Although he had never heard Gabrielli, Thomas Twining offered his opinion. In the first of two letters to Burney, he reports the reaction of the Reverend Hey:

Colchester 19 February 1776   Thomas Twining to Charles Burney

He is sadly disappointed in Gabrielli – Well! He seems to think her a cold, artifici[al] singer – not in the genuine style of ye 'cantar che nell'anima si sente'. Rauzzini he idolizes – Why all this ? – Why, only just that you mayn't spit in his face when you meet him.[33]

In response to an obviously ardent but now lost missive from Burney in support of Gabrielli, Twining responded with the following:

Colchester 7 March 1776   Thomas Twining to Charles Burney

Thank you for detail, & discriminations, about Gabrielli & Rauzzini. Expression, & *the being in earnest* is so essential to my musical pleasure, & beauties of that kind, so much more captivating to me than beauties of execution, voice, polish & embellishment, that tho' I have no doubt but I shou'd receive much pleasure from the excellencies you mention, & allow all Gabrielli's superiorities, yet I conceive it more than possible that I might still prefer Rauzzini on the whole; I mean admitting the exact truth & justice of all you say of them both. The most captivating adagio I ever heard yet was Millico's; but I never cou'd get anybody to be of my opinion except my friend Hey.[34]

For Twining the issue was one of emotion, and he obviously suspected that Gabrielli was a brilliant but cold singer who would fail to
move him.

When he came to formulate a considered judgement for his
General History, Burney, as he was wont to do, attempted to explain
away the singer's relative failure. He focused his argument on the
issue of Gabrielli's cold, about which both supporters and detractors
held firm views. He exonerated her from the charge of feigning sick-
ness, and in turn accused the London audience of failing to acknowledge the possibility of genuine illness.[35] The irrational attitude of the
English opera-going public towards illness was notorious. During his
stay in Munich in August 1772, Burney had noted the comments of
Mingotti (a singer with management experience at the King's
Theatre) who claimed that she had frequently been hissed by the
London audience for having such ailments as a toothache, a cold or a
fever, 'to which the good people of England will readily allow every
human being is liable, except an actor or a singer'. She admitted that
'*pseudo* colds and fevers' were commonplace but insisted that it was
'just possible for these people to have *real* disorders'.[36] Whilst admitting that Gabrielli's voice was 'not powerful', Burney reported that
there were 'a few fair and discriminating critics' (among whom was
evidently his wife!), who had discovered 'a superior sweetness' in the
natural tone of the singer's voice, an 'elegance in the finishing [of]
her musical periods or passages', and 'an accent and precision in her
divisions' that placed her above 'every singer of her time'.[37]

Brooke's preferred choice of opera for Gabrielli's debut would
surely have been a setting of *Didone* by Sacchini, continuing the successful series of *Il Cid*, *Perseo* and *Motezuma*. For some reason, this
was not possible, and the unhappy compromise, described by Fanny
Burney as a 'half-pasticcio', was that Sacchini should compose the
recitatives and '*All the part* of La Gabrielli'. It is possible that Brooke's
problem was with Rauzzini. All four airs sung by this singer are desig-
nated as having been composed by himself, which might suggest that
he had objected to having to sing Sacchini's music. (As we shall see,
relations between Rauzzini and Sacchini were apparently beginning

to deteriorate.) By conceding that Gabrielli would have to make her high-profile debut in a pasticcio, Brooke was having to retreat (albeit temporarily) from her policy of favouring the one-composer opera.

Such was the sensation caused by Gabrielli's first appearance that for once little attention was paid to Sacchini's music. A great deal depended upon the success of his opening aria for the superstar singer ('Son Regina'), because comparisons were certain to be made with Agujari's performances of Colla's setting. Indeed, by choosing this particular libretto, comparisons were being invited. Under pressure to produce something to equal the performance of the Pantheon star, Sacchini miscalculated badly. To discerning London critics, Gabrielli's voice was rich, her vocal lines could be beautifully phrased, she could sustain notes an 'imasing long time', and she had a thrilling soft tone, but, although precise in her 'divisions', she could not match the brilliance and power of Agujari. Sacchini, however, focused attention on precisely this aspect of her singing (see example 5). Sacchini was widely praised in London as a melodist, and even to modern ears his vocal writing can sound Mozartean for short periods. After the promising opening to 'Son Regina', the composer reverts immediately to sterile passagework, Gabrielli's performance of which failed to convince. A further embarrassment was that Gabrielli's songs had been sung 'with a neatness so nearly equal [to Davies], that common hearers could distinguish no difference'.[38]

Although she recovered from her traumatic start, Gabrielli failed to live up to the expectations of the London audience.[39] On the other hand, the season was a great financial success, her presence guaranteeing the King's Theatre a period of intense publicity of the kind that was certain to generate income.[40] The Hoare & Co. accounts for the season show a sharp increase in receipts over the previous year. This was indeed a significant turning point. Just as Manzuoli had done in 1764, Gabrielli clearly demonstrated that the path to financial solvency lay with superstar singers, and the scene was set for a series of such recruitments, including Pacchierotti, Rubinelli and Marchesi, and eventually Catalani. Of more immediate concern, Gabrielli's season had been a brilliant riposte to the Pantheon.

Ex. 5 Sacchini's aria 'Son regina' from the pasticcio *Didone* (London, 1775)

Gabrielli's sensational season marked a turning point in the fortunes of the opera house. With financial stability now achieved, the King's Theatre began to develop into a flourishing concern, a fact recognised by critics and supporters alike. Brooke, moreover, was steadily gaining in confidence as a manager. Indeed, the forceful manner with which the first crisis of the new season was resolved suggests that she was beginning to gain a degree of ascendancy over her singers.

Finding a worthy successor to Gabrielli was always going to be difficult, but it soon became evident that Brooke's choice, Anna Pozzi, was likely to fail. She arrived in the autumn of 1776 and first impressions at least were favourable. She was deemed 'young, handsome, and possessed of a voice uncommonly clear, sweet, and powerful'.[1] Twining was visiting London, and Burney tried to persuade him that he would like her. He replied: 'I shall forgive her a great deal, if she will but get at my entrailles now & then.'[2] Pozzi, however, was obviously inexperienced, both as a singer and an actress, and she was superseded by Cecilia Davies 'before the season was far advanced'.[3] This was to place a very kind interpretation on her undignified demotion, for seldom can a 'first' singer have been ditched so rapidly as was the unfortunate young Italian. Mount-Edgcumbe was blunt: 'though handsome and possessing a most brilliant clear voice (bel metallo di voce) she was at that time so unformed, both as a singer and an actress, that she totally failed in her first opera'.[4] The work in question was *Astarto re di tiro*, a feeble pasticcio, described by one critic as 'an indifferent, unconnected, and unfinished production'.[5] It was dropped after only a few performances, even though the young singer was reported to have received 'every possible encouragement' on her first appearance.[6] Her demise in *Astarto* was followed by a holding operation – several performances of Rauzzini's *Piramo e*

Tisbe from the previous year's repertoire and a new comic opera, but, as is made quite clear in newspaper advertisements, the company was rehearsing for Traetta's *Germondo* with Rauzzini and Davies. First performed on 21 January, it marked the effective start of the *opera seria* season.[7]

The most straightforward interpretation of these events is that Brooke, acting with speed and a measure of ruthlessness, abandoned Pozzi as soon as her inexperience became apparent. A more sinister explanation would be that, having realised that a mistake had been made, she actively set out to sabotage her own singer. Of course she would not have done this without having a readily available replacement, but Davies was in London. In these circumstances, past rancour was put aside, and the English singer recruited as a replacement. The speed with which the adverse critical consensus was reached left no room for argument. On the night of the debut, George Bussy Villiers wrote: 'the new Woman does not strike me much'.[8] Only two days later, the damning verdict of the 'judges' was agreed:

Grosvenor Square 4 November 1776   George Bussy Villiers to
Lady Spencer

> You have no great loss in missing the operas at present; the first woman has I believe a fine Voice, & the Judges say in time she will make a great singer, but she does not know how to manage it to give it the least expression in the World, & her Figure is inconceivably awkward, tho' she is now learning to dance.[9]

An almost instantaneous verdict on the part of critical opinion was possible, because rehearsals were often opened to interested observers like the Burneys, and because singers were encouraged to introduce themselves at private soirées before the opening night. In the weeks before a major debut, speculation about the figure, personality and musicality of a new performer became intense. An exaggerated expectation of success could cause problems as Gabrielli discovered, but anticipation of failure was harder to cope with. Speculation about an imminent flop could be organised by a cabal of jealous rivals, or it could arise out of spiteful but aimless gossip, but obviously it could also stem from a genuinely inadequate performance at rehearsals. It would usually be in the interests of opera managers to combat adverse advance publicity, but on occasion, as perhaps was the case with Pozzi, it could be made to work to their advantage.

A letter from 'A Detester of Oppression' published on 16 January casts further light on the affair. The anonymous writer observes that the young Italian singer, 'over here at the persuasion of a master of music universally known and admired' (Burney), first appeared 'to great disadvantage' in 'a nonsensical patch'd up farrago, called a *Pasticcio*', in which she nonetheless received applause. In the new opera *Germondo*, she 'got up her part, and, after having gone through many rehearsals, was, by the composer himself, judged to be the only woman who could do justice to a character which was, by the celebrated Trajetta, composed entirely from his knowledge of her singing powers'. Despite the fact that the composer had written a leading role in his first London *opera seria* specifically for her, he was over-ruled by Brooke. The writer is exceedingly indignant at the singer's fate, describing her as 'a forlorn woman', debarred from displaying her abilities by 'the blind leaders of that playhouse'. All her hopes had been destroyed by 'those self-created umpires of the public taste'. What most irked Pozzi's defender was that the opera managers were imputing her disgrace to 'the public'.[10] The outcome was that Pozzi suffered the indignity of a demotion rather than an outright sacking, perhaps to forestall any legal action over her contract.

Certain aspects of this anonymous attack are consistent with its having come from the Garrick camp. The continuing hostility between the two rivals is very clear from the coldly formal manner in which Garrick addressed Brooke in a letter of 20 April 1776. Some time before, she had lent him a book that she herself had borrowed. Upon receiving her complaint about his failure to return it, Garrick had contacted the original owner, who seemed unconcerned. He now informed Brooke that his mind had been relieved of 'a most disagreeable concern', namely that 'it at once excuses you from the unpleasing task of writing Angry letters, & me from the mortification of receiving them'.[11] If the newspaper attack on the 'blind leaders' of the opera house was made on Garrick's behalf, then hypocrisy was the hidden charge. Brooke had accused Garrick of 'oppression', through his refusal to stage her works, and also, in effect, of setting himself up as a self-appointed 'umpire of public taste'. She in turn was destroying the hopes of this poor woman. Now retired, Garrick was able to attend opera performances himself, and he was present at Pozzi's debut. Little of the performance pleased him: 'I was allur'd last Saturday with the Gout upon me to the Opening of the Opera, where I cannot say, that I receiv'd any great pleasure from the Singers or the Dancers.'[12]

The retention of Rauzzini as *primo uomo* caused few obvious problems. During his three seasons at the King's Theatre, his reputation had grown steadily. As Burney pointed out, nothing so quickly attracted London audiences as 'a *great* and powerful' voice, which this singer did not possess, yet by 1775 his more muted merits were widely acknowledged.[13] Fanny Burney was pleased to find that he 'gains ground' with the public daily and that 'the more they hear, the more they like him'.[14] A discordant note was struck by one anonymous reviewer, according to whom Rauzzini seemed 'to grow fantastically vain of the public favour', to the extent that he was not 'sufficiently guarded and careful in some of his actions'.[15]

It is possible that this comment refers to a very obscure episode in the history of the King's Theatre at this period, the apparent cooling of the friendship between Rauzzini and Sacchini. Referring to the celebrated plagiarism controversy of 1782, Burney wrote that Rauzzini, once a 'fond friend' of Sacchini, had become 'his most implacable foe', to the extent that he was claiming authorship of many of Sacchini's songs.[16] Although there is very little evidence as to the origins of this bitter dispute, there are some indications that all was not well between the two musicians as early as the 1775–6 season. A few days after the première of Rauzzini's opera *L'ali d'amore*, the following strange letter was published in the London press:

Whereas last Thursday, at the new opera called 'Le ALI D'AMORE', a
man of a very shabby appearance, who sat in the first row of the upper
gallery, cried out several times, 'Bravo, Sacchini!' as applauding the
music, but in the mean time with a malicious intention of defrauding
Signor Rauzzini of the merit of it; I think myself obliged, in justice to
that enchanting singer, as well as ingenious composer, to declare in the
most solemn manner, that I had no hand in his successful opera, having
himself set every note of it, without the least assistance on my part. The
ill-looking fellow who mentioned my name, was evidently the emissary
of some envious moles, who cannot bear the splendour of Rauzzini's
fame; but their scheme is no less weak than wicked; for all such as have
any knowledge of musical compositions cannot be strangers to the high
reputation Rauzzini's productions have gained all over Italy. Were I the
author of the music of Le Ali d'Amore, I should be extremely proud of
making it public; since I really found in it such brilliant fanciful novelty,
such exquisite taste and true harmony as would reflect a never-failing
lustre on the most eminent composer. Which opinion I am confident,
no good musician will attempt to controvert. Nor will the public call in
question my impartiality, when thay shall know, that Lord Kelly commended the music of Rauzzini's new opera in the highest terms, and
exactly confirmed the judgement I passed upon it.

ANTONIO SACCHINI

Great Suffolk Street

5 March 1776[17]

During his years at the King's Theatre Sacchini outshone all other
composers, and Rauzzini in particular appeared completely outclassed. It is quite possible that the letter was not written by Sacchini
at all but concocted by a supporter of Rauzzini to combat the allegation that his music was nothing more than second-hand Sacchini.
Resentment over the relative failure of his operas perhaps contributed to the initial breach between the two men. It may be significant
that during the 1776–7 season, the last of the castrato's ascendancy, no
Sacchini opera was staged at the King's Theatre.

The repertoire presented during the 1776–7 season was not highly regarded. In part this was because Brooke's plan to recruit Paisiello had been thwarted, when on 16 June 1776 the composer received a better offer for a three-year contract in Russia. According to his auto-biography, he was only able to accept this, after excusing himself from a post that he had already accepted in London.[18] In his absence, the opera *La frascatana* scored a notable triumph with nineteen per-formances. His late withdrawal left Brooke urgently seeking a replacement. Several factors favoured Traetta, even though he was better known as a composer of *opera seria*. Through Ozias Humphry, Brooke would have known of Maria Cosway's reports on the favour-able reception accorded to one of his most recent operas. Gabrielli too would have been in a good position to advocate his merits, having given the premières of three of his operas in Russia, *Antigone* (1772), *Amore e Psyche* (1773) and *Lucio vero* (1774). Traetta's first opera for the King's Theatre was *Germondo*, given its première on 21 January 1777. Brooke seems to have obtained the libretto directly from Goldoni in Paris, for which she apparently paid the considerable sum of £95. Traetta achieved only modest success in London. *Germondo* was given only five performances, its music being described as 'very good, but . . . too much in one style'.[19] Worse was to follow. *Telemaco* led one critic to savage Traetta as 'the most tiresome, heavy and noisy composer, that ever shocked the ears of a British audience'. Another reviewer attempted to explain the work's lack of success by pointing out that the recitatives, airs and choruses were in 'an original, manly and expressive style' that seemed 'to astonish and frighten the audi-ence', who had become accustomed to 'the feeble strains of Rauzzini'.[20] Burney, while acknowledging Traetta as 'an able master of good reputation', felt that his reception had been diminished by the popularity of Sacchini with the London public.[21]

The lengthy review of the season which appeared in the first issue of Le Texier's *Journal Etranger* in June 1777 is a significant milestone in the history of operatic criticism in London, because it presents a sub-stantial critique of King's Theatre productions by someone whose sympathies lay clearly with the advocates of reform in *opera seria*.

When he arrived in London in 1775, Le Texier had a high reputation as a brilliant one-man reciter of plays. As a Frenchman with a life-long passion for theatre and opera, he would have known of the ideals of the opera reform movements.[22] He quickly became acquainted with Garrick and for a few years the relationship between the two seems to have been a warm one. The Frenchman addressed him in his letters as 'mon cher maître' or 'mon cher père' and Garrick responded with 'mon cher fils'.[23] Although little is known in detail of the dealings between the two men, their relationship is potentially of some significance. So close are some of Le Texier's views to those that Garrick is believed to have espoused, that the question arises as to whether the English actor played any direct part in their formulation, or at least in encouraging their promulgation. It is certainly possible that by lending tacit support to the publication of the piece, Garrick saw a way of renewing his attack on Brooke, albeit on aesthetic grounds. But even if he was not a direct party to it, he had good reason to welcome Le Texier's assault on the King's Theatre. The Frenchman's own motivation for setting himself up as an opera critic was perhaps to put himself in a position to be considered as manager when the King's Theatre next changed hands.

To place Le Texier's piece in its proper historical context, it will be necessary to review briefly the circumstances of Garrick's earlier attempt to promote reform at the King's Theatre. It is widely acknowledged that his advocacy of a natural acting style, coherence in the presentation of character, and stage management practices aimed at enhancing the dramatic illusion was a major influence on the development of opera on the Continent.[24] Yet in London, no more than a mile from his Drury Lane theatre, the Italian opera establishment remained uninterested in debating ideas about acting in opera, let alone in putting them into practice.[25] The little that is known for certain of the great actor's views on Italian opera suggests that he was markedly cool towards *opera seria* as a genre, and he certainly did not regard the acting abilities of its stars very highly. During his Italian tour he heard Gabrielli and, like so many, was at first impressed with her:

Naples 24 December 1763   David Garrick to George Colman

I was last Night at their great Theatre, which is a most Magnificent one indeed; I was really astonish'd at first coming into it – it was quite full, & well lighted up – but it is too great, & the Singers were Scarcely heard – the famous *Gabrielli* pleas'd me much; she has a good person, is yᵉ best Actress I ever saw on an Opera Stage, & has yᵉ most agreable voice I ever heard; she sings more to yᵉ ear, than to yᵉ heart.[26]

Even at this stage, he was foreshadowing the damaging criticism that was to be made a decade later in London, that her singing was unemotional. Only a few weeks later, however, his initial enthusiasm had cooled considerably:

Naples 5 February 1764   David Garrick to Charles Burney

I have heard the famous Gabrielli, who has indeed astonishing powers, great compass of voice and great flexibility, but she is always yᵉ same, and though you are highly transported at first with her, yet wanting that nice feeling of yᵉ passions (without which everything in yᵉ dramatic way will cease to entertain) she cannot give that variety and that peculiar Pleasure which alone can support the tediousness of an Opera – in short, the Musick, vocal and instrumental, has lost its nature, and it is all dancing on yᵉ slack rope, and tumbling through yᵉ hoop.[27]

The essence of Garrick's objection to Italian opera is neatly expressed in his last point: he considered that it had become a circus-like spectacle, rather than a drama in which human emotions are represented in a natural (and thus) compelling manner. It is interesting that Mozart, writing to his father on 19 February 1778, echoed closely Garrick's feeling that Gabrielli's performance did not really bear repeated hearings. Having reported the rather contemptuous view that she was a mere 'Rouladen-macherin', he observed that any initially favourable impression would not last longer than the fourth time she sang. Her defects included a lack of *messa di voce* and an inability to sustain; overall, she sang with skill ('kunst') but no understanding ('verstand'), or, as Garrick put it, to gratify the 'ear' rather than the 'heart'.[28] However, as is very clear from the account of her reception in London, many in the King's Theatre audience were precisely more interested in the former than the latter quality.

The generally hostile attitude of the opera-going public in London to the kinds of reforms advocated by Garrick was demonstrated only too clearly by reactions to Guadagni in 1770. Burney wrote that when the singer first came to England 'his ideas on acting were taken . . . from Garrick, who . . . took . . . much pleasure in forming him as an actor'.[29] By the time that he returned to the King's Theatre as *primo uomo* in the 1769–70 season, he had become a powerful stage presence: 'his figure was uncommonly elegant and noble; his countenance replete with beauty, intelligence and dignity; and his attitudes and gestures were so full of grace and propriety, that they would have been excellent studies for a statuary'. In the title role of *Orfeo*, his 'impassioned and exquisite manner of singing' the celebrated air 'Che farò' acquired him 'very great and just applause'.[30] A member of the audience reported:

> Went in the Evening to the Opera of Orfeo – the King & Q. there –
> House remarkably crowded – Opera very pleasing – So far French, as to
> admit into it Dancing & chorus – the rest, pure Italian – Grassi shone &
> Guadagni – 'twas over by Nine. The Scenery of Hell magnificent – So
> also that of the Temple of Love – I have never seen there such a
> Spectacle. The Dancing excellent.[31]

Notwithstanding his initial triumph, Guadagni soon began to antagonise the audience, and it is very significant that what most annoyed them was his attempt to put into practice values that he had surely learned from Garrick. He appeared determined to preserve 'the dignity and propriety of his dramatic character, by not bowing acknowledgement, when applauded', and he refused to destroy the 'theatrical illusion' by returning to repeat an air, 'if encored at the termination of an interesting scene'. The King's Theatre audiences, however, continued to interrupt his performances with applause and calls for immediate encores. An attempt to resolve the crisis made matters worse. The famous castrato decided to address the audience in the hope of persuading them to amend their behaviour.

Remarkably, it seems that Hobart, the then manager of the King's Theatre, joined in the hissing that this action provoked. During the court case the following year over the unlicensed opera sponsored by Mrs Cornelys, Hobart admitted as much:

> Mr Kennyon [Kenyon] then asked if Guadagni was not insulted during the course of last season, and whether Mr Hobart did not more than once join in hissing him; Mr Hobart replied, that one night when Guadagni made an insolent speech to the audience, he (being in the gallery) joined with the whole house in hissing him, because he had hired him to sing and not to speak, but to the best of his knowledge he had hissed him at no other time during the season.[32]

The result was a fiasco with the audience so offended that Guadagni was thereafter regularly hissed. Burney later recorded Guadagni's complaint of 'illiberal treatment from the public, who, when he sung in the opera of Orfeo . . . hissed him for going off the stage, when he was encored, with no other design than *to return in character*'.[33] This unfortunate episode demonstrated an uncomfortable truth for would-be opera reformers in London: that King's Theatre patrons accepted and even welcomed practices which were intrusive and damaging to the coherence of the drama.

Garrick was widely believed to have approved of Rauzzini's acting performances, yet the mere fact that this piece of gossip was circulating might lead to the conclusion that this was an unexpected exception to his general view that the standard of acting among opera stars was low. When Le Texier launched his scathing attack on acting standards at the King's Theatre in 1777, it surely had Garrick's full approval.

Le Texier's first essay on the 1776–7 season marks a radical departure from the hitherto undistinguished tradition of Italian opera criticism in London. Reviews of King's Theatre productions published during the 1770s are on the whole uninformative. Rapturous puffs in which everything is 'exquisite' or 'admirable' and savage hatchet-jobs in which everything is 'tedious', 'mediocre', 'trite' or 'tiresome' are exactly alike in one respect: the reader is given only the vaguest idea of the grounds upon which the judgements are reached. The focus is largely upon matters of reception: how large and brilliant the audience was; which singers went down best; which arias were encored. The librettist (Bottarelli) is often attacked for the inadequacy of his work, and there are occasional complaints about the management of the house, and comments on the activities of cabals. Against this background, Le Texier at least comes across as someone with a well thought-out point of view; he sees *opera seria* as a potentially dramatic art-form, which has been rendered extraordinarily monotonous and undramatic, by formal elements in it (such as the *da capo* aria), by acting styles (such as the over-use of gesture) and by performance practices (such as the prevalence of intrusive applause). (The full text of his essay is given in Appendix 3a.) His critique begins by listing the operas that have been performed during the past season, and he notes that comic opera has been more in vogue than serious. He is severely critical of ballet in London and attributes its low state to the audience, which by comparison with that in other countries he deems too indulgent. Everything is forgiven, and there is thus no incentive to improve. Le Texier recommends that ballets be related in their subject matter to the plots of the accompanying opera, a small step in which direction had occurred in Traetta's *Telemaco*.[34] A visitor to the opera on 15 March also reported that 'for the first time on the English stage', there had been 'singing and dancing at once, after the manner of the French opera at Paris'.[35] This shows that Parisian-style ballet in opera was still on Brooke's agenda, but that since *Il Cid* in 1773 little progress had been made in establishing the idea firmly. Arguing in favour of dancing in opera, the Frenchman strikes a patronising tone, perhaps the characteristic which most annoyed those with whom he had dealings. The opera directors, he loftily pronounces, are doing their best, but their motivation is their personal interest, as much as their desire to please the public. This last point, implying some kind of private agenda, would appear to be directed against Brooke, and it could have been made on Garrick's behalf.

The high cost of Italian opera is noted. Principal singers, who already command large salaries in their own country, ask for still more to come to England, a country widely known to be expensive for foreigners, and where there are perceived to be risks to health and the singing voice from the climate. Le Texier takes up the idea of an academy, proposed by Burney as recently as the summer of 1774.[36] In time, he argues, such an institution will enable the London opera house to do without foreigners, especially since Davies and Prudom have already shown that English singers can successfully replace Italians.[37] Le Texier of course admits the continuing necessity of importing castrati in the absence of a local 'manufacture', but by restricting overseas recruitments to one or two male sopranos, it ought to be possible to save a great deal of money, and the directors would thus be less constrained in what they could offer. Le Texier claims to be sympathetic about the costs involved in production, but he then proceeds to accuse the managers of negligence in details of productions, instancing the use of a dozen 'street urchins' as nymphs. The sub-text of this passage about the high cost of opera is as follows. Brooke was arguing that the King's Theatre should be allowed to stage plays, because, as an opera house alone, it was uneconomic. Le Texier, on Garrick's behalf, was pointing out that opera need not be quite as expensive as it was.

The most successful opera in the recently ended season was Paisiello's *La frascatana*. By staging a work written as recently as 1774, London was finally demonstrating enthusiasm for a truly contemporary *buffa* repertoire. Le Texier writes with enthusiasm about the ensembles which end Acts I and II. It would be greatly preferable if this type of writing gained more general currency over arias, which are so often 'monotonous, out-of-place and unnatural'. Paisiello's finales in this opera consist of 'a series of scenes which follow each other', and which are well adapted to the dramatic situation. Le Texier is lyrical in his praise of them:

> there are none of these sad *da capo*s, no fastidious repetitions, everything progresses, everything moves forward, the plot, the acting, the music, everything comes together, the interest builds, the action is sustained, it develops, and it focuses the attention of the spectator, who is equally occupied with what he sees and with what he hears, on the

general uniting of all the different sentiments, which, expressed in forceful, energetic and elegant choruses, allow one to experience simultane-
ously the charm of felicitous harmony in the beauty of their music and
the pleasure of the interest in the variety of the action.

This is of course a description of the extended multi-partite *opera
buffa* finale. Le Texier exaggerates somewhat when he describes this
kind of writing as 'absolutely new'.[38] He is far from rejecting the aria
in its rightful place and acknowledges the pleasure to be experienced
in listening to 'great agility' in the performance of difficult passages
or 'cadenzas powerfully and accurately done'. Yet so often the all-
important quality of naturalness is 'outrageously violated by impro-
prieties'.

Le Texier next considers the individual performances of the
leading singers. He is at pains to stress that any critical remarks he
might be about to make are for the good of the opera house and the
greater success of its singers, a sign perhaps that the idea of taking
over the management of the King's Theatre had already occurred to
him, but a sign also that he was seriously deficient in the diplomatic
skills necessary for successful opera management. At around the
time of his downfall in 1780, Burney noted that the Frenchman was
'little minded by the performers, with whom he had quarrelled, &
who all hated him cordially'.[39] Heedless of the extent to which he
would inevitably annoy the opera establishment, he goes down the
list of singers. There is praise, but periodically he wields the knife
with elegance.

Rauzzini has 'a high degree of talent', 'an attractive voice', 'a taste-
ful manner of singing' and 'a charming manner'. He is also good at
declamation, but he should try to rid himself of the national (Italian)
habit of making 'misplaced gestures which express nothing and are
wearisome for the audience'. This unnatural acting style is one of Le
Texier's pet hates and in his view is one of the chief reasons why *opera
seria* is so monotonous and insipid. Actors in Italian comic opera are
generally 'exaggerated' and 'grotesque' in their manner of performance, but Trebbi has this defect less than most, even though he too
over-uses gestures. He has 'a very attractive voice'. Although very

much better suited to comic opera, he has taken serious roles, for which the public should be grateful to him. Savoi has the purest of voices, and when he takes the trouble to sing well, it gives so much pleasure that he should be invited to do so more often! Fochetti and Micheli come across as wishing to please, a characteristic that allows performers of less than impressive talent to succeed. Fochetti plays jealous roles well, while Micheli would be well advised to stick to 'rôles bouffons', for which he has an excellent 'countenance'. He has humour in his acting as well, which would be agreeably natural if he did not overplay his characters. Davies has shown that in borrowing from the Italian manner of singing, it is possible to give great pleasure 'without capturing completely the national idiom'. Sestini has elegance, humour and an attractive figure, but again she has a tendency to use gesture excessively. She sings with facility but could perhaps control her voice better in the upper register. The young Prudom has had a successful debut but has since fallen back a little. She has everything necessary to succeed but needs to work. In her case, Le Texier seems genuinely worried that he will appear too severe on a young singer. His speaking the truth about 'an attractive and interesting young lady' gives the clearest proof, he claims, of his impartiality. The younger of the two Farnese sisters, with good advice, could become an actress; the elder has only taken minor roles so far. Of the dancers, Le Texier approves of Vallovy and regrets the absence of his wife through 'illness', in fact pregnancy.[40] Baccelli is improving quickly and will soon become one of the foremost dancers of her age.

Having evaluated the individual performers, Le Texier expounds his main theme, which is the way in which the inherent drama of opera is so often ruined by lax acting practices. As a prime example, he cites the failure of opera singers even to learn their parts properly. Constant interruptions from the discordant voice of a prompter reciting loudly and word-for-word the text of the libretto are insufferable. With a little more care, singers would need to have recourse to his services only on occasion. In any event, the prompter should learn to pitch his voice so that only the singers can hear.

Another problem is the practice of making 'deep bows' to acknowledge every burst of applause. Could there be anything more ridicu-
lous, he asks, than to ruin the dramatic coherence of character in this
way? Even arias are liable to be interrupted by spontaneous clapping
when particular passages are felt to have received a meritorious performance. Le Texier is unable to conceal his amazement at the practice. The blame, he concedes, should not be put only on the singers,
who are strongly encouraged to believe that this behaviour pleases
the audience. Whenever a star leaves the stage, someone invariably
claps. Le Texier suggests a method of forestalling intrusive applause,
citing the case of a hypothetical singer, readily identifiable as
Guadagni, much beloved of the public, who has not been seen for
some time and to whom the audience wishes to express great appreciation. Ought it not be possible, he argues, for the singer, before
commencing his part, 'to strip himself of the character which he is
charged with representing' and for a moment to 'become himself', in
order to acknowledge as respectfully as possible the applause, taking
the opportunity to indicate that 'from the moment that his role
begins', he will not be able to suspend its execution 'without the
complete destruction of any kind of dramatic credibility'?

In supporting Guadagni's attempt to put into practice Garrick's
advice on sustaining the dramatic illusion of a piece, Le Texier was
aligning himself with the advocates of opera reform, but, as he seems
to have realised, the chief obstacle to change, especially in matters of
performance convention, was the entrenched conservatism of the
London audience. In his view, the alliance between an indulgent
audience and its pampered favourites had become thoroughly
unhealthy, and by today's standards he was probably right. But any
would-be opera reformer in London had to contend with the powerful appeal of a very different kind of drama, of which Gabrielli's
debut had been the outstanding recent example. The aristocratic
patrons who flocked to the opening night of *Didone* were far less
interested in the drama of the plot, than in the intensely personal,
human drama of the celebrated singer's first appearance. This was
opera as pure spectacle: intense prior interest; a packed house; the

streets outside thronged with disappointed would-be spectators; booing; cheering; a regal entry; ogling of the star's person and dress; vocal gymnastics; bursts of applause, even in the middle of pieces. Garrick's view, reiterated powerfully by Le Texier, was that there was no hope of sustaining plot-related drama in this circus-like atmosphere. Without credible expression of human emotion or development of character, opera for Garrick quickly became tedious, and not even the vocal quality of a Gabrielli could disguise this dramatic poverty for long.

With so intense a focus on the vocal qualities of the star singers among London critics and audiences alike, there was very little incentive for individual performers to seek to improve their acting skills. Le Texier's strictures on this subject, notwithstanding the acknowledged eminence of the great actor whose views he was advocating, seem to have fallen on stony ground. A good acting performance on the London opera stage remained very much the exception rather than the rule. It is interesting to compare the reception of Gabrielli's interpretation of the part of Dido with that of Mara, the next great singer to perform the role at the King's Theatre. Undoubtedly at Mara's request, the 1786 pasticcio version incorporated Sacchini's setting of 'Son regina'. One member of the audience wrote:

> She . . . is in all respects a far better tragedy Queen than I had expected.
> For she really plays as well as sings. But I had imagin'd that she w'd
> merely walk on, sing her song, and then walk off without ever stretching
> out an arm or kicking up a heel. On the contrary, she was a very Didoish
> sort of body.[41]

This opera-goer's manifest sense of surprise that the star singer should have taken the trouble to develop a dramatic interpretation of her character, rather than rely on a vocal interpretation alone, is very telling. From Le Texier's oft-repeated criticism that opera singers employed routine gestures too frequently and sometimes (even in *opera buffa*) in too exaggerated a fashion, it is possible to surmise that many performers were aware that some attempt at an interpretation of character was required of them, but, in the absence of a powerful figure like the modern producer, had to rely on a limited range of stereotyped actions.

To conclude his essay, Le Texier makes a few remarks about technical matters and the orchestra. Colomba (who was both painter and machinist) is praised for his novel method of imitating lightning in the storm scene of Traetta's *Telemaco*. The orchestra consists of good-quality performers led by a violinist of distinction (Giardini), but it lacks, he pointedly remarks, 'the ensemble so necessary for good performance'. In particular the wind instruments often err through 'inaccuracy', which is especially indefensible in aria accompaniments. When he became manager himself, Le Texier, with a characteristic lack of realism, tried to sack the entire orchestra. The leader Cramer, humouring him, agreed that the wind players were, except for the oboist, 'insufferable'.[42] There are some brief comments on Traetta's new opera, and the review ends with a note that an opera by Bach has been announced, the revival of *Orione* scheduled for May 1777.

For the 1777–8 season which was to be her last, Brooke recruited two singers from Mannheim, Francesca Danzi (soon to be Madame Le Brun) and Francesco Roncaglia. Again, Burney may have been influential in the choice. When he visited Mannheim in 1772, he singled out Roncaglia as one of the vocal performers of the band who 'deserve to be distinguished'.[1] Roncaglia had the added advantage of being known to Bach, having sung in *Temistocle* (November 1772) and *Lucio Silla* (November 1774).[2] Danzi was described by Burney as a singer of unusual promise: 'Signora Francesca Danzi a German girl, whose voice and execution are brilliant: she has likewise a pretty figure, a good shake, and an expression as truly Italian as if she had lived her whole life in Italy; in short, she is now a very engaging and agreeable performer, and promises still greater things.'[3] Her recruitment, as usual with Brooke, was made at least a year in advance. When the Reverend Coxe wrote to Lady Pembroke on 3 February 1777, she had already been hired.[4]

The choice of comic repertoire to supplement the major new *opera seria* productions by Sacchini and Bach shows the results of Brooke's previous correspondence with Ozias Humphry. Scores of two works given their première in Rome in 1776, Paisiello's *Le due contesse* and Anfossi's *La vera costanza*, were now available in London. Humphry was still acting as a conduit for opera repertoire between Italy and London, as shown in the following letter:

Rome 13 December 1777   Thomas Banks to Ozias Humphry

The Musick you wrote about is already prepar'd & I believe waits for an opportunity of being sent. I wrote to Miss Hadfield [Maria Cosway] about it immediately on the receipt of yours. She has lately answer'd me by desiring to know how it was to be sent and I have beg'd the favor of her either to forward it immediately to London by some Gentleman who is going or otherways to send it me, and I would find an Opportunity. Our composers and performers for the ensuing Carneval are already arriv'd [and] we are to have serious Operas at the Aliberti. Anfossi [is] Composer for the Argentina & Valle & if anything turns out Curious & extraordinary I will get it and send it you not going upon my own judgement but that of the generality of people . . .

Miss Hadfield out of all the Opera airs perform'd in Rome last season thinks nothing worth sending for Mrs Sheridan but Amante sventurata; she has prepar'd that & something new at Florence which is now Performing. If I can get some of the Best Serious Airs as soon as the Carneval of 1778 is finish'd I will & they will be agreable present for any Musical Lady.[5]

In addition to commissions for the King's Theatre, there was a steady flow of requests from singers in England for the latest opera airs.

Le Texier's *Journal Etranger* resumed its coverage of Italian opera in London shortly before the start of the 1777–8 season. (The full text is given in Appendix 3b.) In his first essay, Le Texier had set forth a critical overview of the general state of Italian opera in London. The coverage of the new season is in the form of a series of appraisals of new productions, singers and dancers, yet there are many points of more general interest. Le Texier was by this time a well-informed observer of the King's Theatre, but he could hardly pass himself off as an objective commentator. Evidently an emotional man, he allowed his personal circumstances to influence the tone of his reviews. In November 1777, when there was the prospect that he would be invited by Gallini to join his new managerial team, he wrote in a warmly optimistic vein of the prospects for the coming season. Once it became clear that Gallini had been outbid by Sheridan and Harris, Le Texier, having now every reason to assume that his ambitions had been thwarted, reverted to the critical tone of his first essay. Had his journal continued until the end of the season, he would presumably have again ameliorated his stance, once he had been appointed opera manager by the new owners. Only once does he let slip (what must have been well known to his aristocratic readership) that he had personal interests which might be deemed to be affecting his objectivity.

In his first piece for the new season, Le Texier praises the two works he has just heard in rehearsal, Sacchini's *Il creso* and Paisiello's *Le due contesse*. Pointing out that he has not yet seen a full dress rehearsal of either and so is not yet in a position to evaluate the acting abilities of the cast, he discusses the topic of greatest interest to his readership – the new singers. Danzi has a voice of extraordinary range and accuracy and a good figure. She seems somewhat timid, a fault that Le Texier imagines will be quickly corrected when she receives applause in the theatre. Roncaglia, the new *primo uomo*, has put an end to any regrets there might have been over the dismissal of his predecessor. His voice is pleasant, he has good taste and he does not make grimaces. He is slender in stature but has a noble countenance. It has yet to be seen whether his acting will surpass that of Rauzzini, who is rated as one of the 'least bad' actors in the genre. Even in this, one of his more anodyne reviews, Le Texier's contempt for the general level of acting ability of *opera seria* singers remains barely concealed. The Frenchman, clearly taking his cue from Garrick, thought that Rauzzini had some 'charm'.

Le Texier reports uncertainty over the casting of the tenor role. At the time of writing (October 1777), it had yet to be decided whether Trebbi, a good comic, would continue to appear in *seria* roles, ill-suited to his temperament. Adamberger, the new tenor not yet arrived, he understands to be a very good musician and an able singer, but he is small in stature and Le Texier believes his voice to be 'nasal' and 'disagreeable'.[6] The hope is expressed that these imperfections will be less evident in the context of a full theatrical performance. Turning to comic opera, Le Texier praises Giardini's work in arranging Paisiello's *Le due contesse*. There are in fact only two or three added airs, but their selection does him great credit. Todi, *prima buffa*, has not yet rehearsed in costume and so Le Texier is unable to comment on her acting ability. Trebbi, from several gestures that he has observed at a rehearsal, is still rated highly. Rossi, the bass, even from a brief glimpse passing him in the street, seems a natural comic.

Le Texier concludes that an excellent season is in prospect, with singers of quality and good composers. With the prospect of his own possible involvement in mind, his earlier criticism of the orchestra now gives way to conventional praise: under the direction of Cramer, it leaves nothing to be desired. Finally, the money which the directors have just spent 'in repainting the entire auditorium' is clear proof of their desire to please the public.[7] Despite his personal motivation for taking so optimistic a view, Le Texier had not got it wrong. The King's Theatre was about to launch one of its most successful seasons of the late eighteenth century, and his preview captures something of the sense of excitement prior to the opening night.

In his next issue, Le Texier rounds out his picture of the leading singers. The charm of Roncaglia's voice and manner of singing continue to please. Danzi is now recognised as a performer of unusual ability. Le Texier expresses himself well satisfied at the news that she has already been engaged at the Milan opera house for the 1778–9 season. A few years in 'charming' Italy, 'the mother country of all that is called music', may be all that is needed to turn her into the most astounding vocalist he has ever heard. Le Texier even discerns potential in her acting. The Frenchman's views on Danzi and Roncaglia are very much in accord with their early public reception:

23 November 1777   Mr Harris to his son

Last night I was at the Opera, composed by Sacchini; it is admirable. Your ladies may like to hear about the voices. The woman Danzi is a good actress and singer particularly in the Bravura style, where she mounts into the clouds and always descends in safety. Roncaglia, the man, has not a strong voice, but is one of the most elegant cantabile singers I ever heard.[8]

Only later did attitudes to both singers cool considerably.

A major factor in Danzi's reception in London was her ability to sing in the highest register. Le Texier professes himself astonished at the accuracy and cleanness with which she could sing the five tones above the normal compass of the soprano voice, and he compares her voice favourably with the 'small, piercing tones' of Agujari at a similar altitude.[9] With such an intense critical focus on the voice, it is hardly surprising that there should have been especial interest in singers who could perform in the highest registers. Burney compared De Amicis, Agujari and Danzi in this respect, but he disapproved of composers who insisted on writing what were known as 'cork-cutting notes', citing the case of a singer who had burst a blood vessel and died, after a Neapolitan composer had 'injudiciously and cruelly' written such a passage for him.[10] This advice was ignored, as the London audience was eagerly anticipating Danzi's high g′′′. Sacchini duly obliged in *Creso*, the opera in which she made her debut on 8 November. The aria 'Quest'alma sventurata' was carefully written to display her voice. Sacchini writes scales, arpeggios, and the little dactyl figure used by Mozart in the 'Queen of the Night' (see example 6). At first, the voice is prudently supported, but later the composer removes the instrumental doubling down an octave, leaving Danzi alone on her highest note. Contemporary witnesses were in agreement that she both ascended and descended in safety.

Even in such an obvious display aria, Sacchini remained alert to the need to depict darker emotions with suitably chromatic harmony. In a contrasted passage setting the word 'palpitar', he modulates to the subdominant minor and uses a characteristic series of dominant minor ninths and diminished sevenths, with rich string orchestration (see example 7). Twining thought such passages the mark of a very fine composer:

19 December 1778   Thomas Twining to Charles Burney

The *only* opera composer who, of late years, has given me any *high* degree of pleasure, is Sacchini. Others hit off a good song now & then. In Sacchini there is *almost always*, something to keep you awake; in inferior parts, when he lets your feelings rest, he amuses your ears with uncommon effects, & passages of unhackneyed harmony, & melody.[11]

At some point, either Danzi or Sacchini had second thoughts about her highest note. In his next opera *Erefile*, Sacchini restricts Danzi to a high f′′′.[12]

Turning to the subject of ballet, Le Texier begins by noting the

Ex. 6 Sacchini, *Il creso* (London, 1777): excerpt from the aria 'Quest'alma sventurata'

Ex. 6 (cont.)

Ex. 7 Sacchini, *Il creso* (London, 1777): excerpt from the aria 'Quest'alma sventurata'

qualities of the leading dancers. There is a characteristic put-down of Banti: she has brilliance and humour in her dance, but 'she would be well advised not to keep her mouth open . . . in so affected a manner, since, although she has the prettiest teeth in the world, it would be more pleasing to see them periodically, rather than the whole time that she is dancing'. His comments on the opening ballets of the season are of real interest. Ballet in London was on the verge of far-reaching change with the arrival of Noverre and the *ballet d'action*. Le Texier's main objection to ballet as it was still being presented at the King's Theatre in late 1777 was that it was mere spectacle, lacking meaning in the context of the accompanying opera. There were two possible responses: to give each ballet its own story-line in the manner of a *ballet d'action*; or to integrate ballet into opera. When he took over as manager, Le Texier promoted the latter option, but in this review he seems to be favouring the alternative. The opening 'serious' ballet fully deserves its title, yet though full of pirouettes and entrechats, it is 'without plan or design and thus without interest'. Such a ballet is merely a showpiece for the talents of the principal dancers. This passage in the review amounts to a clear plea for ballet with plot in the manner developed so successfully by Noverre. Le Texier fears that the second ballet of the season, Simonet's adaptation of Rousseau's widely admired *Le devin du village*, will fail, notwithstanding the fact that it has a plot, because the English audience will not be able to understand it. He admits that the selection of 'charming' airs is effective for those that already know the original opera; 'we French', he writes, 'are enchanted to hear the airs of an opera that we have so long loved, and which we know by heart; we can recall the plot; indeed we sing the words as soon as we hear the ritornellos'. Yet he has doubts as to whether the London audience, not knowing the original opera, will be able to understand the ballet. Simonet ought therefore to have paid more attention to the taste of his English audience. This was a piece of sheer hypocrisy, as Le Texier himself was fiercely critical of that taste.

Subsequent reviews by Le Texier contain notices of *Vittorina*. This work was Piccinni's only commission for the King's Theatre and it should have been a première of distinction. In his brief preview, he merely notes that there are charming numbers in the score which recall the composer of *La buona figliuola*. When it opened, however, the opera flopped completely, receiving only two performances. The recent suggestion that it failed because it fell outside the expected conventions of its genre is fully supported by Le Texier.[13] In trying to account for the lack of interest in this 'so-called comic' opera, he argues that, far from being an *opera buffa*, *Vittorina* is a sentimental work, and indeed almost 'du genre larmoyant'. Its plot seems also to have been deemed unsatisfying and its music not well adapted. The general verdict on the work was that it was 'sad', with some severer critics adjudging it 'tedious'. Its instant failure demonstrated once again the risks involved in challenging the conservative tastes of the aristocratic London audience.

By the time that the first March issue of *Journal Etranger* was published, Le Texier knew that Gallini's bid for the King's Theatre had failed. He continues to give credit where it is due, but this review gives the impression that its author was stemming with difficulty a torrent of abuse. Sacchini is praised for his new opera *Erefile*. As usual, Le Texier approves of the choruses, especially those of the prisoners, performed from 'the bottom of a subterranean prison with glimmering light'. Having by now had plenty of time to assimilate Sacchini's use of the chorus in his operas, critical opinion was mixed. There was no reason to doubt their popularity as music. In 1780 Lady Clarges, writing to Susan Burney, wished she could pass a month with her: 'we w^d sing Sacchini's choruses all day long'.[14] The reviewer in the *Public Advertiser* on 9 February 1778 thought the chorus 'O tu che siede in cielo' equal to the most famous ones of Handel, being composed in 'a very learned masterly stile', and observed that it was received 'with the warmest applause'.[15] Others concurred with Burney that the stylistic mixture of opera and oratorio did not mix: 'too great a part of it is taken up with the chorusses, which tho' confessedly fine, from their numbers, give the piece more an *oratorical*, than an *operatical* complexion'.[16] For Le Texier, the issue was the manner in which this potentially powerful theatrical moment had been ruined, because the chorus was 'stripped of any sense of authenticity', having been performed detestably by five or six miserable children, who sang out of tune and offended against decency by pushing forward, laughing and generally acting like street urchins in the most disgusting manner. 'Let us not', he continues, 'go into detail', because there would be too much to say and 'in our circumstances we might be suspected of bias'. This is his sole admission of personal interest, and, seemingly not wishing to pursue the point, he moves swiftly on to the singers. Danzi has fulfilled all his expectations and after a few years in Italy will be '*la prima donna* de l'Europe entière'. Her performance in the celebrated oboe aria in *Erefile* is astonishing. Le Texier, however, expresses disquiet over the reception accorded to her husband, the oboe player, in London. Roncaglia has sung with his usual perfection. Because of his youth, he has yet to acquire an impressive theatrical manner. At this point, Le Texier seems unable to contain himself any longer, and he launches into a diatribe, which is clearly aimed beyond Roncaglia as an individual. All his frustration with *opera seria* pours out:

> there is hardly any preoccupation with the attraction of the [acting] performance; visual delight is so cruelly neglected in favour of aural pleasure, and that which could move the heart or beguile the spirit is so little esteemed, that it seems to be enough for a performer to sing well in cantabile passages, to be brilliant and astonishing in bravura passages, to perform with dexterity a pretty turn of phrase and to get through a cadenza satisfactorily . . . what blindness! what barbarity!

Other critics agreed that Roncaglia was a singer of moderate accomplishment only. Burney described his voice as a mere 'voce di camera', and thought his performances lacked pathos and execution.[17] Mount-Edgcumbe was severer still: 'his figure was good, and he was far from ill-looking: his voice sweet, and his style easy and *grazioso*: but he was languid, feeble and insipid, and withal extremely affected'.[18] Le Texier is equally scathing about Pozzi's performance in Anfossi's comic opera, *La vera costanza*, the finale to the second act of which is hailed as a masterpiece. The failed *prima donna* has an attractive voice; 'if only she would open her mouth a little more when singing and apply herself to achieving a better pronunciation, a greater variety of ornamentation, and a more pleasing way of ending musical phrases, and [realise] the necessity of some variety in her gestures which are slavishly and unhappily always the same, then she might become interesting'. Rossi, however, is a good *basso caricato*, if somewhat exaggerated. Signora Jermoli alone receives unreserved praise.

In his next review, Le Texier notes that Gasman's comic opera *L'amore artigiano* has not gone down well, which he attributes to the numerous and substantial changes made to the successful Italian version. For once this was no exaggeration. Amazingly, one of the 'changes' was an attempt by Brooke to invert the order of the two acts, a decision that was greeted with derision in the press. A correspondent, writing in the *Morning Post* on 11 March, observed with heavy irony: 'Neither is it very material to the sense, or dramatic conduct of the piece to observe, that the second act began on the drawing up of the curtain, and was succeeded by the first; as neither of them suffered any thing from this preposterous inversion of all order.' Most of the audience, he claimed, merely thought that the opera had been changed, and 'the few who were in the secret were tolerably indifferent to the order in which the acts were given them'. Brooke coolly replied: 'The transpositions were made the first night, at the request of a principal performer, in order to place that beautiful piece of music, the serenade, in a stronger point of view; but the Managers, thinking the transposition hurtful to the whole, have restored it to its original form.' The correspondent retorted: 'What can be said more *severely* of a dramatic composition, than that, after trying sometimes the second act first, and sometimes the first, it is still *sub judice*, which way it acts best?' That such a change could have been contemplated for a moment speaks volumes for the cavalier attitude towards the libretto that prevailed at the King's Theatre, even under Brooke. As the original complainant put it: 'If the music and dances are tolerable, the reception is secured. Character, dialogue, and sentiment are quite out of the question.'[19] These were the prevailing attitudes that would-be reformers like Le Texier had to confront.

A long review of a new ballet ensues, during the course of which Le Texier completely loses control. Highly critical of the manner in which a so-called 'Strasbourg' allemande had been danced, he launches into a paean of praise for his native region of Alsace. Strasbourg is a hot-bed of musical and Terpsichorean talent. The workmen in the streets are skilled part singers. It is written into the contracts of house servants that they be excused two or three times a week to go dancing. Strasbourgers come into the world dancing, so to speak, as their mothers slip out of balls to give birth. In short, readers of Le Texier's periodical were left in no doubt that the attempt to capture something of Alsatian style and character by Banti and his wife had been a total failure. The Italian opera establishment (including the Parisian dancers) doubtless regarded such outbursts, whether or not intended as ironical, with derision and anger. A second ballet receives a more favourable notice, and there is praise for Noferi, the guitar player employed to accompany the dances, and for Simonet, who is felt to have mounted a successful season of dance with limited means.

Le Texier's aesthetic views remained consistent throughout the year of his periodical. Rarely does he criticise a composer, and he gives full due to singers (like Danzi) of real accomplishment. The full weight of his scorn is reserved for poor acting and indifferent production. The reliance on stock gestures, unthinkingly repeated in every situation, and the inability to suit facial expression to the dramatic context were what he most deplored in singers. These faults, when added to production gaffes and inauthentic costumes, resulted in what the Frenchman saw as the complete destruction of dramatic credibility. In *opera seria*, he often identified choruses as the most successful dramatic elements of productions. In *opera buffa* there was a larger element of successful drama, notably in the fast-moving action finales. Le Texier evidently felt the time was right for radical reform, but the real weakness of his position was that so few opera patrons appeared to agree with him. His year of opera reviewing doubtless played some part in Sheridan's decision to hire him as manager for the 1778–9 season, but he had seriously antagonised the Italian opera establishment, and he found little support for fundamental change in an organisation that was reaching new heights of popularity.

The season which drew such a mixed response from Le Texier has been described as 'one of the most successful artistically in the later history of the King's Theatre'.[20] Above all, it was the première of Bach's *La clemenza di Scipione* which brought the Brooke–Yates years to such a distinguished conclusion:

> On Saturday last the new opera of *La Clemenza di Scipione*, composed by Mr Bach, was performed for the second time, with the greatest applause, to a crowded and brilliant audience. We congratulate the present managers on finishing their reign with such a *chef d'oeuvre* as this admirable opera; and we most earnestly recommend it to their successors, never to let a winter pass without employing this great master in composing at least one opera; this being, in the painter's stile, 'the best time of the master'.[21]

It was good advice, but *La clemenza di Scipione* was to be Bach's last work for the London opera house. Le Texier has regrettably little to say about it, merely praising the aria in Act II, sung by Danzi to the obbligato accompaniment of Le Brun (oboe), Cramer (violin), Cervetto (cello) and Florio (flute). Perhaps by now he knew that he was to be appointed by Sheridan as manager for the next season and felt it prudent to cease giving hostages to fortune.

Even before the start of the final season at the King's Theatre, the Brooke–Yates management team was considering a return to the theatrical world. Early in 1777 Richard Yates applied for a licence to open a theatre in Birmingham, and a bill to this effect was presented in the House of Commons on 26 March. It was scheduled for discussion on 22 April. Garrick, who had been lobbying for Yates, wrote to Edmund Burke to thank him for his support.[1] Burke had been sympathetic at first 'despite a very powerful recommendation' from some of his constituents, and he sided with Yates, but, in the face of direct pressure from a group of his supporters with Birmingham connections, he was pressured into adopting a more neutral stance. He nevertheless reassured Garrick about the outcome: 'But I believe, as far as I can see, that Yates is in no great danger. The House seems to be with him; & assuredly I do not mean to be a very mischievous Enemy to him.' Garrick replied: 'Ten thousand thanks my dear Burke for Your very kind letter – God forbid that all ye Patents in the World should injure Your Interest, where you are so much in Duty and kindness [bound].'[2] After the debate, however, the bill was defeated.[3]

Shortly after the failure of the bid to open a theatre in Birmingham, Brooke finally published *The Excursion*, bringing to a very public and bitter head her long-standing quarrel with Garrick, who is satirised with some venom. What makes the attack particularly personal is a lampoon of the actor's speech patterns. Well known for the clarity of his diction on stage, Garrick had received some criticism for the way in which he delivered his lines, with 'natural' pauses in the flow, as opposed to the older rhetorical style with its continuous delivery. Brooke exaggerates this characteristic to imply that the actor was being evasive when offered a script by the heroine (i.e. herself).

Mr Hammond, one of the characters, agrees to take the young heroine's work to Garrick, but on his return he reports that the actor has loftily dismissed her meritorious tragedy: 'Why – a – um – true – this play of your friend's – You look amazingly well, my dear sir – In short – this play – I should be charmed to oblige you – but we are so terribly overstocked.' To this evasion Hammond retorts: 'You have read the play, I take for granted [?]' Garrick again equivocates: 'Why – a – um – no – not absolutely read it – Such a multiplicity of affairs – Just skimmed the surface – I – a – Will you take any Chocolate, my dear friend?' The actor's rejection of her work had long been Brooke's complaint; now she was taking her revenge.[4]

In the summer of 1776, Garrick retired from the stage, and as her novel had not yet been published, Brooke, without apparently toning down the severity of her characterisation of Garrick, felt it prudent to add a footnote. She noted that 'this great theatrical luminary' had 'disappeared from his orbit', and she drew a clear distinction between his acting abilities and his managerial practice: 'As the writer honours his talents, though she disapproves his illiberal maxims of government, she has unaffected pleasure in predicting, that the various excellencies of his performance will be remembered with delight, when the errors of his management, though fatal to literature, shall be consigned to oblivion.' She wished him 'a calm and honourable retreat' but pointedly expressed the hope that 'new Garricks' might arise 'under the auspices of a manager who has sufficient genius to be above envy, and sufficient liberality of mind to be incapable of avarice'.[5]

The reason why *The Excursion* was still being withheld from publication in early 1777 was that Garrick, perhaps anxious to get the opera house team out of London, was supporting the Birmingham licence application. Once the proposal had been rejected, there was no longer any reason to delay publication. The opera managers may indeed have wondered whether Garrick's support was all that it seemed. When the novel finally appeared in July 1777, Garrick was furious:

17 July [1777]   David Garrick to Frances Cadogan

I hope you have seen how much I am abus'd in y^r Friend Mrs Brook's new
Novel? — she is pleas'd to insinuate that [I am] an Excellent Actor, a so
so author, an Execrable Manager & a Worse Man — Thank you good
Madam Brookes — If my heart was not better than my head, I would
not give a farthing for the Carcass, but let it dangle, as it would deserve,
with It's [*sic*] brethren at ye End of Oxford Road — She has invented a
Tale about a Tragedy, which is all a Lie, from beginning to ye End — she
Even says, that I should reject a Play, if it should be a Woman's — there's
brutal Malignity for You — have not ye Ladies — Mesdames, *Griffith,
Cowley & Cilesia* spoke of me before their Plays with an Over-
Enthusiastick Ecomium?   what says divine Hannah More? & more
than all what Says the more divine Miss Cadogan? . . .

   I never knew Madam Brookes —

   What a Couple of wretches are y^e *Yateses* Brookes's partners — I
work'd with Zeal for their Patent — wrote 100 Letters, & they were
Stimulating Crumpling all ye while to Mischief, & they deferr'd ye publication till this time, that I might not cool in their Cause — there are
Devils for You.[6]

What so aroused Garrick's wrath was his realisation that the publication of *The Excursion* had been deliberately delayed in order not to
jeopardise the Birmingham campaign. The actor's friends quickly
rallied to his support. Frances Cadogan replied: 'I beg of all loves, you
will not call Mrs Brooke *my friend*. Had she been so, I would now dis-
claim her for ever.'[7] To Burney, worthy of respect despite his association with Brooke, Garrick observed coolly: 'Your Friend Madame de
Brook has tickled my Toby for Me.'[8] Published reviews were mixed.
The lampoon of Garrick was duly noted and deplored by his supporters. A critic hostile to Brooke wrote: 'The piece is not better, nor can
hardly be worse, than the general trash of modern Novels. The story
is an absurd and improbable one; but the Author seemed resolved to
keep all her *invention* to be lavished upon the principal design of the
work; which was to flatter Mr Sheridan, to puff off Mrs Yates, and to
abuse Mr Garrick.' The reviewer took strong objection to her 'unpro-
voked virulence against Mr Garrick', whose 'merit is so infinitely

superior to her malice'.[9] Hannah More, writing to Garrick on 15 November, described this piece as 'the best paragraph' the reviewer ever wrote.[10] The long pro-Garrick piece in the *Monthly Review* is believed to have been written by the actor himself.[11] The quarrel was becoming a minor *cause célèbre* in London literary and theatrical circles.

The hostility of the review in the *Town & Country Magazine* would not have come as a surprise to Brooke, because in her novel she had been severely critical of this publication's monthly *Téte-à-Téte* [sic] column because of the scurrilous nature of its revelations.[12] A barbed critique was published in August 1777, and this was followed the next month by a satire on the three opera managers, pointedly in the very column slammed by Brooke: 'A Téte-à-Téte between the King of Quavers [Richard Yates] and the Heroine of Romance [Frances Brooke]'. As we have already seen, the title 'King of Quavers' was bestowed on Richard Yates by Garrick himself in the epilogue written to mark the return of Mary Ann Yates to Drury Lane in 1774. In the intervening years, the ironic title had stuck. A satirical verse sung at a masquerade promoted by Mrs Cornelys (who had good reason to feel antipathy towards the King's Theatre after her abortive attempt to stage a rival opera had failed) was published in 1776:

> There rum Dicky Quaver for ever at strife,
> Having tam'd his Italians, is tamed by his wife;
> There Shylock plots deep to distress Tommy Lee,
> And the smug Dr Sharp-chin cries *bar* in a glee.

The 'taming' of the Italians may be a dig at the summary demotion of Pozzi the previous month, while the parsimonious Yates (Shylock) had been in dispute with William Lee over the rent for his concession at the King's Theatre.[13]

The 'Téte-à-Téte' satire is in three short scenes. In the first, Brooke and Richard Yates amuse themselves thinking of the reaction to the novel. King Richard [Yates] observes: 'David [Garrick] will be ready to hang himself.' The Heroine of Romance [Brooke] replies: 'I have owed David [Garrick] a long grudge for refusing my piece, which you know was replete with sentiment, pathos and character.' There is an allusion to the recent failure of the Birmingham licence application, and then the two indulge in speculation as to why Garrick has never been a candidate for parliament. King Richard points out: 'he is no orator – he hums and has [meaning to 'hum and ha'] just as you have depicted'. The Heroine of Romance attempts to deliver a soliloquy in the manner of the Queen of Quavers [Mary Ann Yates], 'throwing herself into a dramatic attitude', to which King Richard responds with an operatic 'Bravo, Bravi, Bravissimo'. The Heroine of Romance regrets that she does not possess the powers of the Queen of Quavers. Not so, rejoins King Richard: 'She can scarce read . . . I am obliged to drive the parts into her, as it were, with a sledge hammer.' Hearing the approach of the Queen of Quavers, King Richard rapidly changes the subject: 'Do not forget to insert the Italian phrases I wrote out of Baretti.' The Heroine of Romance replies: 'No; they shall certainly find a place in my novel, if I lug them in by the head and shoulders, they are so pretty, so soft, and so expressive.' The Heroine of Romance leaves and the Queen of Quavers now enters, having overheard some of the preceding conversation. King Richard attempts to placate her by announcing that he is 'planning our winter operation in the Haymarket'. The Queen of Quavers, however, is furious, calling King Richard a 'mere dead weight' as an actor, and saying that he would long ago have been discarded but for her influence. 'From this moment', she continues, 'that self-conceited scribbler [Brooke] shall never enter my doors', to which King Richard retorts: 'Consider, my dear . . . how she has puffed for us.' In the final scene, the Heroine of Romance returns (similarly having overheard some of the preceding scene) and in turn has to be placated by King Richard.

The satire as a whole draws on the public perception of the three opera managers. Richard Yates, a buffoon vacillating between two strong-willed women, is reminiscent of Fanny Burney's vignette of him in 1774.[14] The artificial insertion of Italian phrases into Brooke's novel had already been attributed to his influence in the *Town & Country Magazine* review: 'We presume she [Brooke] is indebted to her erudite friend the operatical manager, who has lately been obliged to talk, nay swear, in Italian, in spite of his teeth.'[15] Several themes – the supposed illiteracy of Mary Ann Yates; the managers' reliance on Baretti for their Italian; Brooke's activities in writing puffs for King's Theatre productions – were shortly to be taken up and developed in a much more substantial satirical work.

The Remarkable Trial of the Queen of Quavers, published by J. Bew in early 1778, is satire on a grand scale – the volume is nearly 150 pages long. Given its timing, its use of the Queen of Quavers character and its subject matter, it is hard to see this as anything other than a pro-Garrick piece, a fierce response to *The Excursion*. There were other interests early in 1778 who might have had reason to attack the Brooke–Yates team, notably Le Texier and Gallini, the losing bidders in the struggle to take over the King's Theatre. Yet there is nothing in *The Remarkable Trial* to suggest that a sale was imminent, and its mock trial 'At the Assize' is dated 9 December 1777 when the three managers were still firmly in charge of the opera house. As a response to *The Excursion*, however, the satire makes excellent sense. Brooke had fiercely criticised Garrick's abilities as a manager and (perhaps unwisely) had allowed the attack to become personal with her lampoon of the actor's speech patterns. The author of *The Remarkable Trial* ruthlessly dissects the managerial performance of the three opera impresarios and indulges without restraint in vitriolic personal attacks on their characters and (in the case of Brooke) on her physical deformity. The choice of the 'quavering itch' (an unaccountable liking for Italian opera) as the disease for which the managers on trial are being held responsible was a neat riposte to Brooke's satire of Garrick's supposedly hesitant speech. As becomes plain, 'quavering' is drunkenness as well as the musical disease. In his final summing up, the satirist, speaking through the judge, is at pains to point out (lest any reader has been misled by the assaults on castrati and other conventional butts of scorn) that Italian opera and its performers are not his real targets; the villains of the piece are the trio in the dock, the opera managers. In the process of destroying their characters, the satirist allowed few of their close associates to escape unscathed, although a lighter, more jocular tone is preferred for the lesser targets. Highly partisan though it is, the satire is a valuable source of evidence about the managerial practices of the King's Theatre during the latter stages of the Brooke–Yates partnership.

The three prisoners-at-the-bar are the three opera managers. The 'Queen of Quavers', obviously an apt title for the regal Mary Ann Yates, was retained from the 'Téte-à-Téte' satire, but Richard Yates now becomes 'Dicky Blunderall', a buffoon like so many of his most celebrated theatrical characters. The harshest treatment is reserved for Brooke; the gently ironic 'Heroine of Romance' becomes the altogether sharper 'Goody Crooks', a play both on the element of self-righteousness in her character and on her bodily deformity. The accusation is that the inhabitants of the moon (i.e. England) are being affected by a 'quavering itch', a love for Italian opera so strong that it results in the inversion of normal, sane values. Responsibility lies with the controllers of the 'lunatick empire' (the King's Theatre). The adversarial format of the courtroom allows the satirist two means of attack: frontal assault from the prosecution; withering irony and snide comments from the defence.

The prosecutor begins with a conventional target; no fewer than 'seven exotick animals' (castrati) have lately been imported from the Continent. By early 1778 there were indeed an unprecedented number of castrati in England: Rauzzini; Tenducci; Savoi; Roncaglia; Coppola, described by Burney as 'a languid and uninteresting soprano';[16] and Manzoletto, who was currently appearing at the Pantheon. He admits that he has to explain why the 'quavering itch' has such a powerful hold on the inhabitants of England. The answer, it seems, is that the three managers have indulged in witchcraft. In Richard Yates's case, the evidence, seemingly consisting of allusions to parts played during his long theatrical career, appears incontrovertible: he has a 'familiar' disguised by a crooked finger; he has the brazen head of Friar Bacon, the liver and heart of a Jew, is ignorant of the Lord's Prayer, practises lycanthropy by assuming the form of an ass or that of a bull with long horns, and boils herbs in a suspicious manner. Mary Ann Yates is altogether more formidable. Prone to violent rage, she leaves behind her 'the smell of brimstone' as the Witch of Endor. She is, moreover, a drunk: 'the Queen of Quavers is so far from being *Mistress of the Bottle*, that the bottle may be most justly termed Mistress of the Queen of Quavers, the truth of which she takes care to confirm every afternoon, always appearing at that time as dizzy as a goose, and as tipsy as a witch'.

The fiercest assault, however, is reserved for Brooke, in whose chamber numerous suspicious objects have been discovered. The crowning proof is her physical appearance: 'To all this I shall add, that the witchcraft of Goody Crooks cannot fall short of proofs, nor admit of any dubiosity, the vengeance of Heaven, which she visibly carries on her back, being such a cogent argument of her criminous conscience, as no man in his senses will pretend to oppose.' Described by her friend Fanny Burney as 'short, broad, crooked, ill-featured, and ill-favoured', Brooke was easily cast as a hag. The prosecutor quotes Otway:

> *In a close lane*, as I pursu'd my journey,
> I spy'd a wrinkled hag with age grown double;
> Picking dry sticks, and mumbling to herself:
> Her eyes with scalding rheum were gall'd and red.
> Cold palsie shook her head, her hands seem'd wither'd,
> And on her crooked shoulders had she wrapp'd
> The tatter'd remnants of an old strip'd hanging.

The exceptionally personal nature of this attack suggests that of the three managers Brooke is the real target of the satirist.

Having blackened the characters of the three prisoners, the prosecutor now examines their qualities as opera managers. Enter, as first witness, Lord Fiddle-Faddle, a vapid, aristocratic opera-goer, badly affected by the itch. He evaluates the singers recruited for the 1777–8 season in a short, punning parody of the kind of opera reportage found in private letters:

> Execrable singers this season – extremely so – Signora Dunce [Danzi] never in tune – ten thousand times worse than Signora Uglesina [Inglesina] – by G- she is – Signor Wrong call ye [Roncaglia] – poor

creature! no voice, no action, and no figure: as to Signor Scanderbeck [Adamberger] the tenor, he has the same dismal tone of voice with the bellman of St Sepulchre – a bad omen for Dicky![17] Signora Buboni [Buroni] horrid![18] Signor Crapula [Coppola] *pejor pessimo*[19] – His recitative and his air cantabile in the last opera, sounded precisely like the dying speech of a rat starved in a hole.

This is very topical, as Danzi, Roncaglia, Adamberger and Coppola all made their debut in Sacchini's *Creso* on 8 November. The appearance of Buroni results in a minor anachronism; the trial is dated 9 December, but the singer did not make her debut in Piccinni's *Vittorina* until a week later. It was normal practice, however, for rehearsals to be open, and for judgements to be formed *before* the opening night. The prosecutor concludes his examination of Lord Fiddle-Faddle with a dig at the opera managers' habit of submitting unlikely-to-be-granted applications for licences. The noble lord is advised to frequent the House of Lords, rather than the opera house, to which he replies: 'I never opened my mouth in Parliament, but I must now break the ice: I am determined to move for a license to perform Operas on Sundays.'

The next witness is Miss Giddy, a subscriber to the opera. Since Burney, as Brooke's musical advisor, is about to come under fire, it is tempting to see in this young character a lampoon of one of the Burney girls – Fanny, Esther or Susan. Fanny, shy, somewhat prudish in character, and a friend of Brooke's seems to fit the character best: Miss Giddy claims her teacher is Signor Giuseppino Miccio [Millico][20] – Fanny had been infatuated with this singer;[21] Miss Giddy blushes when it is suggested that she is in love with 'that delicious sugary fellow my dear Rauzzini' – Fanny was fond of Rauzzini;[22] when asked if she can speak Italian, Miss Giddy offers four words – Fanny was learning the language but was embarrassed to speak it in public.[23]

In his opening remarks, the counsel for defence admits the existence of the 'quavering itch' but attributes it entirely to natural causes. He ridicules any suggestion of necromancy: 'Who could be so weak as to imagine that the Subtle Tartarean Monarch would make a league with two insignificant old women, as the Queen of

Quavers and Goody Crooks, and take for his partner such a thick-sculled patch as Dicky Blunderall?' In turn, each of the managers receives an ironical 'defence'. Richard Yates's avarice is noted; Orpheus, at least, returned from the underworld: 'whereas Dicky will be sure of being kept there, and hugged and caressed by Mamon, in return for the peculiar devotion with which he reverences him in this world'. Counsel confesses that Mary Ann Yates has been known to be drunk, but the devils who attend her 'are mere Printer's devils, belonging to a certain newspaper, whom she employs occasionally to prop the sinking interest of her Monarchy, and to lay a Varnish over her rotten abilities'. (As in the Tête-à-Tête satire, this is a reference to Brooke's practice of writing puffs.) If she has a fierce countenance and a 'morose and peevish manner', it is only to 'curb the forward assurances of Dick'. The 'vindication' of Goody Crooks starts by rejecting the poem as beneath contempt. The interpretations placed upon the items found in her boudoir are rejected with heavy irony: there is no reason to believe that the *'shift of necessity'* stands for 'one of her ragged smocks', nor the *'looking-glass of darkness'* for her 'spectacles', nor the *'dry-stickes'* for her 'legs'. Her four broomsticks are for sweeping the apartment of the Queen of Quavers, for 'Goody is only Maid of Honour to the Queen of Quavers, and withal so extremely attached to her royal Mistress, that she is continually *bending down* for the service of her gracious Sovereign'. To explain away the ointment found her room, Goody Crooks is fortunate to have 'an evidence of incredible weight', namely 'the most eminent Quack [Italian opera expert] in this metropolis' – 'the famous Signor Joseph Bear-hate-ye [Baretti]'. The Italian had once been arrested for stabbing an assailant and for a while had been in danger of being hanged for murder. The defence counsel labours this point: 'his *striking* abilities . . . he has such a *sharp* and *pointed* way of arguing, never fails to *knock down* his adversary & *to cut him to pieces*'. Baretti, it is claimed, will 'swear any thing' on Brooke's behalf. The final item to be explained is a 'subtle magical disquisition', which, however, is nothing more than an Italian opera, as the inscription on the elegant title-page makes clear: *'Opera di rappresentarsi sopra il Teatro di'.*

The discovery and identification of the opera libretto leads the defence counsel into a diatribe against Metastasio, the purpose of which is to prepare the ground for an attack upon Burney. Supporters of Metastasio rarely produce the grounds for their admiration, except, that is, for 'a certain musical Doctor, who, in his learned travels, has thought it proper to inform the public, that he had the extraordinary good luck of staring at Signor Met-ass-t-ass-he-ooo at Vienna; whereupon he takes occasion to assure us, that this most sublime author has the nose precisely in the middle of his face, and that he never speaks but his mouth opens'.[24] After an attack upon the lack of realism in Metastasian plots, counsel returns to Burney:

> But ere I quit this head, I must admonish a certain Doctor Mus not to be too rash and preposterous in his panegyrics: let him acquire at least a small tincture of Italian literature, before he attempts to puff the works of any Italian author. Fulsome elogies founded upon the bare *ipse dixit* of an insignificant travel-monger are mightily ridiculous.

Brooke's reliance on Burney and his travel books was obviously well known to the satirist.

The defence next seeks to rebut the allegation that the 'extraordinary success' of the current 'operatical undertaking' is due to necromancy: on the contrary, 'the improvement of the prisoners' fortune and the prosperity of their finances are entirely owing to their superior industry, and to the prudence of their economical plan'. 'It is therefore proper to take notice', he continues, 'that they have increased the number of the boxes and crammed the subscribers in, like anchovies in a barrel.' Future plans for increasing revenue still further include the idea of placing 'a piss-pot in every box for which each Lady will be obliged to pay a guinea'. Here the satirist was perhaps getting in a dig at the passage in *The Excursion* where there is talk of going to see the opera *Motezuma*. The heroine's chaperone, Lady Hardy, is described as belonging to 'a certain set' who look on going to public places as 'so much time lost from the important business of the card-table'. It was certainly not *Motezuma* which drew this 'accomplished dowager' to the opera, even though '*all the world was to be there'*, but the death of her friend which had meant the cancellation of a card party. 'The Opera was therefore her *pis-aller*' (choice of last resort).[25] While on the subject of 'taxes, impositions and extorsive measures' Richard Yates must also be given his due. It had been the custom with former managers to tip the orange girls at the end of the season; but 'crook-fingered Dick has altered the story, and does every year hook a guinea out of the pocket of each of those poor women'. Even the singers and dancers, it is claimed, 'are all reduced to half pay', with Signor Wrong-call-ye (Roncaglia) receiving 'no more than five hundred pounds'. (There seems to be no other evidence that this was so.)

Having introduced the topic of singers, the defence moves on to consider how the opera managers have dealt with their leading castrati. The most important development in the 1777–8 season had been the decision to replace Rauzzini by Roncaglia. The satirist seems to have been aware of tension between Rauzzini and the opera managers during this period, for there follows an elaborate tale concerning the hiring of Roncaglia. The scene is set with Rauzzini complaining that the shaky state of his finances is forcing him to repair to the country and that during his absence his adversaries will seize the chance to turn Mary Ann Yates against him. She, however, gives him a ring and promises to come to his assistance if he sends it to her. The implied attachment between a castrato and a woman – Yates is described during this conversation as 'playing with his curls' – was a commonplace of opera satire. In the event, Rauzzini's forebodings are fully justified; the opera subscribers speak out against retaining him for the following season. Yates immediately informs her favoured castrato. He, however, ignores her letters, until, in difficult financial circumstances, he is forced to send Mr Scoundarelli (Bottarelli, the librettist) to the opera manager with her ring in order to stop his replacement by Roncaglia. Bottarelli, however, pawns the ring, and Yates, not having heard from Rauzzini, signs 'the fatal warrant, that is, the engagement of Signor Wrong-call-ye'. Shortly afterwards, Bottarelli drops the pawnbroker's receipt, and it is found by Richard Yates who takes it to his wife. 'She perceiving some letters on it . . . orders her Secretary of State, and Maid of Honour Goody Crooks to peruse the contents.' The pawnbroker confirms the authenticity of the receipt, whereupon Mary Ann Yates, pronouncing 'dire imprecations and foul maledictions on all the tribe of the Castrati' gets thoroughly drunk. The plot of this story is highly fanciful, and yet there are elements of reality: the influence of the opera subscribers in the decision to refuse a fourth season for Rauzzini; and the risky game of bluff and counter-bluff that went on between singers and managers during recruitment periods. Above all, the tale reinforces the satirical persona of Mary Ann Yates as a domineering, illiterate drunk, and that of Brooke as subservient to her friend.

Next it is the turn of Sacchini:

> But in regard to the direction of Operas, the prisoners have undoubtedly discovered a great share of sagacity; and to shew it in every step, they have employed for Composer the famous Signor Sack, being the most diligent man in his profession capable of bringing forth an operatical brat, with the expedition of an elephant, who carries her young no longer than two years: and because novelty is the soul of music, this ingenious and ingenuous Signor Sack always takes care to make people believe, that his old compositions are entirely new, and therefore his last *crazy* Opera he palmed on the public for a fresh production, although set and performed at Rome about eighteen years ago.[26]

The failure to renew Giardini's contract as leader of the orchestra for the 1777–8 season is noted: Mary Ann Yates 'expelled' him because he was 'perpetually *Jarring* in the harmonical mansion, and rebelliously encroaching on the royal prerogative'.

Summing up, the defence argues that 'the managerial conduct of the prisoners at the bar, deserves the highest ecomiums'. He is so confident of their acquittal that he requests £50,000 in damages. Witnesses for the defence are now summoned. Bottarelli, author of the recently published *The New Italian, English, and French Pocket-Dictionary* (London, 1777), is quizzed and ribbed about his work. Joseph Baretti is summoned and is discovered with a knife 'half-a-yard' in length, which causes momentary panic in the courtroom.

Discussion of Baretti's colourful past gives the satirist the chance to introduce a passage in fulsome praise of Garrick, whose support had been instrumental in his acquittal: 'Did not Mr G_____k prove, in many instances, your most generous Benefactor? Did he not mend your *dirty* situation a number of times? and was it not entirely owing to his influence, and efficacious patronage, that you once had the good luck of slipping your neck?'

In his final summing up, the judge is at pains to stress that the target of the satirical trial has not been Italian opera as a genre, or the King's Theatre as a venue, or the singers and composers employed there. In a sweeping and generous absolution he praises the Italian opera community:

> I shall mark down the names of all those foreign musicians, who, by their probity as well as by their abilities, deserve to be made Denisons of the Moon:
>
> *Singers*
> The celebrated Pacchierotti, Roncaglia, Tenducci, Ansani, Signora Sestini, Signora Todi, Signora Danzi, Signora Rosa Baglioni, Signor Lovattini, Signor Germogli, Signor Rossi, Signor Rovedini, etc. etc.
>
> N. B. the heavy sarcasms given in evidence by Lord Fiddle-Faddle, against the truly excellent Signor Roncaglia, and the much admired Signora Danzi, can have no sort of influence over our opinion, since we know very well, that his Lordship, being troubled with the Quavering Disease, was entirely out of his senses.
>
> *Composers*
> Bach, Piccinni, Anfossi, Paisiello, Giordani and Barthelemon.
>
> *Instrumental Performers*
> Lolli, Abel, La Motte, Cramer, Pugnani, Vachon, Fischer, Mr Le Brun, Noferi, Agus, sen. and jun., Marella, Salpietro, Storace and Morticelli.
>
> *Teachers of Musick*
> Signor Piozzi, Signor Quilici, Signor Picciarelli and Signor Leopoldo Micheli.

Dancing Masters
Signor Gallini, Monsieur Gallet, Monsieur Fierville, Signor D'Elpini, Mademoiselle Baccelli, Monsieur and Madame Vallovy, Signora Tinti.

These lists contain the names of most of the singers and composers involved in the 1777–8 season, together with names from the recent past (such as Lovattini) and from the immediate future (Pacchierotti and Ansani). There are three notable absentees – Sacchini, Rauzzini and Giardini – presumably missing because of their close association with the managers.

Before the verdict is pronounced, hostile character witnesses are called. Mr Punch, speaking against Richard Yates, lets loose a final shaft at the failed Birmingham licence application. A publisher, Mr Octavo, denigrates Brooke as a writer. His words of condemnation of her literary *oeuvre* focus the reader's attention on the ultimate reason for the whole satire: 'She once wrote for me an Almanack, wherein she mistook every particular, the event always proving the reverse of what she had marked down . . . so that the next year I was obliged to sell all her Almanacks to a Grocer in Cheapside, as I did her other productions.' The verdict is 'guilty' and the sentence 'death'. The ultimate penalty, however, is commuted. Two fitting punishments are suggested, the first of which is aimed specifically at Brooke 'to transport the Kingdom of Quavers with all its retinue, into, *A-merry-key* [America] for the purpose of exhibiting Italian Operas before the Right Honourable Congress'. The message is unambiguous: Frances Brooke, who had lived in North America between 1763 and 1768, should return there. Failing that, 'a tax of one penny per quaver' would be 'just sufficient to pay off the National Debt'.

The Remarkable Trial of the Queen of Quavers brought to a spectacular conclusion the personal side of the long Garrick–Brooke controversy. As an onslaught on a specific management team, the piece stands outside the mainstream of Italian opera satire in England. The author was well acquainted with the King's Theatre, and this knowledge enabled the attacks to range over the whole opera establishment of the later years of the three managers, including their leading composer, their leading castrato, their libretto translator and their artistic advisers. Severe though the invective is, the satirist could not deny (and did not seek to deny) that the opera managers had made a real financial and managerial success out of their five years in control of the King's Theatre. Coming from such a source, this judgement must be accepted, and it is in line with all other contemporary comment. The satire thus makes a nice counterbalance to *The Excursion*, in which Brooke felt obliged to acknowledge fully Garrick's powers as an actor. The *Queen of Quavers* satire is similarly directed against three professionals whose success was by now incontrovertible. Its date of publication (probably January or February 1778) made it highly topical, and yet it just failed to appear in time. The agreement to sell the King's Theatre to Sheridan and Harris (of which there is no hint in the satire) was made public in February 1778, and this would have much diminished its impact. It does not seem to have received much critical attention. In the *Monthly Review* for May 1778 it is described as 'A most virulent attack on the masculine, feminine, and epicoene directors and performers of the opera, probably the production of some incensed Italian, and chiefly calculated for the meridian of the Orange coffee-house.'

The financial records of the opera house at this period suggest that the general competence and flair of Brooke's regime was eventually rewarded by a positive balance sheet, once the crisis over Agujari had been overcome. The discovery of several bank accounts used by the managers has shed much light on the details of the finances of Italian opera in London in the 1770s, a subject about which little has hitherto been known for certain. Until the 1772–3 season, Hobart banked at Drummonds, where there had been an opera account for many decades. The Brooke–Yates partnership abruptly terminated this long association, opening an account at Hoare & Co., which they used for three and a half seasons (see Appendix 1a). For the 1777–8 season, their last at the King's Theatre, they opened an account with Mayne & Graham of Jermyn Street, but since this partnership went bankrupt in the early 1780s, the accounts must now be regarded as lost. In 1778 Sheridan and Harris returned to Drummonds, opening an account which lasted for the year of their partnership (see Appendix 1b). Jonathan Garton, treasurer of Covent Garden, became involved with opera finances that year, and his own, much larger account includes transactions clearly made on behalf of the King's Theatre (see Appendix 1c). Pacchieriotti's account at Coutts & Co. is also useful for identifying the amounts he was paid and the dates on which he received payment (see Appendix 1d). A single sheet of opera-related payments for 1780 in the William Salt Library contributes a few further details of salary payments (see Appendix 1e). These new sources do not overturn the central conclusions reached by the authors of the recent study of the King's Theatre,[1] but they do suggest that the finances of the opera house in the later 1770s were in a generally healthier state than hitherto believed.

THE HOARE ACCOUNT

This was opened in the joint names of James Brooke and Richard Yates, and it became effective in the summer of 1773, when the first subscriptions for the following season were received. It can best be described as a working account, with money from subscriptions and box office being paid in and salaries for performers and others being paid out. In no sense, however, does it provide a full balance sheet; a significant proportion of the transactions (for example payments to orchestral musicians) must have been made in cash. Many opera employees appear in these ledgers, if only briefly. Most are singers and dancers, but there are also composers and librettists, orchestral leaders, recruiters, agents and bankers, lawyers, a painter and machinist, a publisher, a treasurer, a prompter and a man responsible for lighting. The account was kept approximately in balance, but in the spring of 1777 transactions began to dwindle. There is virtually nothing for the 1777–8 season, during which the managers were using the Mayne & Graham account. The small deficit which remained when the King's Theatre was sold in 1778 was paid off on 21 January, when the account was terminated.

The Hoare ledgers demonstrate conclusively that at this period opera singers and dancers were paid in three instalments: (1) in late December/early January; (2) in late March/early April; (3) in late June/early July. In this respect, the system differed slightly from that of the 1780s, when payments were made rather later. Each payment was retrospective, for three months' work completed. This rather simple basic schedule was of course liable to alteration for numerous reasons, among which were: single payments to couples or even whole families (particularly common with dancers); payments to individuals with a double responsibility, for example, a leader/composer (like Giardini), or a singer/composer (like Rauzzini); salary instalments reduced because of the prior payment of an advance; final salary payments reduced because the individual chose to take the risk of a benefit; reduced payments to performers who arrived late or left early and who therefore received only a proportion of their notional annual salary; payments to short-term replacements or stand-ins for those who fell ill. All these complications notwithstanding, it is usually possible to work out what was (at least notionally) a season's salary, by taking the largest payment made on one of the normal settlement dates and multiplying by three.

The opera accounts in Drummonds for the season 1768–9 are sufficiently detailed to show that the payment system used by the Brooke–Yates management was already established practice.[2] This season was unusual in that there was no *opera seria* at all. Lovattini, the star of the comic troupe, received £900 in three instalments, on exactly the dates on which they were due – 31 December, 31 March and 30 June. The leading woman, Guadagni, sister of the celebrated castrato, together with her husband Felice Alessandri, the composer, received jointly £700 in three instalments on 31 December, 31 March and 1 July. The bass, Morigi, received £300 in three instalments on the same dates. Other salaries are less completely documented and inevitably more speculative. A winter payment of £116. 13s. 4d. to the dancer Slingsby suggests a salary of £450, which accords with a later newspaper report of his career salary level.[3] The performers of this celebrated comic troupe certainly earned their money. Exceptionally, there were just over seventy performances of *opera buffa* that year.

In the following season-by-season discussion of the Hoare ledgers, an attempt will be made to show how the bank account reflected the changing fortunes of the opera house.

THE 1773–4 SEASON

Millico's triumph in *Il Cid* in January 1773 made him the obvious choice as *primo uomo* for the new season. His salary of £1,200 (estimated from the spring payment of £400) was in line with the current norm. The summer payment of £100 only may mean one of several things: that there was part payment from cash-in-hand; that the singer's contract specified a reduced salary payment in return for a benefit; or even that the singer agreed to a reduced payment, in the hope of re-engagement. In the uncertain conditions of the previous decade, singers like Mazziotti and Manzuoli had demanded that their contracts be guaranteed before their departure from Italy, thereby demonstrating the fact that non-payment was seen as a real possibility.[4] At the winter and spring payment dates, singers had a powerful sanction over the managers – if they were not paid they could wreak havoc on the remainder of the season by refusing to perform. But on the final payment date, performers were in a much more vulnerable position, even though their contracts were legally enforceable. At this stage, it was open to the managers to offer a private inducement to take a July reduction in return for the prospect of future engagements. Except for the very top performers like Manzuoli and Gabrielli, the uncertainties of sustaining a career were such that some might have felt it worthwhile to retain the goodwill of a major opera house and go quietly in the hope of future work. Any such agreement would certainly have been kept strictly private. As far as the public were concerned, the Brooke–Yates partnership never reneged on a contracted salary, apart from the special case of Davies. Indeed, Susan Burney's comment in response to Sheridan's problems in the spring of 1780, that "twas quite a new thing here that there sh^d be so much trouble for the Performers to get their salaries paid', is convincing evidence that in the recent past an engagement at the King's Theatre had been a financially secure option.[5]

Another explanation for Millico's reduced summer payment is that the singer left England before the expiry of his contract. Johann Christian von Mannlich records that Millico turned up in Paris in July 1774, admitting openly that he had abandoned the King's Theatre. Millico was claiming that he had received a letter from Paris, informing him of Gluck's death, and that when he heard that the news was untrue, he was so overwhelmed with joy that he travelled night and day to reach France. He is reported as describing his departure from London thus: 'I left all my engagements in London, with the firm resolution of fulfilling them upon my return. I wrote to all my friends and backers before my departure, that unavoidable matters had been necessitating my return to Paris for some time, but that I gave them my word that I would not sing.'[6] It seems that with his star in England on the wane, Millico had simply abandoned his contract and hastened to Paris.

Davies was the first Englishwoman to be offered a season at the King's Theatre as *prima donna* and her salary is thus of unusual interest. The Hoare accounts, however, present something of a conundrum: winter and spring payments of only £200, which might suggest the surprisingly low salary of £600. Her recruitment was an imaginative move, but one not without risk, since the reaction of the conservative King's Theatre audience to an Englishwoman singing in Italian was not entirely predictable.[7] However, the winter payment to Davies, unusually, is annotated with the comment '2 at £100', which could mean that her overall salary level was £800–£900 (£100 a month). One thing seems clear: money was at the root of the 'perpetual Quarrels' between the singer and managers to which Fanny Burney referred in April 1774.[8] It would have been a matter of great resentment if, as the undoubted star of the season, she should have been in receipt of a salary only half or three quarters that of Millico. The composer Sacchini received two payments of £150 on 30 December and 7 April. Since he produced one opera for each third of the season: *Lucio vero* (première on 20 November 1773), *Perseo* (première on 29 January 1774) and *Nitteti* (première on 19 April 1774), it is reasonable to conclude that the annual salary he received as house composer was £450, but the final payment is missing. December and March payments of £43. 6s. 8d. to the leader Celestino suggest an annual salary of £130, but again the final payment is missing.

THE 1774–5 SEASON

This was a lean year for the opera house. Takings were substantially down, and since the managers were not willing (or allowed) to run up a large deficit in this account, generally fewer salary bills were met from it. Where the additional money came from is not known. Although salary estimates are necessarily less certain, in several cases there is external evidence to confirm the projected total. Payments to

Rauzzini are complicated by the fact that the revised version of his opera *Piramo e Tisbe* was given its London première on 16 March 1775. His annual salary of £1,100 is clearest in the accounts for his third and final season as *primo uomo* at the King's Theatre in 1776–7. Schindlerin was a flop, but her payment of £233. 6s. 8d. at the end of the season suggests an intended salary of £700. As we know from the Humphry correspondence, Lovattini's fee was £900, exactly the sum he had received in the 1768–9 season. The Hoare ledgers record the spring and summer payments, but the absence of any winter payment (even one reduced because of the singer's delayed debut) is clear enough proof that this account was not the sole source of payments to singers. The summer payment of £166. 13s. 4d. to Sestini, the *prima buffa*, indicates a salary of £500, which accords exactly with a later newspaper report of it.[9] Sacchini received £150 on 11 February, clearly for his opera *Motezuma*, which had received its première four days earlier. This confirms the 'going rate' for a full-scale piece by the composer, but the accounts give no clue as to whether he received any further remuneration as house composer. No regular payments to a leader can be identified, but a small sum given to Celestino hints at his continued presence in this role. The other major payments relate to the Davies lawsuit, notably £333. 6s. 8d., the first instalment of her unpaid £1,000 salary. Perhaps as significant, however, is the payment to Fish Coppinger, the lawyer.[10] His settlement date was early February. In 1775, when the legal battle with Davies was already half a year old, he received £650, the next year £700 and the year after that £650. Obviously not all of this relates to the Davies case, but these payments contributed to the general decline in the financial position.

THE 1775–6 SEASON

The superstar Caterina Gabrielli's fee was reported in a London newspaper as being £1,500 plus carriage and house.[11] Spring and summer payments of £500 confirm this. The smaller payment of £279. 13s., made on 2 January, probably relates to an advance, since

Brooke is unlikely to have wanted to risk asking this particular singer for a reduction on account of her illness and the notoriously late cancellation of her debut. Trebbi, the new *buffo*, received a respectable salary of £600. The house composer was Vento, who in total seems to have received an amazing £500. Three payments to him of £116. 13s. 4d. on the usual dates appear to show that his basic salary as house composer was £350, below the rate enjoyed by Sacchini. However, on 22 February a 'Mr Vento' received £150. Whether the use of the title 'Mr' rather than 'Sig' is indicative of a second, hitherto unknown Vento is not at all clear. If this man was the composer, his annual total would have exceeded even that of Sacchini. Such a salary would of course have included payment for work done on pasticcios and playing the harpsichord, but it would nonetheless still be a remarkable one. The librettist for Vento's two new operas (*Il bacio* and *La vestale*) was Badini, who received £25 for each. Three payments to Celestino might lead to the supposition that he was still leader, but a similar number of payments to Salpietro confuses the situation. The violinist Giovanni Salpietro had long had some connection with the King's Theatre, but his wife was a singer, and it is possible that she took some (otherwise unrecorded) roles this season.[12]

THE 1776–7 SEASON

The salaries of Rauzzini (£1,100) and Trebbi (£700) are clear from their winter and spring payments. Trebbi this season sang some *opera seria* parts, which may explain his increase. The run-down in the Hoare account in the spring of 1777 leaves us with an incomplete picture; no summer payments are recorded, because in-payments of cash ceased. Pozzi's failure is represented in her single payment of £137. 10s. Her replacement Davies received one payment of £250, perhaps part of a deal for £750 for completing the season (about six out of eight months). The new composer Traetta perhaps received an even better basic rate than his predecessors, assuming his spring payment of £166. 13s. 4d. to indicate a notional salary level of £500. The winter payment of £16. 13s. 4d. was perhaps the residue of the salary after a payment of £150 for his first opera. Traetta in fact completed three operas, one for each third of the season, as Sacchini had done in the 1773–4 season. The payment of £95 to Goldoni on 6 December is of interest. Brooke had for several years been trying to get opera libretti. The fee was perhaps for *Germondo*, which received its première at the King's Theatre on 21 January 1777, and possibly also for *Vittorina*, given the following year. Two payments to Piccinni, the first on 1 January 1777 (£16. 13s. 4d.) and the second on 30 April (£20. 7s. 4d.), seem much too small and much too early to relate to *Vittorina*, which did not receive its first performance until 16 December 1777. It is more likely that they were payments for substitution airs. The new leader was Giardini. If his spring payment of £100 indicates a salary of £300, it was a big increase over what was paid to Celestino.[13]

MORTGAGE

In February 1774, the managers took out a mortgage on the King's Theatre with Henry Hoare to the value of £4,500, at 5 per cent interest per annum.[14] Unlike the huge financial millstone that Sheridan took on, this was a modest sum. The first interest payment in February 1775 was for £225. In 1776 Hoare allowed the managers to move to a retrospective system, perhaps in a bid to ease their immediate financial problems. On 3 February the banker was paid £112. 10s., which had been due the previous August, and the second instalment was postponed. However, a clear indication of the growing prosperity of the King's Theatre comes on 21 May 1777, when the managers repaid £1,000 of this loan. After the sale of the opera house in 1778, the mortagage was repaid in full, Hoare receiving £3,567. 14s. 2d. (the remaining £3,500 plus interest).

RECEIPTS

The pattern of receipts is fairly consistent over the four seasons. The tradition had been established during previous managements that subscriptions could be paid either directly into the bank nominated by the proprietors, or else to the treasurer at the King's Theatre. Only subscribers who opted for the former method would be listed by name in the bank records. To judge by the last years of the Hobart opera accounts in Drummonds, relatively few opted to do this. In the three seasons prior to the purchase of the King's Theatre by the Brooke–Yates team, subscription figures recorded in Drummonds were: 1770–1: £462 (twenty-two subscribers); 1771–2: £399 (nineteen subscribers); 1772–3: £525 (twenty-five subscribers).[15] By far the larger part of the subscription income was paid direct to the theatre and did not pass through the bank account. The Hoare & Co. opera account also lists a few individuals who paid their £21 subscription direct to the bank. Other subscriptions collected by the managers were paid in as lump sums. For example, towards the end of 1773, Richard Yates on three occasions paid in £105 (five subscriptions). From November, box office money began to come in. These much larger sums certainly include further subscriptions. It is striking how closely the receipts in the Hoare account mirror the dramatically changing fortunes of the opera house. Cash lodged during the 1773–4 season amounted to *c.* £8,800. The following year saw the total plunge to *c.* £6,600. With the legal dispute set to cost the managers £2,000, the scale of the crisis is easy to understand. Gabrielli's season saw a big improvement with *c.* £9,750 lodged. The takings for the 1776–7 season amounted to *c.* £7,250, but since the Hoare account was not used for any summer payments, this sum was doubtless a smaller than usual proportion of the overall take in what was evidently a relatively prosperous season. Crucial to interpreting these total figures is the question of what proportion of annual income went through this account. Leaving aside the troubled 1774–5 season, the money that was paid into the Hoare account (or that would have been paid in the last season had the account continued) averages around £9,000 a year. It is demonstrable, however, that important areas of expenditure are not included, notably payments to orchestral musicians, *figurants*, the daily running costs of security men, dressers, porters and scene changers, and at least some substantial payments to performers (such as Rauzzini). Payments to orchestral musicians alone could have come close to £1,500, taking 'upwards of thirty' to indicate an orchestra of around thirty-two at fifteen shillings a night for sixty nights.[16] A conservative estimate of this cash element of the opera house economy would be £3,000 to £4,000, which would put the managers' operating budget at around £12,000 to £13,000 during the three successful seasons for which there is evidence. To explain this healthy state of affairs, several factors need to be considered.[17] The addition of stage boxes in 1773 increased capacity to a limited extent. The satirical observation that the Brooke–Yates team crammed their patrons in 'like anchovies in a barrel' may have had some basis in truth, to judge by persistent newspaper reports of extremely crowded houses early in 1778. An additional two hundred tickets sold on the five most popular nights of the season, plus an extra one hundred on the ten next most popular nights, could alone have generated £1,000. The widespread view that the King's Theatre was in a healthy financial state above all implies that an all-important *continuity* of income had been achieved. The Sheridan–Harris opera account for the 1778–9 season shows a healthy general level of receipts, rarely falling below £200 per performance. The overall picture of the late 1770s is thus of a theatre, limited in capacity, but with an ever-more healthy occupancy rate, as Italian opera entered one of its most prosperous phases in London. This is the background to the rapid series of expansions of capacity that occurred in 1773, 1778 and 1782. Had Sheridan and Harris in 1778 been in a position to confine their debt to the £4,000 spent on expanding the theatre's capacity, there is little doubt, as Price, Milhous and Hume argue, that they could have operated at a profit.[18]

THE DRUMMONDS ACCOUNT

Readers of the brilliant analysis of Sheridan's spectacular but catastrophic style of management in *Italian Opera in Late Eighteenth-Century London* by Price, Milhous and Hume will not be surprised to learn that his opera accounts for the 1778–9 season are strikingly unlike those run by the Brooke–Yates management. The Hoare &

Co. accounts may present only part of the picture, but they are tidily run and allow us to establish with reasonable certainty details of salary levels. The account opened by Sheridan and Harris at Drummonds is by contrast chaotic. It is evidently part of a much wider network of financial dealings, which for this one year embraced a monopoly of all three major London theatres. Disorganised though it is, it enables us to place the finances of the opera house during the Brooke–Yates partnership in a clearer perspective.

The theory that Jonathan Garton, Thomas Harris's treasurer at Covent Garden, was involved in the financial management of the King's Theatre in the 1778–9 season is fully borne out by his Drummonds account.[19] The ledger is prefaced with the note: 'either to draw & subject also to the Drafts of Mr Jona: Garton' – in other words, Garton, as well as Sheridan and Harris, could draw money. The situation is complicated by the fact that Garton himself ran an account at Drummonds from which some opera payments were made. His own account is very substantial and his interests evidently extended widely. That he was paying musicians prior to his involvement with the King's Theatre is evident from his 1777 ledger; during the months of February, March and April, there are payments to Arne, Leoni, Lamotte, Tenducci and Cervetto. The first signs of activity relating to the opera house come in the 1778 ledger. In October, advances were paid to Pacchierotti (£150) and Adamberger (£25), and a bill from the Bolognese agent Vergani of £40 was settled. The opera account itself opens in late November, and thereafter box office payments are entered 'by cash rec^d of Jonathan Garton'. From that point, out-payments cease from Garton's own account and begin in the opera account, which ends in July 1778; the final receipt is on 15 July and the last payment (to Jermoli) is on 22 July. The balance left was £8. 8s. 8d., a sum that was to sit unused for several years. At the end of July, opera payments resume from Garton's account, and large sums are paid out to performers: Baccelli £166. 13s. 4d. (30 July); Cramer £50 (7 August); Slingsby £126 (10 August); Zucchelli £73. 6s. 8d. (12 August); Pacchierotti £383. 6s. 8d. (17 August); and, last of all,

Bernasconi £183. 6s. 8d. (16 October). This was the start of the late payment of singers' fees that was to become such a hallmark of the Sheridan regime. There is also one apparent advance – £50 to Trebbi (2 October). The final opera payment is to Le Texier on 27 December, perhaps the day of his summary dismissal.[20] The pattern of the ledger in late 1779 seems to indicate that the financial set-up for the new season was to be as before, but opera payments suddenly cease at the beginning of Garton's 1780 ledger, no doubt the moment at which Sheridan assumed sole control of the King's Theatre and instituted new arrangements. Continuing payments from Garton to Luppino (the taylor), Colomba (the machinist) and Hayling (the light specialist) probably relate to work undertaken elsewhere. The managers' strategy was thus to use the opera account for as long as there was money in it and to rely on Garton's account for the period before and after the season. The total of £1,500 paid out in advances and late salary settlements by Garton may well represent part of the operating loss of £3,000 which Sheridan later claimed to have sustained for that season.[21] Garton himself was not ultimately liable for this loss, as, on a subsequent occasion he asked for security before advancing money to enable Sheridan to pay Pacchierotti.

The closing months of the opera account illustrate starkly the impossible position into which the managers had fallen. Sheridan and Harris had purchased the King's Theatre for £22,000, of which £10,000 was a down payment and £12,000 a mortgage. To cover the £10,000 they had sold renters' shares, which gave the right of free admission for a term of twenty-one years. In effect they were giving up some £500–£1,000 income for each of these years. Receipts from the shares, however, had apparently not covered the full amount (some £2,000 was still outstanding), and to make matters still worse, the end-of-season salary settlements were approaching.[22] If the King's Theatre was to remain solvent without subsidy, all of these debts were going to have to be met from ticket receipts in May and June, an obvious impossibility. Faced with the approaching crisis, Sheridan opted to juggle his funds. Throughout the season, Garton had been paying in cash taken at the twice-weekly performances.

Suddenly in late April, lodgements cease. There are several possible explanations for this. Under the previous management, it had been the practice for the treasurer Johnson to settle a significant number of accounts from reserves of cash-in-hand. It is possible that during the months of May and June 1779, as creditors for the season submitted their bills, Sheridan and Harris switched to the earlier method, making a sufficient number of cash payments to diminish the flow of credit into the account (which in any case usually tailed off towards the end of the season). Alternatively, Garton might himself have withheld the money to cover his earlier advances. But the most plausible explanation is that the absence of receipts relates to the larger debt crisis and that the money was needed urgently elsewhere. Sheridan and Harris did succeed in postponing one commitment; the £3,000 mortgage payment was successfully deferred.[23] Even so, by ceasing to lodge money, the managers quickly ran their opera account at Drummonds badly into the red. The bank would not allow this situation to continue for long, and so a loan was taken out. On 19 June, the very day that security for a £2,000 loan was posted,[24] two payments of £1,000 appear in the opera account, and ten days later a further £1,000, bringing it back into balance. It is impossible to know whether Sheridan and Harris had used box office money in May and June to cover the remainder of the purchase price and then been forced to borrow £2,000 to balance the opera account, and in one sense it hardly matters. What is certain is that debts were mounting out of control. One further step was necessary to keep the Drummonds account in balance; most of the large salary payments had to be postponed until after the ledgers were closed in July. In the end, a neat balance of £8. 8s. 8d was left in the account, with massive debts simply transferred elsewhere.

The most interesting aspect of the Drummonds account is the pattern of receipts. Over the course of the season the regularity of lodgements is notable. Around Christmas there were fewer, and they diminished rapidly in April for one or other of the reasons given above, but for the rest of the year, Tuesday and Saturday performances were usually followed by Wednesday and Monday lodgements. In March, all the lodgements followed this pattern. Nightly receipts hardly ever fall below £200. If the lodgement of £500 after a performance of *Zemira ed Amor* represents a single night's takings (rather than an accumulation), the King's Theatre would have been crammed to bursting point. In all, £13,500 was paid in. One question of obvious relevance is whether the £3,000 lodged in June to balance the account equates with the total box office receipts after late April. Prior to the 21 April payment, total receipts had been £9,500. Some twenty performances remained (excluding benefits). Taking a pessimistic view (average ticket sales of only £100 for the remainder of the season), £2,000 would have come in during May and June, augmenting the total annual receipts to £11,500. But there are few early warning signs in the Drummonds account of so sharp a down-turn, and, bearing in mind also the intense loyalty of Pacchierotti's following, a more realistic estimate might be an average take of £125 to £150, resulting in £12,000 to £12,500 for the year. As with the Hoare accounts, it is necessary to consider whether the money banked represents the overall take. Johnson, the deputy treasurer, withdrew around £2,000 during the course of the season. One or two sums taken out by him could represent salary instalments, but the bulk of the cash was probably used for paying orchestral musicians and daily running expenses. The system seems to have been that Garton collected and banked the income, while Johnson withdrew cash to make routine payments. Nonetheless, some cash turnover probably went unrecorded in the Drummonds account. Even if a small sum of £1,000 is allowed for this, then the receipts for the 1778–9 season amounted to no less than £13,500, a total very much in line with estimates for the income achieved during the last three years of the Brooke–Yates partnership. Sheridan later claimed to have lost £7,000 on this season's programme, from which must be subtracted the sum of £4,000 paid for auditorium improvements.[25] If income was £13,000 and the season's loss £3,000, expenditure was around £16,500 – which equates well with the minimum budget suggested during the 1780s.[26] This figure is higher than that suggested by Price, Milhous and Hume, but if the upwards revision is accepted, then the year-by-year costs of the King's Theatre in the late 1770s to the early 1780s, as represented in their table, appear to be rising steadily rather than spectacularly, and it might be argued that this accords better with the essential stability of opera salaries at this period.[27]

There is a very striking contrast between the regularity of salary payments in the Hoare accounts and the chaotic state of Sheridan's settlements with his performers. It is hard to identify any regular payment dates, and the impression is given that accounts were settled as late as possible, sometimes only when the managers were threatened with action. It is thus far harder to derive even notional salary scales. A wide range of opera personnel received at least some payment: Colomba (the scene designer), Weltje (the caterer), Fish Coppinger (the lawyer), Mountford (the carpenter), Hayling (the lighter), Vergani (the broker) and Luppino (the taylor). Cramer, the leader, received £150, in three instalments on 22 January, 5 June and 7 August. Some of the most interesting payments in the Sheridan and Harris opera account are to librettists and composers. Two payments to 'Mr Andries' (probably Antonio Andrei) of £26. 13s. 4d. place him above Badini, who received two payments of £20. Bertoni's single payment of £150 on 16 March is hard to interpret. If it was for a single opera, this was the rate that Sacchini had established. However, Sacchini himself, who composed two operas that season, received two payments of £100, both on 30 April. On 19 July Piccinni was paid £23. 6s. 8d., probably for a small packet of songs. (*Alessandro nel Indie*, which opened the following season, had three airs by the composer.) Finally, the controversial acting manager, Le Texier, received payments totalling over £300.[28]

THE SALT MANUSCRIPT

A single untitled sheet in the 'Sheridan Letters' in the William Salt Library may be added to the document cited by Price, Milhous and Hume as the only financial paperwork that seems to survive from Sheridan's first year in sole control of the opera house.[29] It is not an opera account as such, but the payments and receipts are unquestion-

ably related to the King's Theatre season of 1779–80. It begins on 29
February with a payment of £6,029. 15s. 3d. to Harris, which no doubt
marks his financial withdrawal from the venture and Sheridan's
assumption of sole responsibility. During the course of the year,
there are scattered payments to singers (Pacchierotti, Le Brun and
Bernasconi), a dancer (Guiardele) and the leader (Cramer), almost all
of them late. Total outgoings are £8,460. 5s. Partly off-setting these
payments are a number of interesting receipts, notably money from
the sale of shares in Drury Lane – some at £150 (or less) for ten-year
shares, some at around £230 for twenty-one-year shares. This raises
the obvious possibility that Sheridan resorted in periods of acute
difficulty to some very questionable cross-subsidy (however temporary) between his two ventures. On 16 March is the most amazing
entry: 'By Opera Acct. for 78 & 79 Ballance in Hand – £926. 16s. 4d.'
How Sheridan managed to conjure up such a balance from the previous year's debts is anyone's guess. The possibility of long-delayed
subscription payments cannot be ruled out. The next entry on 12
April is in fact for subscriptions for the current season. Late in the
year, Sheridan managed to sell two opera shares at much below their
original price of £300. Total income is only just over half of expenditure. With its almost random selection of entries, this page typifies
Sheridan's cavalier approach to accounting. Even if complete documentation of his opera transactions were to come to hand, it is probable that no coherent picture would emerge. A charitable view would
stress the incompetence of his financial dealings, but more plausible
is the conclusion reached by Price, Milhous and Hume that he
indulged in shady business practice. His methods seem indeed to
have been those of the classic con-man: late payment of bills, or non-
payment if at all possible; loans taken on an unplanned basis to cope
with problems as and when they arose; rapid movement of funds
from one account to another; cross-subsidies from one venture to
another; and the sale of future income to meet present needs. The
King's Theatre did well to survive Sheridan's proprietorship.

When taken in conjunction with the mid eighteenth-century Drummonds opera account and with other information recently compiled on salary levels, the newly discovered Hoare and Drummonds accounts allow us to establish what different types of singers earned in the 1770s.[1] The following tables present annual salaries, excluding benefits. Salaries in square brackets are derived from information for the same singer from another year. Salaries followed by a question mark are derived from one or two of the winter, spring and summer instalments, as described above. It is worth repeating again the caution that these are notional figures; numerous factors may have led to salaries not being paid in full.

Manzuoli's £1,500 was quite exceptional. Over the period as a whole, the salary level of the *primo uomo* remained very stable at between £1,200 and £1,000. Salaries at the top end of this range went to singers with outstanding reputations (like Pacchierotti); at the lower end of the range Roncaglia, a performer who was regarded as no more than adequate, got the bare £1,000.

Pacchierotti was one of the outstanding singers of his age. As so much information survives about his salary in London in the late 1770s and early 1780s, it will be useful to present it as a case study of how a leading castrato at this period was paid. Even for a musician of his artistic eminence and great popularity, the path from the initial contract to the final payment of salary in full was strewn with obstacles. For a foreigner with only a modest command of the English language, dealing with the King's Theatre under the Sheridan or Taylor management must have seemed a morass of legal and financial difficulties. Little wonder that the singer placed his affairs in the hands of a lawyer.

There is much circumstantial evidence to suggest that Pacchierotti was recruited by Brooke. As Burney pointed out, the

Table 2 *Salaries paid to the* primo uomo *at the King's Theatre*

Season	Singer	Salary	Comments	Source
1764–5	Manzuoli	£1,500		Milhous and Hume, 'Opera Salaries', 42
1765–6	Elisi	[not known]		
1766–7	Guarducci	[not known]		
1767–8	Guarducci	£1,230 ?	Spring payment £410.	Drummonds
1768–9	Guadagni	£1,150		*London Magazine*, 40 (1771), 93
1769–70	[no *opera seria*]		Guadagni is reported to have asked for £1,600.	*London Magazine*, 40 (1771), 93
1770–1	Tenducci	[not known]		
1771–2	Tenducci	[not known]		
1772–3	Millico		Did not arrive until late in the season.	
1773–4	Millico	£1,200 ?	Spring payment £400.	Hoare & Co.
1774–5	Rauzzini	[£1,100?]		
1775–6	Rauzzini	[£1,100?]		
1776–7	Rauzzini	£1,100 ?	Winter and spring payments £366.13s.4d.	Hoare & Co.
1777–8	Roncaglia	£1,000		*The Remarkable Trial of the Queen of Quavers*, 75
1778–9	Pacchierotti	£1,200		See below, p. 201
1779–80	Pacchierotti	£1,200		See below, p. 201
1780–1	Roncaglia	£1,000		Milhous and Hume, 'Opera 'Salaries', 44

Table 2 (*cont.*)

Season	Singer	Salary	Comments	Source
1781–2	Pacchierotti	[£1,200]		
1782–3	Pacchierotti	£1,200		Milhous and Hume, 'Opera Salaries', 45

singer enjoyed a very high reputation in England long before his arrival, as a result of the interest engendered by performances of airs 'after his manner' by Piozzi. There was also a favourable report in Brydone's *Travels*.[2] No documentary evidence concerning the recruitment has yet come to light, but the indications that Brooke was responsible include the following:

(1) Her agent, Wiseman, claimed in late 1777 to have 'fatigue for the year 1778 and 1779'. In plain English, he was saying that he had already undertaken some preparatory tasks for the 1778–9 season (and possible even the 1779–80 season) without payment.[3]

(2) It was Brooke's normal practice to recruit major singers over a year in advance, as was the case with both Rauzzini and Danzi, whose hiring was common knowledge by January or February of the year of their debut.

(3) Mount-Edgcumbe records that Roncaglia's reception at his debut in Sacchini's *Creso* on 8 November 1777 was so enthusiastic that he was immediately offered a contract for the next available season, which was not until 1780–1.[4] This suggests that Pacchierotti had already been hired by the King's Theatre for the next two seasons, and perhaps also that Roncaglia too had future engagements. In general, the recruitment of leading singers was having to be done a long time in advance. Susan Burney describes how in 1780, when Pacchierotti fever was gripping the opera world in London, a group of subscribers circulated a petition 'to beg that after next year when Roncaglia's engagement must take place, they w[d] reengage Sig[r] Pacchierotti to return here for two years more'.[5]

(4) The *Queen of Quavers* satirist, writing late in 1777, includes the names of Pacchierotti and Ansani in a list of Italian opera singers worthy to be made 'denisens of the moon' (i.e. inhabitants of England).

If Brooke was indeed responsible for the great castrato's recruitment, she bequeathed her successors an even more valuable legacy than she herself had received in the person of Sacchini.

As far as can now be determined, Pacchierotti's salary remained at £1,200 throughout his years at the King's Theatre. On 20 July 1779, the singer opened an account at Coutts & Co. with a payment of £400, which was immediately invested in government stock – consolidated annuities at 3 per cent. On this occasion the money could not have been the summer payment for that season, because that was not made until 17 August. In a letter to his partner, Sheridan expressed his concern about his inability to settle with Pacchierotti. It is docketed in a contemporary hand '2 July 1782', but the fact that it is addressed to Harris (who withdrew from the King's Theatre towards the end of 1779) suggests that this is a mistake and that it actually dates from the end of the 1778–9 season:

[mid June 1779]   Richard Brinsley Sheridan to Thomas Harris

Saturday 4 o clock

Dear H.

I'll get these six two hundred and fiftys, exchanged directly for 12. of £150 and more if I can. Garton has also one of [£] 250 and another of £150 besides those he gave me the Receipt for. Which will make £2200. In the mean time I have no possible way to pay Pacchierotti, but by Garton's accepting a Note for his last Payment – which Pacchierotti will take at 2 months – and he wants to leave England tomorrow. Garton has no objection but desires me to write to you first. The Case is you see that He may be sure at least of this money from the above securities before the Note can be due – for Johnson is quite positive that Stone etc. will lend even back to the £300, when once the subscriptions are paid up – and then Garton may have as much of the money as he likes, and I'll empower him to receive it of Stone, but from this Delay I have no other possible way of satisfying Pacchierotti, and it will be the Devil and all to detain him. I have paid Pozzi and another who are going directly to Day. Pray send me a line for Garton.[6]

Sheridan's most pressing concern seems to have been to raise security for the £2,000 loan which was deposited in the Drummond's account on 19 June. The two singers, Pozzi and Manzoletto, were paid on 7 June, which suggests that the letter was written in the second week of that month. His frank admission that he could not pay Pacchierotti proves that Drummonds would not allow him to run the opera account into the red at this late stage in the season. Also of note is the clear implication that part of Sheridan's problems stemmed from subscriptions not yet having been paid up.[7] Garton was willing to make the payment to Pacchierotti, but only after receiving something in writing from Harris, his long-time associate at Covent Garden. Pacchierotti appeared willing to accept a small delay of two months, and in fact he received his money from Garton in mid August. Sheridan's real worry in all this was his fear of being unable to 'detain' the celebrated singer. It is not clear whether he was threatening to leave before the final performances of the season, or (more likely) to renege on the second year of his contract.

The following year, Sheridan got into even deeper financial trouble, and Pacchierotti began to suspect that he would not receive his salary at all. He threatened that unless he and Bertoni were paid by 21 June, they would hire a lawyer 'who is to have the charge of reimbursing himself as soon as possible *by Lawyer's means*'.[8] Susan Burney describes how the singer compiled an 'incendiary letter' to send to Sheridan: 'Pacchierotti sends his compts to Mr Sheridan, and is very displeased to be obliged to call him a Rascal – but his conduct is in everything so irregular he can give no better title to so great Breaker of his Word. D—n him and his way of thinking, which I wish it may bring him to the Gallows.'[9] He then drew a gallows with a man hanging and himself at the bottom of it pulling down the victim's leg. The incident was reported as a piece of humour, but the singer was seriously concerned. A few weeks later, the threat of legal action had worked, and Susan Burney noted Sheridan's assurance that he would in future be more attentive to matters of business with the singer. To raise some additional money, Sheridan extended the season to Saturday 1 July. On 5 July, the sum of £604. 9s. was duly deposited in Pacchierotti's Coutts & Co. account: 'By cash received R. B. Sheridan's bill on Jon. Garton'. This comprised half a year's salary plus a small extra sum, perhaps a nominal payment for the additional performance. According to the page of accounts in the Salt Library, the other £600 (plus £8. 13s. 2d., of interest?) was paid on 5 December. The opera subscribers were furious at Sheridan's behaviour and alarmed at the damage it might cause to the reputation of the King's Theatre. Roncaglia was already hired for the 1780–1 season, but there were doubts about whether Pacchierotti would return the following year, as planned, if Sheridan remained in charge. Lady Clarges wrote to Susan Burney: 'I am sorry that Rascal Sheridan is in Parliament. I dare say *Pac* will hear of it & he will not come, or any body else, perhaps Manzoletto will sing *gratis* as he is so fond of England, it makes me melancholy to think of it, I wish Dr Burney & Sir Thos [Clarges] w^d let us choak Sheridan & be ye managers for next year.'[10]

Pacchierotti himself was having serious misgivings about a further engagement in London. Before leaving Venice, he wrote to Fanny Burney for advice:

2 December 1780   Pacchierotti to Fanny Burney

> I am astonished of Mr Sheridan's undertakins and I found your remarks very judicious on his purpose but pray tell me freely what do you think of him? do you suppose he will succeed well in his schemes? as I have a great Idea of your judgement I shall take your hints for my guide, assured by them not to miscarry.[11]

With the assurance of support from the Burneys, he agreed to return, but he remained deeply apprehensive about how he would cope with a further round of negotiations with the opera manager. In the spring of 1781, some months before he was due to return to England for a second two-year engagement, he confided his continuing uncertainty to Fanny Burney:

18 April 1781   Pacchierotti to Fanny Burney

... as soon as the Performances at Mantua is over I take your advise, &
without esitation shall return to England, where I may consider myself
happy if I can be favoured as formerly by your assistance on which
depends my future tranquillity; for indeed relying only, either on my
prudence, or expirience both could mislead me, particularly in a place,
which is for Foreigners the most intrigate of all, in the World, unless he
is so lucky as to trust his lot in the hands of a Native, who has a peculiar
Fiendship [sic] for him such as I have expirienced from your sensible
heart.[12]

His assessment of the 'intrigate' nature of the London opera world
was fully justified. The new manager proved every bit as evasive over
salary payments as Sheridan had been. In direct emulation of his predecessor's behaviour, William Taylor called upon Pacchierotti to
hand him two bills for his overdue salary payments, one postponing
payment indefinitely. As was by now fast becoming an annual event,
the singer, relaxing in Tunbridge Wells after the season had ended,
wrote to his confidant about his latest problem:

20 July 1782   Pacchierotti to Fanny Burney

Nothing remarcable has happened to me the few hours of my stayng in
the capital, except a very curious transaction with our manager, *not yet
member of parliamen*[t. H]e waited on me when I was out, and asking for
paper pen and ink set down a note in which he thought proper to
include the remain of my payment in two hand Bills one to be payed 5 or
six months after Date, and the other when he pleases. What do you
think of that? My affairs are, you know, in the hands of a lawyer who I
intend to inform with the particulars and I am sure he will give a
warning to Mr Taylor how he must behave in future, but the little Rogue
knows the Court of Laws is shut up now 'till November, and it was the
reason of his using me so unkindly; patience, three times patience since
it is not the worse of my misfortunes.[13]

Later that autumn, various payments emanating from Taylor did
begin to enter Pacchierotti's account, but at the start of the new
season, things went from bad to worse. The chaos was beginning to
spread beyond the finances of the opera house:

9 November 1782   Pacchierotti to Fanny Burney

Money transactions still remains at the same footing – no body is payed and the Opera house is always in confusion. Yesterday it was appointed the general Rehearsal so every body there Morigi excepted ready to do his duty – When we found the house quite overset and all occupyed by Painters, Bricklers, Carpenters, etc, who having taken possession of the Ground did not suffered to yeild it to us so we had no chance but to make a retreat & let them be master of the field, and went away. I had hardly walked a few steps when met with Mʳ Sheridan to whom I tell which had happened and he smiled saying *sad management*. What do you think of that – ha ha ha.[14]

This little picture of Sheridan, sauntering past the great theatre he had done so much to cripple financially, is an apt epitaph on his three years as manager. Pacchierotti adopted an air of resigned, ironical detachment, while waiting for his next chance to institute legal action.

A further postscript to Pacchierotti's struggle to achieve the final settlement of his salary occurs in his Coutts & Co. bank account in the summer of 1783. Payments of £400 on 23 April and 13 May 1782 and 21 May 1783 suggest that his salary was still at the level of £1,200 per season. A surprising receipt on 19 July 1783 is £483. 6s. 8d. 'by cash recd of Lady Mary Duncan's account being the amount of Mr Sheridan's debt'. On 6 August, £83. 6s. 8d. was promptly repaid 'to cash Lady Mary Duncan's account'. This ardent supporter of the singer had apparently taken it upon herself to settle a long outstanding debt of Sheridan's, perhaps from the 1778–9 season. The Drummonds payments for that season plus the full sum given by Lady Mary amount in total to £1,100. The size of the refund therefore suggests that one payment of £183. 6s. 8d. had been made from elsewhere in Sheridan's labyrinthine financial empire. Having been overpaid, it seems that Pacchierotti, acting with a degree of good faith never shown to him by his London employers, immediately refunded the surplus. Although he had to wait a long time for the final payment, Pacchierotti was probably the one person to emerge from Sheridan's regime with a full settlement of all his debts. It was overwhelmingly in the interests of the opera house that the singer should be retained. He had a large and devoted following in London, and his presence ensured excellent houses over extended periods. Once he had given up the King's Theatre, Sheridan could afford to procrastinate on the matter of the singer's final payment. The tactic was unscrupulous, but it worked. The new regime was so anxious to retain the singer that an adoring fan was persuaded to part with the cash. Lady Mary's motive was doubtless to ensure that the singer would return the following year, which, given Taylor's treatment of him, was by no means certain. Burney was involved in the scheme. He wrote to Thomas Twining on 6 September 1783: 'If Gallini's Claims to the Theatre are valid, we shall have the dear Pacchierotti another year, by a Contrivance of mine & another of his Friends – but mum – more in my next on this & other matters.'[15] The long-term stability of Pacchierotti's salary in London is shown by the fact that he was still receiving £1,200 for the 1790–1 season at the Pantheon.[16]

Salaries for the *prima donna*, sometimes high in the first half of the eighteenth century, were apparently in the doldrums during the 1760s. In his hypothetical pay-scale for 1763, Giardini suggested £950 for the *primo uomo*, but for the leading woman, he thought £760 appropriate and even less (£552. 10s.), if she were only a 'middling' performer.[17] A salary of £600 to Davies in her first season is thus not implausible, especially as Schindlerin the following year was perhaps contracted for only £700. The singer's triumph with the London public meant that she was offered £1,000 for her second season, whereupon the managers promptly reneged on her contract. The arrival of Europe's two leading women singers, Gabrielli at £1,500 and Agujari at £1,200, dramatically altered the situation. These super-star salaries pointed the way towards the large fees that were to be paid regularly to Mara, Banti, Billington and Catalani at the end of the century. The first hint of this comes in Mara's letter of 12 November 1783, refusing £1,200, but claiming that 'if Mr Gallini had offered me £1,500, I would have accepted it subject to the usual conditions'.[18] In the short term, however, the salary offered to a high-quality *prima donna* stabilised at around £1,000.[19] Whether Bernasconi really

Table 3 *Salaries paid to the* prima donna *at the King's Theatre*

Season	Singer	Salary	Comments	Source
1773–4	Davies	£900 or £600 ?	Winter payment of £200, '2 at £100'.	Hoare & Co.
1774–5	[Davies]	[£1,000]	Her contract was for £1000 plus benefit.	
	Schindlerin	£700 ?	Summer payment of £233. 6s. 8d.	Hoare & Co.
1775–6	Gabrielli	£1,500 ?	Spring and summer payments of £500.	Hoare & Co.
	[Agujari]	[£1,200]	Her Pantheon salary.	
1776–7	Davies	£750 ?	Pro rata for three quarters of a season at £1,000?	Hoare & Co.
1777–8	Danzi [Le Brun]	[£1,000]		
1778–9	Bernasconi	£550 ?	Delayed summer payment of £183. 6s. 8d.	Drummonds
1779–80	Le Brun	[£1,000]		
1780–1	Le Brun	£1,000		Milhous and Hume, 'Opera Salaries', 44

received only £550 is hard to say on the evidence of the Drummonds account alone. The following year when she was demoted to the rank of *prima buffa*, she may have received only £350, to judge by the single delayed payment of £116. 13s. 8d. in the Salt Manuscript. The only evidence of Le Brun's salary in the 1779–80 season is the much delayed payment of £200, also in the Salt Manuscript. This singer also had to take legal action to force Sheridan to pay.[20]

The high status of top women singers in late eighteenth-century London is reflected in an interesting linguistic convention.

Aristocratic opera subscribers usually referred to male singers by name alone ('Lovattini') or by title and name ('Signor Lovattini'). As has been seen throughout this study, when reference was made to a leading woman singer, a common formulation was the definite article with the surname ('the Gabrielli', 'the de Amicis'). In part this could have been an affectation deriving from perceived French or Italian linguistic usage – Fanny Burney sometimes refers to 'La Gabrielli'. There are connotations of a proprietary nature, as though a woman singer was a commodity to be traded between opera houses, as indeed was often the case. Yet the use of the definite article could also be seen as a mark of distinction, an acknowledgement of a quality of uniqueness.

Little is known about the salaries of comic opera performers in the mid-eighteenth century in England. The De Amicis family asked for £1,000 for its collective contribution to the *opera buffa* season in Dublin in 1762–3.[21] The salaries enjoyed by the *primo buffo* during the 1770s reflect the establishment of comic opera as a major part of the King's Theatre season. It seems reasonable to assume that Lovattini got £900 for each of the seven seasons which he played in London. Carabaldi's reputation placed him on a par with Lovattini, while Trebbi, less distinguished, nonetheless received a respectable salary.

Fewer figures are known for *prima buffa* singers, but the £500 paid to Sestini is confirmed by a later newspaper report.[22]

Dancers' salaries are greatly complicated by the presence of families, but normal levels for the 1770s can be established. The remarkable salary of £1,200 given to Heinel (admittedly only half of which was paid by the opera management) was not repeated, but the fashion for dancing started by this inspirational performer meant that significant expenditure was incurred. The ballet master received a minimum of £500–£600 – the higher sums offered to Pitrot and Simonet may have included payments for other family members.[23] Leading dancers took a similar amount: Fierville £525 and Vallovy £600 (wife and son included). Baccelli's salary of £300 in 1774–5 and £400 in 1775–6 is exactly as noted in a later newspaper report.[24]

If the low fees suggested by Giardini in 1763–4 are typical of

Table 4 *Salaries paid to the* primo buffo *at the King's Theatre*

Season	Singer	Salary	Comments	Source
1766–7	Lovattini	[£900]		
1767–8	Lovattini	[£900]		
1768–9	Lovattini	£900	Three payments of £300.	Drummonds
1769–70	Lovattini	[£900]		
1770–1	Lovattini	[£900]		
1771–2	Lovattini	[£900]		
1772–3			No *opera buffa*.	
1773–4	[Carabaldi]		Did not arrive.	
1774–5	[Carabaldi]	[£850 plus benefit]	Fee requested by singer.	Humphry MSS, HU/13
	Lovattini	£900	Benefit proceeds to the managers.	Humphry MSS, HU/13
1775–6	Trebbi	£600?	Spring and summer payments of £200.	Hoare & Co.
1776–7	Trebbi	£700?	Sang some *seria* roles. Winter and spring payments £233. 6s. 8d.	Hoare & Co.

Table 5 *Salaries paid to the* prima buffa *at the King's Theatre*

Season	Singer	Salary	Comments	Source
1768–9	Guadagni	*c.* £500–£600 ?	Three payments of £233. 6s. 8d. include husband.	Drummonds
1774–5	Sestini	£500 ?	Summer payment of £166. 13s. 4d.	Hoare & Co.
1775–6	Sestini	[£500]		
1776–7	Sestini	[£500]		
1779–80	Bernasconi	£350?	Single payment of £116. 13s. 8d.	Salt MSS

Table 6 *Salaries paid to the dancers at the King's Theatre*

Season	Dancer	Salary	Comments	Source
1772–3	Heinel	£1,200		Burney, *A General History of Music*, II, 878
1773–4	Pitrot (ballet master)	£750	Includes payments to Mimi and Nina Faviere.	Hoare & Co.
	Fierville	£525		Hoare & Co.
1774–5	Lany (ballet master)	£500		Hoare & Co.
	Vallovy	c.£600	Includes payments to wife and son.	Hoare & Co.
	Baccelli	£300		Hoare & Co.
1775–6	Bouqueton (ballet master)	[unknown]		Hoare & Co.
	Fierville	£525		Hoare & Co.
	Baccelli	£400		Hoare & Co.
1776–7	Simonet (ballet master)	£800	Includes payments to wife.	Hoare & Co.
	Vallovy	£600	Includes payments to wife and son.	Hoare & Co.
	Baccelli	£300		Hoare & Co.

mid-century payments to composers, then the 1770s witnessed a striking improvement in their position. The 'going rate' for a Sacchini opera in the early years of the Brooke–Yates partnership seems to have been £150, but it is not clear how this related to his salary as house composer. At this rate (excluding anything for work done on pasticcios or as a harpsichordist) his salary in the 1773–4 season would have been £450, but only £150 the following year when he produced only one new opera. Vento and Traetta appear to have been paid at a broadly comparable level. From being a (financially) insignificant figure, the composer was by the mid 1770s almost on a

Table 7 *Salaries paid to the composers at the King's Theatre*

Season	Composer	Salary	Comments	Source
1763–4	Piccinni	£200	Offered for 2 operas and work on pasticcios.	Price, Milhous and Hume, *The Impresario's Ten Commandments*, 27
		£38	Offered for 1 opera by post.	Price, Milhous and Hume, *The Impresario's Ten Commandments*, 27
	Vento	£142. 10s.	Offered for 2 operas.	Price, Milhous and Hume, *The Impresario's Ten Commandments*, 27
1770–1	[Piccinni]	[£400]	Offered for 3 operas and pasticcio work.	Burney, *An Eighteenth-Century Musical Tour in France and Italy*, 247
1773–4	Sacchini	£450?	Payments of £150 for 2 operas (composed 3).	Hoare & Co.
1774–5	Sacchini	£150	Payment for 1 opera.	Hoare & Co.
1775–6	Vento	£350 or £500?	3 payments of £116. 13s. 4d. plus £150?	Hoare & Co.
1776–7	Traetta	£500?	Spring payment of £166. 13s. 4d. (composed 3 operas).	Hoare & Co.
	Piccinni	£16. 13s. 4d.	For opera airs by post?	Hoare & Co.
		£20. 7s. 4d.	For opera airs by post?	Hoare & Co.
1778–9	Bertoni	£300?	Spring payment of £150 (composed 2 operas).	Drummonds
	Sacchini	£200	For 1 or 2 operas?	Drummonds
	Piccinni	£23. 6s. 8d.	For opera airs by post?	Drummonds

par with the *prima buffa* or leading dancer. Vento, who in 1763 was described contemptuously as a 'pasticiere' when offered a contract for £142. 10s., was a decade later in receipt of a salary three times this amount.[25] Under Sheridan, Bertoni was probably due to receive £300 for two operas, but whether he earned anything more as house composer is not clear. If the two payments of £100 on a single day to Sacchini relate to both his two operas that year, that might indicate a decline in his earning power, although drawing any definite conclusions from Sheridan's financial accounts is a risky business.

Although the details are not always clear, the general trend undoubtedly saw the financial status of composers improve during the 1770s; it is one of the most noteworthy aspects of Brooke's management. The origins of this development perhaps lie in Burney's unproductive but illuminating encounter with Piccinni during his Italian tour of 1770. His experience may well have led him to recommend a fundamental reappraisal of what salary the King's Theatre could expect to pay for a good composer. Acting on behalf of Hobart, Burney offered to Piccinni a salary of £400 for three new operas and 'to arrange and patch up Pasticcios'. Since this was twice the £200 proposed by Giardini, Burney perhaps regarded it as generous. If so, he received a shock when Piccinni asked for £800. The composer, who was obviously quite well informed about operatic life in London, at first scornfully rejected the notion of being 'plagued with the Pasticcios, which would occupy all his leisure and produce him neither honour nor profit'. He then reminded Burney that the earlier offer had been for two operas only. As a further condition, Piccinni pointed out that he would be asking for control over the printing of his own opera songs, which Guarducci had told him was a profitable enterprise in England. On this point Burney disagreed, noting 'how short lived' opera songs were and that only 'the *favourite* songs' were printed, which 'nothing but the number sent to the shops and abroad by a dealer in music could make it worth while to publish'. On the other hand, there were other significant financial benefits to be had in London. Piccinni might employ his leisure hours 'in teaching at a very high price ladies of great quality, or in composing for instruments which would turn to good account'. The composer's rejoinder, however, was that he could make £400 for two operas in Italy without the expense or risk of going to England, which journey he would not undertake for less than £800. He further pointed out that travel was expensive 'if he travelled at his ease, which he had been accustomed to do' and would 'occasion a considerable diminution in the £400 proposed'. By now, seemingly somewhat taken aback, Burney told the composer that 'no one could be so good a judge of his affairs as himself', and that he would not attempt to persuade him to do what he thought 'contrary to his interest and inclination'. Piccinni thought 'the offer might be a good one to a young man not known or established here', but to him 'it was no kind of temptation'.[26] With the benefit of these blunt observations, Burney could now report back to the King's Theatre manager that though he might hire without difficulty a third-rate hack to stitch up pasticcios, he could not expect to hire a major figure like Piccinni for a small sum. When Brooke took over responsibility for hiring composers, she clearly opted (doubtless at the behest of Burney) to spend money on recruiting composers of repute to provide new works for her theatre.

The other factor in the increased rewards offered to composers was that Sacchini was the most important and successful composer in long-term residence at the King's Theatre since the days of Handel. His triumph with *Il Cid* at the start of the Brooke–Yates management demonstrated the potential value of obtaining good-quality operas to stage, rather than relying too heavily on cheaper pasticcios.

The relatively high level of remuneration offered to the house composer during the later years of the Brooke–Yates partnership has some bearing on Gallini's first attempts to recruit Haydn for the King's Theatre in 1783. Burney was deeply involved, writing to Twining on 6 September: 'I have stimulated a wish to get Haydn over as opera Composer – but mum mum – yet – a correspondence is opened, & there is a great likelihood of it, if these Cabals, & litigations ruin not the opera entirely.'[27] On 12 November Burney continued: 'Did I tell you that Gallini's agents shewed me a Letter from

Haydn, in wch he was in treaty to come over for the opera?'[28] In his 'MS Materials Towards the History of German Music & Musicians', Burney recorded the figures under negotiation: 'In 1783, Gallini wrote to him [Haydn] to come over as Composer to the Opera: I saw his answer, he asked £600. Gallini was then in Italy. Since that according to Fischer he had asked him £1,000 for coming over expressly for the opera.' In response to a further enquiry from Gallini in 1787, Haydn demanded £500, a free benefit and the right to perform at the Hanover Square concerts.[29] The salary level initially under discussion for Haydn, a minimum of £500 to £600, equates fairly closely with the norm established by Brooke (which, however, had probably fallen during Sheridan's proprietorship). The active participation of Burney in suggesting to Gallini an appropriate level of payment to Haydn seems a distinct possibility.

Taken as a whole, salary levels during Brooke's period of management reflect general trends in Italian opera. Castrati were still earning the highest fees. Women singers, following the success of Davies and above all the year of the Gabrielli–Agujari confrontation, found their earning power much improved. The important place of comic opera in the London season was reflected in solid salaries for the *primo buffo*, not far below that of the castrato. The growing reputation of tenors such as Adamberger and Ansani is not reflected in the Hoare accounts. In all, principal performers – the *primo uomo*, the *prima dònna*, the *buffo*, the *buffa*, the dancing master, leading dancers, composer and orchestral leader – cost the King's Theatre about £5,000–£5,500 each season. In 1776–7, for example, the following: Rauzzini (£1,150); Pozzi–Davies (*c*. £1,000); Trebbi (£700); Sestini (£500); Simonet (£800); Vallovy (£500); Baccelli (£300); Traetta (£500); Giardini (? £300): in total around £5,300. This overall figure seems to have remained quite stable during the period.

The bank accounts of the King's Theatre during the 1770s confirm the anecdotal evidence of letters, newspaper reports and satires that Brooke made a notable commercial success of the opera house. It was no ordinary achievement. Even to recover costs, she had to overcome formidable obstacles. Prior to its enlargements in 1778 and 1782, the theatre's capacity was probably no more than 1,000. Judith Milhous estimates a mid-century full-house at around 950 'with extreme crowding', to which total must be added an unknown but probably small number of stage boxes.[1] An equally limiting constraint on the theatre's income was the law restricting it to performances of Italian opera, particularly since the season lasted some sixty nights a year only. For four and a half months from July to November, the building remained closed. Had permission been granted for English productions, or even for a greater number of social events such as masquerades, some subsidy for Italian opera would have been possible, but this way of achieving financial stability was denied to successive proprietors. The only ways to increase income from the theatre with the existing restrictions were thus to raise admission charges or to increase the occupancy rate. To have put up the price of tickets would have been to take a big gamble; admission charges had long been established and any increase might well have been counter-productive. A much more promising strategy was to aim for as high an occupancy rate as possible throughout the season. This was Brooke's policy and it clearly worked. Newspaper reports of 'brilliant and crowded' houses were clichés of the puff writers, among whom indeed was Brooke herself, yet early in 1778, such observations are so frequent as to carry conviction. A review of the opening night of Sacchini's *Erefile* is typical: 'the theatre was filled in a few minutes after the doors were opened, or rather crammed; as not only the pit, boxes and galleries were crowded, but the stage, the passages, and the tea-rooms: never was there a more brilliant assembly'.[2] A piece in the *Morning Post* noted that the pit had been 'so thronged with *plumed heroines*, that more than a hundred *fine gentlemen* were obliged to display their *divine* figures on the stage, to the no small inconvenience of the performers, and the dislike of the audience'.[3] A strongly critical letter from Philharmonicus published on 16 March confirms the full houses but churlishly suggests that the managers were achieving them by 'cramming the upper part of the house with a set of miscreants (the sweepings of every Italian warehouse in town)'.[4] In April, Bach's new opera opened to a 'crowded and brilliant audience'.[5] Well-attended opening nights were not difficult to achieve; much more problematic was to retain a high level of interest through to the last weeks of the season in June. By far the best way of achieving this desirable outcome was to hire at least one performer with the necessary personal and musical charisma to attract audiences over a long period. Brooke learnt this lesson through hard experience. The indifference of the public to the Rauzzini–Schindlerin partnership plunged her management perilously close to financial ruin, but the following year Gabrielli demonstrated that a star with personal magnetism could transform the fortunes of the opera house. Her celebrated temperament and the controversies over her voice did not prevent patrons from returning again and again to hear her. Brooke's peremptory dismissal of Pozzi in 1776 is indicative of the fact that she had by now accepted the reality that the financial health of her theatre was largely bound up in the reception accorded the star performers. It seems certain that she was encouraged to take this view by Burney, who had long argued the economic case for the hiring of superstar singers. Commenting on the fortunes of the rival Pantheon, he observed that although Agujari was offered a considerable salary, the investment had paid off, as 'the dividend was more considerable than it has ever been since that memorable aera'.[6] The policy of spending extra money on singers of the highest class was not without risk but it usually worked; the large salaries paid to Manzuoli, Gabrielli and Pacchierotti all proved highly successful investments.

Burney was probably responsible for another aspect of Brooke's managerial strategy – the time and effort she put into locating operas by good composers. The practice of employing one or more 'house' composers and supplementing the programme with works bought abroad was a very effective one. During her final two years in charge she purchased works by Bach, Sacchini, Traetta, Piccinni and Paesiello. The relatively modest quality of this commissioned repertoire should not detract from the significance of the policy change. Whereas Le Texier (and perhaps Garrick) viewed acting styles and audience behaviour as the central problems of Italian opera in London, Brooke, under the influence of Burney, looked to improve the quality of the music. In due course, this policy led to the recruitment of Cherubini and the invitations offered to Haydn and Mozart. The new emphasis on what composers could contribute to the King's Theatre was in part a consequence of the scale of Sacchini's success, something not seen since the days of Handel. After five years, his popularity seemed undiminished, and he still had many active supporters. A letter published in the *Morning Post* on 7 March 1777, at the height of the one season during his London years in which no opera by him was performed at the King's Theatre, was strongly critical of London taste, which was condemned as 'uncultivated' because of its failure to support his works with sufficient enthusiasm.[7] When he returned as house composer in the 1777–8 season, he scored a notable triumph. Spending money on music, it now appeared, made economic sense. If there was to be an outlay of over £2,500 on leading singers (as with the Gabrielli–Rauzzini partnership), an extra hundred pounds or so invested in a composer of repute was likely to be money well spent, if only to ensure the best possible public response to the star performers.

One consequence of this policy was that the culture of the pasticcio began to come under attack. Brooke probably heard from Burney just how dismissive Piccinni had been, when offered a contract specifying some work on pasticcios. She had seen for herself the extent to which Sacchini's *Il Cid* had re-invigorated the *opera seria* tradition in London, after years during which the employment of a good composer was coming to seem virtually superfluous in this genre. The decline of the pasticcio during the period of Brooke's management became obvious during her last two seasons. In the first three of her seasons there were three pasticcios in each; in 1776–7 there were only two, and in 1777–8 one. The total number of pasticcio performances (which naturally depended on the success of the works in question) declined still more rapidly: thirteen, twenty-one, twenty-five, six, one. This is too small a number of seasons to provide unambiguous evidence of a trend, since there had previously been seasons with few pasticcios, but there are strong indications that Brooke, an author herself, favoured the one-composer opera as a matter of policy. The only serious setback came when Rauzzini apparently forced her to turn *Didone* into a pasticcio. This was only an isolated surrender, and in subsequent seasons Brooke, supporting her composers, insisted that new operas by Traetta, Sacchini and Bach should be given largely as their authors intended. Yet the pasticcio was very far from being defunct. Its revival following the 1778 sale reflects the reassertion of an older balance of power, with a strong manager (Brooke) being replaced by a very weak one (Le Texier), and with moderate singers (Danzi and Roncaglia) being replaced by one with charisma (Pacchierotti). Once again, star singers started to insist on their traditional right to incorporate airs of their own choosing.

Brooke certainly spent more on composers than had hitherto been the practice, but her concern was with quality rather than innovation, an attitude she perhaps shared with Burney. It is probable that the major innovation in *opera seria* – the attempt at the start of the 1773 season to introduce some of the ideas of reform opera to London – was instigated by Hobart, but Brooke quickly got involved in the running of the King's Theatre, and she could well have played some part in agreeing a production of *Orfeo*. The fate of Gluck's masterpiece – two performances followed by a reversion to the pasticcio version – demonstrated that reform opera would not succeed in London. Thereafter, despite the continuing emphasis on spectacle and chorus, and occasional attempts to integrate ballet, composers of Italian opera in London showed little inclination to experiment radically with the genre. In making decisions about repertoire, Brooke was obviously influenced by the subscribers to the King's Theatre. The adverse reaction to *Vittorina*, a comic opera deemed too serious, led to the immediate suspension of the production. Brooke was in effect accepting the need to write off money spent on this production in order to achieve the broader goal of keeping her subscribers happy. This was perhaps the central difference between her and Le Texier, whose intervention as a critic in 1777 in favour of radical change was sadly mistimed. His proposals ignored the fact that the finances of the King's Theatre were balanced on a knife edge and that to antagonise the audience would be to court commercial ruin. In an age in which fashion and novelty were powerful selling points, for example in the retail of musical instruments, Brooke's pragmatic submission to the entrenched conservatism of the opera establishment had a clear economic rationale. Change did come, but slowly; the significant influences were experience of productions gained by English visitors taking the Grand Tour, and Gallini's links with the Burgtheater in Vienna.

Throughout her years at the King's Theatre, Brooke never deviated from the view that a programme of popular *opera buffa* was vital to the commercial success of the opera house. For many decades, the repertoire of comic opera performed at the King's Theatre had been distinctly old-fashioned. In the 1770s, London finally caught up with the Continent. Given the location of Brooke's contacts, it is hardly surprising that Rome was the dominant source of supply. Roman operas staged by Brooke (with dates of first performances in Rome and London) included Piccinni's *La donna di spirito* (1770, 1775), Anfossi's *La marchesa giardiniera* (1774, 1775), *Il geloso in cimento* (1774, 1777) and *La vera costanza* (1776, 1778), and Paisiello's *Le due contesse* (1776, 1777). The immediacy of the Roman connection is obvious at a glance. Yet, even as she was urging her contacts in Italy to seek out the newest scores, Brooke did not lose sight of the potential of a good comic work to last. There was apparently never any question of repeating an *opera seria*. Not one of Sacchini's serious works, even the triumphant *Il Cid*, was deemed worthy of revival by Brooke in a subsequent season. (The exceptional revival of Bach's *Orione* late in the 1776–7 season, fourteen years after its London première, was surely intended as a tactic to re-introduce the composer to the King's Theatre audience, prior to his new opera *La clemenza di Scipione* the following year.) But a pattern of repeating successful comic works was beginning to be established. The most successful of the older generation of *opere buffe*, Galuppi's *Il filosofo di compagna*, had lasted several seasons in the 1760s. Piccinni's *La buona figliuola* had been given in the six consecutive seasons before Brooke assumed control. It appeared to be on the verge of extinction, but when she revived it in 1775, she established it as the first Italian opera in London to achieve the status of a canonical work. It was to be well into the nineteenth century before a lasting canon of opera came into being, but Brooke's policy of reviving past favourites is an interesting precursor. Following the success of *La buona figliuola*, she brought back in 1777 the same composer's *La schiava*, which had been given during the five consecutive seasons from 1768 to 1772. Her own most successful *opera buffa* import, Paisiello's *La frascatana* (Venice 1774, London 1776) was revived in several subsequent seasons.

Notwithstanding the attention Brooke devoted to improving the quality and variety of repertoire and to enhancing the dramatic spectacle, there is little doubt that the star singers remained the central attraction of Italian opera in London. A commercial strategy which relied to so great an extent on one or two individual performers was not without great risk; it could be placed in immediate jeopardy by ill-health, which, after fire, was probably what eighteenth-century opera managers most feared. A simple cold, which prevented Gabrielli from making her debut on the appointed night, caused the biggest furore of Brooke's years at the King's Theatre. On such occasions, managers had to cope with the understandable but irrational rage of disappointed subscribers. Yet, as time went on, the King's Theatre began to benefit from a development which reduced the risk of a major catastrophe on this count. This was the growing number of Italian opera singers who elected to reside in England for significant periods. Leading Italian singers could find employment not only at the King's Theatre, but at the Pantheon, the English opera theatres, the concert series promoted by Gallini at Hanover Square, further afield in affluent centres such as Bath, Dublin or Edinburgh, and they were in demand as private guests at aristocratic residences. Had Roncaglia become incapacitated during the 1777–8 season, there were six other castrati, including two with experience of playing *primo uomo* at the King's Theatre (Rauzzini and Tenducci), who could have deputised at short notice. When Pozzi failed, Davies was able to take her place within weeks.

An important strand of the managerial strategy adopted by Brooke was the strict control of costs. Apart from the addition of stage boxes in 1773 and the redecoration in the summer of 1777, no major alterations were carried out, although it should be pointed out that there is no evidence as to what the £4,500 mortgage obtained in 1774 was used for. Italian opera was on the verge of needing a much enlarged auditorium, but Brooke, prudent rather than speculative, opted to develop the existing building to the fullest extent possible without substantial capital expenditure. Harsh economies were made in the operating budget. She cut back on the services of overseas agents. Payments to such individuals in the Hoare ledgers match closely what is known of their activities from the Humphry correspondence: Butler (the emissary), Wiseman (the agent), Vergani (the representative), Barazzi and Wills & Leigh (the bankers), all received payment for services rendered. The recruiter John Gordon was paid in 1773, 1774 and 1776. But few other agents can be identified, as Brooke began to make much greater use of unpaid assistance from men like Humphry, Greville and Hamilton. She also relied more heavily on correspondence. This policy had the added advantage of giving the opera subscribers, through involvement in the process of planning and recruitment, a sense of collective ownership.

To effect the required savings, Brooke seems to have relied on Richard Yates, who, making good use of his long experience of theatres, instituted a rigorous programme of cost-cutting in house management. He soon became notorious for his parsimony. Fanny Burney amusingly revealed this side of his character in her description of his anguish at having to turn away the audience (and the money) after the cancellation of Gabrielli's opening night. A reviewer of Traetta's *Telemaco* noted acidly: 'The scenes, decorations, dances etc, were in the usual paltry manner, strongly marked with the effects of the oeconomical spirit for which Mr Yates seems to wish to immortalise himself.'[8] Such was his reputation for tight-fistedness that legends grew up. Parke recounts an amusing story:

> Sir John Gallini was not the only manager of the King's Theatre who had directed it on a saving plan. He was infinitely exceeded by Y__s, one of his predecessors, whose parsimony was hyperbolically described by a wag in the following manner: This dwarflike manager, who had an eye to every thing, going his morning round in the theatre, came to a hogs-head containing lamp oil, which being nearly empty, he, in order to gauge it to a nicety, leaned over the brim so far that he fell into it, and was from its depth, unable to extricate himself. His cries for help, however, bring one of the lamp-lighters to his assistance, he with his usual thrift, desired the fellow who took him to hang him by his clothes on the large wooden peg above the cask, till the whole of the oil should have dripped from them.[9]

The *Queen of Quavers* satirist even accused him of extorting money from the orange-sellers. Rents charged for concessions escalated rapidly, leading William Lee, long-term holder of the coffee house concession, to complain to the public.[10]

One other factor contributing to the stability of the opera house at this period was the relatively substantial resources which the well-paid Yates couple, together with James Brooke the lawyer, could call upon. The financial problems of the 1774–5 season would have been enough to bankrupt many of the mid-century musician-impresarios at a stroke. The Brooke–Yates partnership had time to learn from its mistakes and recoup the losses. Henceforth, the management of the King's Theatre would be undertaken by men such as Sheridan and Gallini, who, whatever their managerial shortcomings, were much more substantial financial figures than the likes of Giardini.

The final proof that the opera house had become financially successful by the last two seasons of Brooke's management is provided by her fiercest critic. Shortly after Sheridan took over the King's Theatre, Garrick purchased several of the renters' shares that the new manager put on sale. In doing so, he observed that the opera house would prove 'a mine of gold, if conducted with ability'.[11] There was perhaps an element of conscious symbolism in this purchase, an acknowledgement that his quarrel had been with Brooke rather than with the opera house. Although his reported remark might well be taken as a further dig at his rival, it was also in effect a tacit admission that the possibility and even the reality of financial success had been demonstrated by Brooke. Her success had an impact further afield. Dublin, which had hitherto only had a single season of Italian *opera buffa* with the De Amicis family, now staged two full seasons in 1776–7 and 1777–8, for the latter of which Fochetti and Sestini were recruited from the King's Theatre.[12] Perhaps the most telling comment is that of John Williams in *A Pin Basket to the Children of Thespis*. Referring to Richard Yates, he noted that his 'long acquaintance with places of public resort, the caprice of performers, the fraud of door-keepers, etc, enabled him to form such economical *reformation* [at the opera house] that on his relinquishing it, in the language of the City, he receded a *better* man than he came in'. Not many financial backers of Italian opera in the eighteenth century could make that claim.

From a financial point of view, early 1778 was a good moment to put the King's Theatre up for sale. Brooke and her partners received two bids; the £20,000 offered by Le Texier on behalf of Gallini was within days bettered by a bid of £22,000 from the managers of the Drury Lane and Covent Garden theatres. As to why competing managers with no background in opera should have combined to purchase the King's Theatre, Price, Milhous and Hume suggest that Sheridan persuaded Harris to join in 'a grandiose but short-lived scheme for a theatrical monopoly'.[13] By adding the opera house to their existing interests, the theatre managers certainly succeeded in establishing a monopoly of winter theatrical entertainment in London, but the scheme was doomed from the start. To raise the purchase price, they had no alternative but to borrow heavily, even though by doing so they knew they were likely to incur interest payments large enough to plunge the finances of the opera house deeply into the red. For the King's Theatre to have remained solvent, receipts from the next four seasons would have had to have covered interest payments on the £12,000 mortgage as well as the running costs. Harris, the more prudent of the two, quickly withdrew his support, and he later claimed that they had paid 'many thousands more than the property had been at any time before sold for' in anticipation of 'occasionally performing English pieces'.[14]

A different interpretation of the sale is possible if it is seen as the outcome of the intensive campaign to win a licence for a third London theatre that had been going on for much of the 1770s. The persistence of the anti-monopoly lobby at this period has been underestimated. The anonymous petition of 1770, Brooke's reference to the current 'agitation' for a third theatre in 1772, the proposal made by the new partnership in 1773, the 'poetical exordium' of November 1773, which reaffirmed the intention to stage plays, and the document submitted in response to Agujari's appearance at the Pantheon early in 1775, all add up to a sustained drive for change. Indeed, when Sheridan was negotiating to purchase Drury Lane early in 1776, he thought it prudent to try 'to get the King's promise, that while the theatre is well conducted, he will grant no patent for a third'.[15] Garrick was of the view that the King would never agree to one – a comforting but not disinterested thought on the part of the vendor. The campaign had not yet succeeded, but by 1777 Sheridan and Harris had apparently convinced themselves that it soon would. The consequences of a successful application to establish a third theatre at the opera house seemed only too obvious to the monopoly holders. With its social prestige and its advantageous geographical location close to the fashionable new squares in the West End of London, the King's Theatre manifestly had the potential to cause serious damage to the other theatres. Matters came to a head early in 1777, when Le Texier advertised a plan to bring a troupe of French comedians to London. In itself, this was not a particularly threatening development for the theatre managers, but since it represented an attempt to erode the monopoly, it had to be treated very seriously, as the potential precursor to a more damaging competitor. The theatre

managers were by now so alarmed that they decided to make a pre-
emptive strike, by drawing up their own proposal for a third theatre,
to be housed in a completely new building. The plan had scarcely
been formulated when the news of Brooke's decision to sell the
King's Theatre became public. The two managers discovered to their
consternation that a bid from Gallini was being fronted by none
other than Le Texier. It was imperative that this offer be bettered, and
thus £22,000 was borrowed at great risk to enable a decisive bid to be
made. Once the rival team had been defeated, Sheridan and Harris
adroitly refocused their plan for a third theatre on the site of the
opera house. Had a licence been forthcoming, the two managers
might well have made money out of their monopoly, but, as he had
resolutely done throughout the decade, the Lord Chamberlain
refused to grant one. Although they were left to cope with an escalat-
ing problem of debt management, in the short term at least, they
were relatively secure from the threat of a new theatrical competitor.
If, as Price, Milhous and Hume argue, the venture was monopolistic
in intent, then unquestionably it was a reckless and ill-considered
gamble; if, however, the managers made the purchase primarily to
protect their existing interests against the perceived threat of a third
theatre, then their commercial judgement deserves less severe
censure, and the purchase, in effect a hostile take-over to neutralise a
rival, should be accounted a very hazardous, but nonetheless calculated risk.

   A source which throws much light on the 1778 sale is the draft proposal for a third winter theatre drawn up for Sheridan and Harris in
1777.[16] This document (Appendix 2c) expressed forcefully the managers' growing fear that a new theatre was about to be given permission to stage 'some species or other of dramatic entertainment'. Any
such new venture, they argued, was likely to result in the 'absolute
ruin' of one of the established theatres. The document suggests that
there was growing support for a third winter theatre on a number of
grounds: (1) that there had been a great increase in London's population; (2) that the distance of the two theatres from the 'politer' streets
was proving an inconvenience to patrons; (3) that the number of

boxes was too small; (4) that the two theatres were opening too early, causing difficulties for parliamentarians and, more generally, for those who wished to dine at the 'prevailing hour'. Hitherto, such arguments had been successfully rebutted, but now there was a new factor: an 'unusual fashion' for theatrical entertainments among the upper classes. This was an allusion to Le Texier's much-admired private entertainments, performed to great applause in aristocratic households during the early years of his residence in England. Private performances were beyond the reach of any law, but Le Texier's attempt to set up a subscription for the importation of a 'French Company of Comedians' with 'a very powerfull Patronage' marked him out as a potentially dangerous foe. It is claimed that this (seemingly insignificant) proposal was to be the foundation for 'other entertainments', in other words, it was intended as a Trojan Horse with which to breach the monopoly. The scheme was indeed openly advertised as an evasion of the Act: 'The French comedians who are to perform here under the management of Mons. Texier, in order to evade the Act of Parliament passed in the 10th of George II will act by subscription, and the tickets of admission are to be half a guinea each; but no money will be taken at the door.'[17] The question that Sheridan and Harris now had to face was whether they should 'contentedly wait' for some other person to take advantage of the 'prevailing wish' for a third theatre or whether they should pre-empt other bidders with their own proposal. Convinced that the latter course of action was the only one that would give security to their monopoly, they set out their proposals. There was to be a new 'assistant' theatre, which would recruit its performers from the unemployed part of the two existing companies, but which would be conducted on 'a different plan of business'. If possible, the 'dormant patent' was to be used. Various guarantees were offered to current shareholders to convince them of the merits of the plan.

Sheridan began lobbying intensively for his proposals in November 1777, two months before the King's Theatre was actually put on the market. On 6 January 1778, it was reported that he had 'devoted himself much of late to his darling scheme of a third theatre'.[18] Once the King's Theatre went on sale, an obvious alternative presented itself. By bidding for the opera house, the managers would not only thwart a potentially dangerous rival, they would also acquire a site for their own plans. Sheridan and Harris thus took decisive action. They agreed that whatever the short-term cost, their best long-term interests lay in the defeat of the opposing team. The £22,000 that they raised to make the offer thus reflects not only what they thought the King's Theatre was worth as an opera house, but also their appraisal of the damage that it could inflict upon their existing interests, if it were to emerge as the third theatre.

Before the matter was finally settled, a fierce dispute broke out between Le Texier and Brooke over her conduct of the negotiations.[19] On 6 February 1778, the *Morning Post* announced that Le Texier 'in conjunction with a gentle man of character and considerable property' (Gallini), had 'absolutely entered into articles for the King's Theatre' in order to conduct it 'upon the usual plan of Italian *operas*'. As early as mid January, Le Texier had consulted Walpole as to whether he thought it would be advantageous to take over the opera house 'on the present plan'.[20] On 13 February, however, it emerged that Le Texier had taken legal action against the opera managers claiming a breach of contract. Brooke, it was asserted, had signed an agreement of sale, which had been set aside after the receipt of Sheridan's higher bid. The 'opera-house people' were supporting the action and were hoping that the sale would be pronounced invalid because Brooke's husband was 'still in existence'. That notwithstanding their contempt for Le Texier, leading members of the Italian opera establishment were supporting this bid, shows how desperate they were to avoid becoming entangled in Sheridan's theatrical empire. The following day, Brooke attempted to refute these allegations by claiming that she had been totally unaware of Gallini's involvement. She had not heard of any person being involved with Le Texier's application 'except Mr. *Garrick* and Mr. *Colman*'. On 16 February, the *Morning Post* responded with a double attack. The editor observed acidly that someone 'so easily offended at the freedom of newspapers' should be less free with other people's names. The anonymous author of the original paragraph was even harsher. His letter was addressed to: 'Mrs F. Brooke, Manageress of the Opera', demonstrating once and for all that any pretence that the King's Theatre was under the control of Richard or Mary Ann Yates had been dropped. He claimed that the original agreement with Le Texier had been judged 'binding' on all parties by 'the first legal authorities'. He castigated Brooke for her abuse of 'other gentlemen' (Garrick and Colman) and accused her of possessing 'a disposition to insult genius'. (That this was a direct reference to her long-running dispute with Garrick is made clear in a footnote, which refers to 'the violent abuse in this lady's late publication called The *Excursion*'.) The *Morning Post* of 18 February printed Brooke's response:

> What Mrs Brooke's having, in the Excursion, given her opinion, with freedom, in respect to the public conduct of a late theatrical manager, can have to do with the dispute between Mons. Le Texier, and the Managers of the Opera, she knows not; but this she knows, that she is incapable, however ill treated, of writing any thing to the disadvantage of any person whatever, without putting her name to the publication.

She professed amazement that her supposition that Garrick and Colman were concerned with Le Texier's application for the opera house could be construed as abuse.

Le Texier now wrote to the *Morning Post* on 23 February:

> Sir,
>
> I am too much affected by, and interested in, the several paragraphs in your paper, relating some transactions concerning the Theatre in the Haymarket, to remain silent, according to my first resolution; but, out of respect to the sex in general, I restrain myself from expressing my thoughts upon that subject; notwithstanding, as it is essential for me that the truth should appear in its proper light, I declare, for the first and last time, that I have, in my hands, proposals, and conditions of a treaty, made, and written by the hand of Mrs Brooke herself, in the name of Mr Brooke, and Mr and Mrs Yates. They gave me a week for my decisive answer, till Sunday morning, the 25th of January. On Friday, the 23rd, Mrs Brooke had notice from a respectable quarter, which she cannot

deny, and again, on Saturday the 24th, from myself in person, that I was ready to accept the conditions, and that the money was ready. We gave, and received, our respective words of honour, and she told me she expected her brother in town, and that, immediately upon his arrival, she would appoint a time for the execution of the contract.

On Monday, the 26th, they met clandestinely, and signed, at nine o'clock on Tuesday morning, another contract with the purchasers, for 1000 guineas more. This I can and will prove, whenever it shall be found necessary, in another place, being absolutely resolved to take no more notice of any misrepresentation that may appear in the public papers, declaring that nothing shall proceed from me that is not signed with my name.

I am also very sorry to have seen the names of Mr Garrick and Mr Coleman mentioned so often in this business; and I think myself obliged honestly to declare that they have never been concerned in this treaty in any manner whatever.

> I am, Sir,
> Your humble servant,
> Le Texier

Sheridan and Harris entered the debate to rebut the allegation that their offer was made clandestinely.[21] Brooke's final response was published on 25 February:

Mrs Brooke having seen . . . a letter signed *Le Texier*, complaining of misrepresentation . . . thinks it necessary to say there have been no misrepresentations . . . but what appear to have proceeded from himself or his friends. He not only knew of the treaty with Messrs Sheridan and Harris, but that the first application had been made . . . by those gentlemen; indeed, both applications were sufficiently public, and had been the subject of general conversation many days before the agreement with Messrs Sheridan and Harris had been signed. Mrs Brooke certainly did not give any word of honour to Mons. Le Texier, as he supposes; on the contrary, she told him she believed Mrs Yates was at that instant, Saturday night, January 24th, treating with Mr Sheridan, which was really the case. The paper he alludes to . . . was written and sent the *first* of January, so that, from his own account, his decisive answer should have been given the *eighth*. But as he has mentioned honor, Mrs Brooke begs

leave to observe how little his declaration in that letter respecting Mr
Garrick and Mr Coleman is reconcilable on that principle with his having
mentioned one of those gentlemen as the friend on whom he depended
to support him in the purchase, * and the other, as having applied to him
with the intention of bringing English plays to the Opera House.

*Quaere [note by the editor] Does not this border a little on the
improbable, when it is well known to the Managers that Mons. Gallini
was the man who had the money ready to complete the above purchase?

What is not clear is whether Brooke's dispute with Garrick
influenced the sale in any substantive way. It is certainly hard to
believe that she was unaware of Gallini's interest, even though his bid
was being fronted by Le Texier. In the context of these machinations,
it is worth pointing out that Mary Ann Yates was Sheridan's own
leading lady. Although his relationship with her was at times difficult,
it perhaps gave him an additional advantage.[22] The legal action was
settled out of court. The *Morning Post* on 13 March reported: 'The
dispute between Messrs Sheridan and Harris, and Mons. Le Texier . . .
is at length finally and amicably adjusted; the latter has given up all
pretensions to it [the King's Theatre], and the former, in consequence
thereof, have appointed him superintendent of the Italian Opera at
that theatre.' The celebrated sale of the King's Theatre to Sheridan
and Harris thus went ahead unopposed, with Le Texier neutralised
and Gallini out in the cold.

The only chance that Sheridan and Harris had of making the
King's Theatre sufficiently profitable to cover interest payments was
if a licence could be obtained for its theatrical use. Sheridan quickly
informed potential subscribers that his original proposal for a third
theatre in a new building had been abandoned in favour of the opera
house. The revised plan was discussed in a piece entitled 'Theatrical
Intelligence' in the *Public Advertiser* on 13 February. The author
(Sheridan himself or an associate) claimed that members of the
nobility had recently expressed a desire to have a theatre where prices
are *raised*, to ensure a more select company, and that since the building of a new theatre was proving far too time-consuming and costly
an option, the decision had been taken to approach Richard Yates

with a view to the purchase of the King's Theatre for the purpose. Few informed readers can have been taken in by so cynical an explanation of recent events. The hope was expressed that it would be possible for 'those Nights which are not appropriated to the Italian opera' to be used for other purposes. These included 'select plays' once or twice a week, for which the best performers from both houses (Drury Lane and Covent Garden) would be recruited. (In the original proposal it had been the 'unemployed' members of the two theatrical troupes.) 'Young nobility', moreover, were to be encouraged to participate in amateur theatricals. On the remaining nights of the week, there were to be ridottos, concerts, masked and fancy balls. A new suite of rooms laid out for card parties was also under consideration. 'The whole', it was claimed, would form 'a more *general and entertaining Coterie* than any that has yet been established'. Most important of all, it would be open to 'subscribers only'. Sheridan's application to the Lord Chamberlain would make interesting reading. The theatre managers had strongly opposed Brooke's ideas for presenting plays at the King's Theatre; now one of their number was arguing precisely the opposite case. In the *Morning Post* of 2 March, a further report speaks of plans for 'a superb suite of rooms, similar to those at Bath' for the reception of subscribers in the mornings, with a 'grand band of music' to play the whole time.

Sheridan's ideas for the greater exploitation of the opera house emerge clearly in James Lewis's plans for 'a New Theatre, designed for the Opera', published in his *Original Designs in Architecture* (London, 1780).[23] On the plans for the opera house, Lewis wrote:

> Our Theatres being upon a very small scale, compared with those of other principal cities in Europe, about two years ago [in 1778] a report prevailed that a New Theatre was intended to be built by subscription, which might serve as well for all Dramatick Performances, as Concerts, Assemblies, Masquerades, &c. And the proprietors of the Opera House intending to purchase several adjoining houses and ground, to render the theatre eligible for the various purposes mentioned, suggested the idea of making a design adapted to the situation of the present Opera House, with the principal front towards Pall Mall.

The plans clearly date from the period of Sheridan's abortive attempt to expand the remit of the King's Theatre. Lewis's plans show that the intention was to enhance the public space outside the existing auditorium. At least five large rooms were proposed, one of which contained 'almost as much square footage as the auditorium itself'.[24] These rooms were intended to provide the elegant surroundings for cards, coffee and dancing, as reported in the newspapers. Lewis's plans notably fail to allow for any significant increase in audience capacity, and this is entirely in line with the report that Sheridan wished to raise ticket prices to ensure a more select company. In effect, the King's Theatre was to double as a high-society venue, where aristocratic and wealthy patrons could take coffee in style, play cards, and participate in balls, masquerades and even amateur theatricals. Sheridan's thinking was clearly influenced by the sucessful package of relaxing entertainment being offered at the Pantheon. He was evidently hoping that the high cost of opera could be subsidised by a range of more profitable activities. It was an ambitious scheme, but it came to nothing when the Lord Chamberlain again refused a licence for anything other than Italian opera. The managers now had a monopoly of the two theatres and the opera house, but crucially they lacked the permission to exploit the potential of the latter. Ironically, Sheridan and Harris found themselves in exactly the same position as Brooke in 1773, with an opera house to run, but with little or no experience of Italian opera.

After giving up her interests in the King's Theatre, Frances Brooke continued with her life-long quest to win recognition as a dramatist, and her persistence eventually paid off.[25] A new tragedy, *The Siege of Sinope,* was performed at Covent Garden in the 1780–1 season, despite Samuel Johnson's celebrated put-down of the work. She had repeatedly asked him to look over the new play, which he had refused to do, saying that she herself could easily see if anything were amiss in a careful reading. 'But Sir', said Brooke, 'I have no time. I have already so many irons in the fire.' 'Why then, Madam', replied Johnson, 'the best thing I can advise you to do is, to put your tragedy along with your irons!'[26] When *Rosina* was finally staged at Covent Garden with

music by William Shield, it scored a resounding success, fully vindi-
cating her confidence in it. The inclusion of an aria by from Sacchini's
Rinaldo acknowledged the significance of her debt to the composer,
to the success of whose operas the revival of the King's Theatre
under her management owed much. Summing up the life-time
achievement of her friend, Fanny Burney wrote: 'Mrs Brooke had
much to combat in order to receive the justice due to her from the
world . . . nevertheless she always ultimately obtained the consideration that she merited.'[27] Struggle ending in success certainly seems an
apt epitaph for her years at the King's Theatre.

Appendix 1a   The accounts of Richard Yates and James Brooke at Henry Hoare & Co. (1773–1777)

Ledger 89   (fol.245ᵛ)

1773		Expenditure	£	s	d
Oct	23	To Mʳ Fochetti	10		
		To Luigi Mattei	28		
		To Mʳ Bartolomeo	25		
		To Gaetano Mariotini	10		
		To Mʳ Metralcourt	6	6	
	25	To Stella Lodi	20		
Nov	3	To Thoˢ Luppino	30		
	19	To John Gordon	140		
Dec	21	To Jaˢ Canter	66	13	4
	24	To Thoˢ Luppino	65	3	
	27	To Cath Galli	100		
		To Francois Fierville	175		
		To Bartolomeo Schiroli	85	5	
		To Marchetti Mattei	35	1	8
		To Vincenzo Fochette	32	5	
		To Eligio Legi Celestino	43	6	8
		To Peter Du Baulieux	8	6	8
		To John Asselin	20		
	28	To Jaˢ Sergeant	15		
		To Anᵗ Pitrot	216	13	4
		To Joˢ Agus	13	6	8

1773		Expenditure	£	s	d
		To Sophia Daigueville	20		
	29	To Eliz. Buckinger	17	10	
	30	To An^t Sacchini	150		
		To Miss Davies 2/100	200		
		To Jo^s Millico	400		
	31	To J^{no} Gordon 100 & 25	125		
1774					
Jan	20	To Leop^d Michelli	33	6	8
	22	To Chris Scott	50	7	6
Feb	10	To Oliver Farrer	700		
	13	To Ja^s Brooke	1195	14	11
		Total	4037	6	5

Ledger 89   (fol.246)

1773		Receipts	£	s	d
Jul	27	By Lady Scarsdale	21		
Aug	13	By Duch^s of Leeds	21		
Oct	6	By Duch of Bedford	42		
	14	By R^d Yates	105		
Nov	8	By Cash	105		
	9	By D^o	105		
	15	By R^d Yates	143		
	20	By Lord Bruce	21		
	22	By Cash	506	5	
	29	By D^o	268		
Dec	4	By D^o	500		
	9	By D^o	476		
	24	By D^o	175		
1774					
Jan	10	By Sir Laurence Dundas	42		
		By Thos Dundas	42		

1774		Receipts	£	s	d
	17	By Cash	610		
	31	By D°	698	19	
Feb	17	By D°	1281	19	6
		Total	5163	3	6

Ledger 89   (fol.246ᵛ)

1774		Expenditure	£	s	d
		Broᵗ over	4037	6	5
Feb	21	To John Martingdale	242	17	
	23	To Lawrence Laforest	251	4	6
	28	To Joseph Heyling	73		
Mar	5	To Mʳ Woodfill	23		
	9	To Thoˢ Yatman	41	2	6
	12	To George Wheeler	76		
	14	To John Edwards	35	5	
	24	To E. L. Celestino	43	6	8
		To Thoˢ & Lancelᵗ Leverton	88	18	
Apr	5	To Signʳ Schirole	190		
		To Signʳ Michelli	33	6	8
		To Mʳ Fierville	175		
	6	To Miss Davies	200		
		To Mʳ Pitrot	266	13	4
		To Miss Buckinger	17	10	
		To Signʳ Gardi	55	8	4
	7	To Signᵃ Galli	100		
		To Signʳ Sacchini	150		
	8	To Signʳ Millico	400		
		To Mʳˢ Daiquville	20		
	9	To Mʳ Fierville	41	12	
	18	To Wᵐ Bowen	24		
	25	To Joˢ Hayling	72	19	6
		To Mʳˢ Daiquville	43	11	
	26	To Thoˢ Allam	27	8	
		To Mʳ Martindale	71	13	

1774		Expenditure	£	s	d
May	5	To Wm Fenton	65	4	4½
	7	To Step Parvis	25		
	10	To LaForest & Co	212	10	6
	12	To Mr Gordon	67		
	25	To Thos Yateman	37	10	
		Total	7208	6	9½

Ledger 89   (fol.247)

1774		Receipts	£	s	d
		Bro^t over	5163	3	6
Mar	4	By Cash	926	15	
	21	By D^o	525		
Apr	14	By D^o	969		
	29	By D^o	315		
May	17	By D^o	353		
Jun	4	By D^o	436	17	
	6	By bill on Browns & Co	105		
		Total	8793	5	6

Ledger 91   (fol.324)

1774		Expenditure	£	s	d
		Bro^t over	7208	6	9½
Jun	6	To Peter Crawford	132	11	9
	11	To Parry Mellish & Co bill to Gore & Co on acco^t of Sigⁿ Sestini	100		
		To Henry Johnson	60		
	13	To Signora Lodi	50		
	15	To Mr Schiroli	40		
		To Mr Marchetti	50		
	18	To F^r Brookes bill to H. Johnson	63		
	20	D^o to R^d Brooke	100		

1774		Expenditure	£	s	d
	25	Dᵒ to H Johnson	20		
	28	To Mʳ Felix	21	13	4
		To Mʳ Daiquville	33	6	8
		To Sigʳ Mariottini	50		
	30	To Miss Buckinger	17	10	
		To Monˢ Pitrot	266	13	4
		To Signʳ Fochetti	84	10	
		To Signʳ Bocchini	52	16	8
		To Signʳ Bozzoni	64	8	4
		To Signʳ Michelli	33	6	8
Jul	1	To Mʳ Marchetti	84	15	8
		To Signʳ Schiroli	160		
	2	To Signʳ Gardi	20		
	5	To Millico	100		
	23	To Rᵈ Brooke's bill	50		
Aug	31	To a Lʳᵉ from Turin	7		
Sep	12	To Keck & Laminit's bills	651	13	4
	15	To Lany's bill to Sir Jnᵒ Lambert	100		
	26	To Sir Jnᵒ Lambert's bill for Money pᵈ to Mons Lamp	30		
Oct	3	To Mʳ Simonin	121		
Nov	17	To Thoˢ Allam	42		
	26	To Jaˢ Butler's bill to Hart & Co	200		
1775					
Jan	2	To Hʸ Johnson	100		
		Total	10107	19	6½

Ledger 91 (fol.325)

1774		Receipts	£	s	d
		Brought over	8793	5	6
Oct	1	By Cash	63		
	18	By Dᵒ	120		

1774		Receipts	£	s	d
	24	By the Duchess of Bedford	42		
	27	By Lord Bruce	21		
Nov	8	By Lady Mary Coke	21		
	12	By Cash	500		
	15	By Geo Pitt	21		
		By Geo Pitt Jun	21		
		By John Pitt	21		
		By Lord Scarsdale	21		
		By Cash	149		
	18	By Lady Spencer	21		
Dec	1	By Lord Spencer	21		
	7	By Cash	500		
	10	By bill on H. Hoare & Co	21		
			10356	5	6
			10107	19	6½
		Balance	248	5	11½

Ledger 91   (fol.325^v)

1775		Expenditure	£	s	d
Jan	4	To Mr Frederick	20	11	9
	13	To H^y Johnson	100		
Feb	1	To Sig^r Rauzzini	100		
	6	To Fysh Coppinger	650		
	10	To H^y Hoare Jun for 1 y^{r}s Int^t on 4500 due 5 inst^t	225		
	11	To Ant^o Sacchini	150		
Mar	31	To Sign^r Fochetti	74	5	
		To Signora Farinella	50		
		To Sign^a Cestini	50		
		To D^o	126	13	4
		To Mons Lany	106	13	4
		To Monsr Vallouis	149		
		To Mad^m Baccelli	100		
Apr	1	To Sign^a N. G. Celli	10	13	4

1775		Expenditure	£	s	d
		To Signa Galli	66	13	4
		To Sign Lovattini	300		
	6	To Sign Rauzzini	207	14	
	7	To Sigr Pasini	73	6	8
		To Siga Schindlerin	133	6	8
	26	To Sigr Rauzzini	114		
May	10	To Oliver Farrer	120		
	20	To Hen Johnson	105		
Jun	22	To Mad. Schindlerin	233	6	8
	23	To Mr Baccelli	100		
	26	To Signa Farinella	80		
		To Signr Pasini	100		
		To Monsr Vallouis	200		
		To Mons Lanny	166	13	4
		To Signa Kellick	78	1	8
		Total	3990	19	1

Ledger 91 (fol.326)

1775		Receipts	£	s	d
		Brought over	248	5	11½
Jan	30	By Cash	400		
Feb	2	By Do	300		
	4	By Do	550		
	20	By Do	700		
	22	By Do	300		
Mar	8	By bill on G. Moretti	156	8	6
	10	By Cash	600		
	31	By Do	300		
Apr	11	By Do	400		
	27	By Do	577	15	
		By Do	283		
		By R. Brooke's bill debted by mistake 23 July	50		
May	31	By Cash	300		

1775		Receipts	£	s	d
Jun	6	By bill on Chambers & Co	105		
		Total	5270	9	5½

Ledger 94   (fol.195ᵛ)

1775		Expenditure	£	s	d
		Brought over	3990	19	1
Jun	27	To Sigʳ Fochetti	70		
		To Cecilia Davis	333	6	8
		To Sigᵃ Sestini	166	13	4
		To Signᵃ Sestini	50		
		To Mʳ Stracchini	6	13	4
	28	To Monsʳ Fay	21		
	29	To Monsʳ Luge	14		
		To Signʳ Rauzzini	175		
		To Signʳ Lovattini	300		
		To Miss De Baulier	10		
	28 [*sic*]	To Signʳ Celestina	11	16	8
		To Mad Ducluzel	13	6	8
	30	To Mrs Tilley	11	13	4
Jul	1	To Sigᵃ Gally	66	13	4
		To Higginson & Co	10		
	6	To Sir John Lambert's bill on accᵒ of Fraˢ Fierville	50		
	14	To Sign Columba	52	6	8
Aug	24	To Donat Vergani	70		
	29	To Vergani's bill	190		
Dec	6	To Oliver Farrer	333	6	8
	9	To P. Crawford	148	6	8
	26	To Bearer	25		

1776					
Jan	1	To Monˢ Fierville	175		
		To Signor Celestino	50		
		To Signor Fochetti	87	8	

1776	Expenditure	£	s	d
	To Signor Cestini	33	6	8
	To D°	80		
	To Higginson & Co	11	13	4
	To An^t Stracchini	6	13	4
	To Signor Columba	116	13	4
	Total	6680	17	1

Ledger 94   (fol.196)

1775		Receipts	£	s	d
		Brought over	5270	9	5½
Sep	22	By Duch^s of Bedford	42		
Oct	31	By R. Rigby	21		
		By Lady Mary Coke	21		
Nov	2	By Lord Bruce	21		
	7	By Cash	1000		
	9	By Lord & Lady Pelham	42		
	27	By Cash	610		
Dec	6	By D°	525		
	19	By D°	553	5	6
		Total	8105	14	11½

Ledger 94   (fol.196^v)

1776		Expenditure	£	s	d
		Brought over	6680	17	1
Jan	2	To Monsr Helm	11	15	
		To Sig^r Onofrio	30	14	8
		To Sig^r Salpietro	22	6	8
		To Monsr Bouqueton	77		
		To Monsr Chaubert	16	13	4
		To Madg Louille	30		
		To Sign^a Francesca	30		
		To Sign^a Gabrielli	279	13	
		To Sign^r Badini	25		

1776		Expenditure	£	s	d
	3	To Signor Vento	116	13	4
		To M. Baccelli	88	2	8
		To Mr Agus	13	6	8
		To H. Hoare Junr ye In^t on			
		4500 due 5 Augt last	112	10	
		To Mons Auge	14		
	4	To Sig Savoi	65		
		To Sign Rauzzini	104	3	4
		To Sign Trebbi	66	13	4
	5	To F. Gabrielli	20		
	8	To Mad Debremont	10		
	9	To Mrs Daigville	20		
	23	To Cec^a Davies	450		
Feb	5	To D^o	333	6	8
	10	To Sig^n Rauzzini	100		
	13	To Hen^y Johnson	100		
	16	To John Martindale	78	17	
		To S. Trebbi	100		
	19	To Fish Coppinger	700		
	22	To Mr Vento	150		
Mar	15	To Fi Coppinger	27	14	
	25	To H. Hoare J^n Int on 4500			
		due 5 Feb last	112	10	
Apr	1	To Mons Auge	14		
		Total	10000	16	9

Ledger 94   (fol.197)

1776		Receipts	£	s	d
		Brought over	8105	14	11½
Jan	20	By Cash	210		
	31	By Ja Brooke	63		
Feb	1	By Cash	250		
	5	By D^o	333	9	6
	12	By D^o	1000		

1776		Receipts	£	s	d
	26	By D°	700		
Mar	13	By D°	700		
	25	By D°	700		
		Total	12062	4	5½

Ledger 94   (fol.197^v)

1776		Expenditure	£	s	d
		Brought over	10000	16	9
Apr	1	To Miss Higginson	11	13	4
		To Mad Baccelli	133	6	8
		To Sig^n Trebbi	200		
		To Sig^n Cestini	158		
		To Sig^n Savoi	74	15	
		To Mr Agus	610	2	
		To Mons Helm	42		
		To Mons Daigeville	13	6	8
		To Sig^n Fochetti	100		
		To Sig^a Cardarelli	20		
		To Mad Lany	21		
		To Sign^r V. Sestini	33	6	8
		To Sign^r Badini	25		
		To Mons Choubart	16	13	4
		To Sign Colomba	116	13	4
	2	To Sig^n Rauzzini	266	13	4
		To Sig^n Celestino	20		
		To Sign^a Tinti	44	9	6
		To Sign^r Salpeitro [sic]	33	6	8
		To Sign Vento	116	13	4
	3	To Mad. Lowry	10		
	4	To Mons Bougueton	105		
	6	To Sign F. Gabrielli	80		
	8	To Monsr Fierville	175		
	9	To Mad S. Louillie	30		
	11	To Monsr Henry	10	7	4

1776		Expenditure	£	s	d
	25	To Sign^a Gabrielli	500		
May	11	To O. Farrer	26	10	11
	20	To Mad Baccelli	50		
Jun	7	To S. Columba	86	13	4
	20	To F. Barazzi's bill	59		
		To D^o	71		
	28	To Mr Gordon	200		
		Total	12857	16	4

Ledger 94 (fol.198)

1776		Receipts	£	s	d
		Brought over	12062	4	5½
Apr	1	By Cash	265	19	6
	23	By D^o	600		
May	6	By D^o	430		
	20	By D^o	420		
Jun	3	By D^o	725		
	17	By D^o	300		
			14803	3	11½
			12857	16	4
		Balance	1945	7	7½

Ledger 94 (fol.198^v)

1776		Expenditure	£	s	d
Jul	1	To Monsr Auge	14		
		To Monsr Duprez	11	8	4
		To Monsr Fierville	175		
		To Monsr Helm	42		
		To Monsr Choubert	16	13	4
		To Sig^r Salpietro	33	6	8
		To Mad Lany	21		
		To Sig^a Cardarelli	49	10	
		To Mad. Baccelli	83	6	8

1776		Expenditure	£	s	d
		To Sign^r Fochetti	80		
		To Sign^r Trebbi	200		
		To Mad Sophie	30		
		To Monsr Henry	13	10	4
		To Sign^r Celestino	30		
		To Sign^r V. Sestini	33	6	8
		To Sign^a Sestini	15		
		To Mad Daigville	15		
		To Fra Gabrielli	100		
		To Sign^r Rauzzini	255	12	8
		To Mad. Demainvillers	14	4	8
	2	To Sig. Vento	116	13	4
		To Miss Higginson	11	13	4
		To Sig^a Gabrielli 500 & 20	520		
		To Sig^r Savoi	79	10	
		To Sign^r Tinti	90		
	15	To Sign Agus	13	6	8
	17	To Mad^e Lowry	10		
		To Wiseman's bill	40		
Aug	2	To Rougier's bill	106	1	
	13	To H. Hoare J^r & o Farrer for ye In^t due 5 inst	112	10	
Sept	25	To D^o for D^o on 4500 on	00		
Nov	1	To Wills & Leigh's bill	80		
		Total	2597	13	8

Ledger 94   (fol.199)

1776		Receipts	£	s	d
		Brought over	1945	7	7½
Jul	1	By Cash	200		
			2597	13	8
			2145	7	7½
		Balance	452	6	6½

Ledger 94   (fol.199ᵛ)

1776		Expenditure	£	s	d
		Brought over	452	6	6½
Nov	4	To Monsʳ Vallovy	173	15	
		To Wills & Co bill	2	15	6
	6	To Mʳ Vallovy	26	5	
	12	To Mary Ann Yates	200		
	13	To Sʳ Pʳ Denis	300		
Dec	6	To Sir John Lambert's bill on			
		accᵗ of Signʳ Goldoni	95		
1777					
Jan	1	To Signʳ Savoi	63	5	
		To Signᵃ Cestini	45	3	4
		To Monsʳ Lucquet	14	10	4
		To Monsʳ Ferrere	16	13	4
		To Mʳ Piccini	16	13	4
		To Mʳ Auges	13	6	8
		To Signʳ Rauzzini	366	13	4
		To Signʳ Zucchelli	40		
		To Mons Ravilly	17	13	4
		To Signʳ Fochetti	80		
		To Signᵃ Zuchelli	26	13	4
		To Signʳ Trebbi	233	6	8
		To Mons Simonet	221	8	4
	2	To M. Giuliani	22	16	8
		To Val. le Cadet	18	1	8
		To Madame Durare	17	13	4
	3	To Signʳ Trajetta	16	13	4
	4	To Sigʳ Michelli	33	6	8
	6	To Monsʳ Felix	17	13	4
		To Mad. Lany	10		
	9	To Monsʳ Fay	21		
	10	To Sʳ Agus	13	6	8
	27	To Signʳ Giardini	79		
Feb	19	To Mad. Egleprese	21	6	8

1777		Expenditure	£	s	d
	24	To P. Crawford	130		
		To D^o	16	4	10
		Total	2822	11	8½

Ledger 94   (fol.200)

1776		Receipts	£	s	d
Nov	2	By R. Stonhewer	21		
		By the Earl of Ailesbury	21		
	4	By Cash	717	18	
	7	By D^o	500		
	19	By Lord & Lady Pelham	42		
Dec	2	By Cash	500		
	28	By D^o	500		
	31	By D^o	200		
1777					
Feb	3	By D^o	630		
	12	By D^o	525		
			3656	18	
			2822	11	8½
		Balance	834	6	3½

Ledger 98   (fol.270^v)

1777		Expenditure	£	s	d
Feb	27	To Fysh Coppinger	650		
Mar	5	To John Berry	200		
	11	To H^y Hoare J^r & O. Farrer			
		1/2 ye Int to 5 inst^t	112	10	
Apr	2	To Sig^n Rauzzini	366	13	4
		To Sig^n Giardini	100		
	3	To Sig^n Trajetta	166	13	4
		To Sign^a Pozzi	137	10	
		To Sign^a Sestini	30		

1777		Expenditure	£	s	d
	5	To Sign^a Columba	94	9	8
	8	To Mad^m Lanny	21		
	16	To Monsr Vallovy	10		
	30	To Monsr Piccini	20	7	4
		To Monsr Ange	16	13	4
		To M Baccelli	100		
		To Sign^r Sestini	106	13	4
		To Sign^r Savoi	60		
		To Monsr Ferrere	16	13	4
May	1	To Monsr Simonet	266	13	4
		To Mad. Eglesprese	13	6	8
		To Mad. Durare	13	9	4
		To Monsr Lucquet	17	13	4
		To Sign^r Massimino	33	6	8
		To Sign^r Trebbi	233	6	8
		To Sign^a Zuchelli	40		
		To Sign^r Zuchelli	26	13	4
		To Sign^r Fochetti	50		
		To Monsr Felix	21		
	2	To Monsr Revilly	11	7	8
	3	To Sign M. Farnese	59	3	4
		To Sign^a L Farnese	58	3	4
		Total	3053	7	4

Ledger 98   (fol.271)

1777		Receipts	£	s	d
		Brought over	834	6	3½
Mar	3	By Cash	900		
	13	By Mr Brooke	63		
	17	By Cash	400		
	24	By D^o	600		
	26	By D^o	100		
Apr	21	By D^o	700		
		Total	3597	6	3½

Ledger 98 (fol.271ᵛ)

1777		Expenditure	£	s	d
		Brought over	3053	7	4
May	5	To Miss Davies	250		
		To Mʳ Agus	8	1	8
	12	To Mʳ Fay	21		
	17	To Signʳ Micheli	33	6	8
	21	To Hʸ Hoare Jʳ	1000		
Jul	1	To Vallovy le Cadet	23	6	8
Aug	5	To Henry Hoare Jʳ 1/2 yʳˢ Int to yᵉ day	87	10	
Sep	16	To Dᵒ for Int of money short debted on 1000 pᵈ off 21 May	14	13	10
		Total	4491	6	2

Ledger 98 (fol.272)

1777		Receipts	£	s	d
		Brought over	3597	6	3½
May	14	By Cash	800		
1778					
Jan	21	By Dᵒ	93	19	10½
		Total	4491	6	2

Appendix 1b The customer account ledgers of Sheridan and Harris (1778–1779)

1778 R-Z: DR/427/79

('Either to draw & subject also to the Draft of Mr Jona: Garton')

1778		To cash paid (creditor side)	£	s	d
Dec	3	W Bernascoy	100		
	26	Bellamy & Co	200		
	28	W Lacy	500		
	29	W Harewood	200		
		Thomas Harris	200		
	31	R B Sheridan	200		
		John Mountford	100		
		Total	1500		
		To new ledger	715		

1778		By cash rec[d] of Jonathan Garton (debtor side)			
			£	s	d
Nov	20	D°	160		
	24	D°	84		
	27	D°	250		
	28	D°	203		
	30	D°	200		
Dec	3	D°	271		
	7	D°	350		
	14	D°	347		
	16	D°	150		
	22	D°	200		
		Total	2215		

1779 R-Z: DR/427/83

('Either to draw & subject also to the Draft of Mr Jona: Garton')

1779		To cash paid (creditor side)	£	s	d
Jan	1	Mr Johnson	30		
	2	Thoˢ Harris	200		
	5	Mr Johnson	100		
		Dᵒ	50		
		Mr Cripps	125		
		Mr Woods	125		
	9	Mr Johnson	70		
	16	Mr Johnson	150		
	19	Mr Andries	26	13	4
		Mr Michela	33	6	8
		Mr Banti	100		
		Mr Revedino	25		
	20	Mr Pacchierottie	283	6	8
		Mr Colombe	103	6	8
	21	Mr Adamberger	108	6	8
		Mr Rossi	76	13	4
	22	Mr Slingsby	120		
		Mr Simons	200		
		Mr Cramer	50		
		Mr Jermoli	84	5	
		Mr Pozzi	74	1	4
	25	Mr Zuchelli	60		
		Mrs Zuchelli	73	6	8
Feb	2	Fish Coppinger	630		
	3	Mr Texiere	50		
		Dᵒ	60		
	6	Mr Micheli	67	4	6
	12	Mr Colomba	101	11	
	17	Mr Rossi	10	10	
	20	Mr Texiere	100		
Mar	3	Hugh Dine	500		
	12	Mr Webber	1000		
	13	Mr Weltzie	50		

1779		To cash paid (creditor side)	£	s	d
		Mr Johnson	150		
	16	Mr Bartoni	150		
	17	Mr Badini	20		
	18	Mr Weltzie	100		
		Mr Creaser	20		
		Mr Weltzie	50		
	19	D°	60		
	20	Mr Johnson	30		
	23	Mr Adamberger	20		
	24	Mr Colomba	40		
	25	Miss Tinti	33	12	
	26	Mr Stoquelar	50		
	30	Harris & Sheridan	1000		
Apr	6	Mr Johnson	135		
	7	Mr Weltzie	30	13	
	8	Mr Colomba	32	5	7
	17	Mr Mountford	100		
	19	Mr Luppino	25		
		D°	21	16	6
	20	Mr Evans	300		
	27	Mr Micheli	57	17	
	30	Mr Sacchini	100		
		D°	100		
May	8	Mr Evans	100		
		Mr Johnson	100		
	19	Mrs Vidini	16	13	4
	22	Mr Colomba	30		
		Total	7710	9	3

1779			£	s	d
Jan	1	By Ballance from Old Ledger	715		
	6	By cash rec^d of Jonathan Garton (debtor side)			
			300		
	11	D°	300		
	13	D°	600		

1779			£	s	d
	15	D°	400		
	19	D°	200		
	27	D°	200		
	29	D°	630		
Feb	1	D°	300		
	8	D°	250		
	15	D°	400		
	22	D°	250		
	24	D°	300		
Mar	1	D°	280		
	3	D°	500		
	8	D°	210		
	10	D°	210		
	15	D°	225		
	17	D°	250		
	22	D°	260		
	29	D°	300		
Apr	12	D°	200		
	14	D°	330		
	19	D°	150		
	21	D°	235		
May	22	D°	336		
		Total	8331		

1779		To cash paid (creditor side)	£	s	d
May	29	Mr Bernasconi	37		
		Mr Adamberger	80		
		Mr Smith	300		
Jun	3	Mr Slingsby	120		
		Mr De Burgh	315		
		Mr Micheli	33	6	8
	5	Mr Revilly	30		
		Mr Stoquelar	116	13	4
		Mr Cramer	50		
	7	Mr Manzoletto	75		

1779		To cash paid (creditor side)	£	s	d
		Mr Columba	70		
		Mrs Pozzi	66	13	4
		Mr Andries	26	13	4
	21	Thos Harris	80		
		Mr Smith	500		
		Mr Hilman	504	11	9
	24	Mr Hayling	46	5	8
	25	Mr Johnson	630		
	26	D°	70		
Jul	1	Mr Johnson	206	13	4
		Mr Texiere	20		
	3	D°	30		
		D°	15		
		Mr Macnaughton	18	12	
	5	Mr Johnson	200		
		Mr Cranfield	8	6	6
		Mr Badini	20		
	6	Mr Johnson	100		
	7	D°	60		
		Mr Texier	15		
		D°	15		
		Miss Mathews	15	6	8
	8	Mr Ratchford	10	19	6
	10	Mr Johnson	166	13	4
		Miss Ross	11	10	
	12	Mrs Inville	9	11	8
	13	Mrs Bernasconi	150		
		Mr Johnson	43		
	15	Mess^r Dagville & Co	21	18	4
	19	Mr Piccini	23	6	8
	22	Mr Revilly	20		
		Mr Jermoli	150		
		Total	12,192	11	4
		Balance	8	8	8

1779			£	s	d
Jun		balance	8831		
	2	By cash rec^d of Jo Garton	300		
	3	D°	120		
	5	D°	300		
	19	D°	1000		
		D°	1000		
	29	D°	1000		
Jul	15	D°	150		
		Total	12,201		

Appendix 1c   Selected entries from the account of Jonathan Garton at Drummonds Bank (1778–1779)

1778 E-H: DR/427/77

1778		To cash paid	£	s	d
Oct	13	Mr Colomba	20		
	20	Sig Pacchierotti	150		
	24	Mr Vergani	40		
	31	Mr Adamberger	25		
Nov	2	Mr Luppino	30		
	23	Mr Luppino	20		

1779 E-II: DR/427/81

1779		To cash paid	£	s	d
Apr	29	Mr Giardini	17	10	
May	22	Mr Giardini	13	19	6
Jul	22	Mr Salpietro	30		
	30	Mr Micheli	33	6	8
		Mrs Bacchelli	166	13	4
Aug	7	Mr Cramer	50		
	10	Mr Slingsby	126		
	12	Mrs Zuchelli	73	6	8
	14	Mr Colomba	100		
	17	Mr Pacchierotti	383	6	8
Sep	27	Mr Luppino	100		
Oct	2	Mr Trebbi	50		
	16	Mrs Bernascony	183	6	8
Nov	13	Mr Luppino	100		
Dec	27	Mr Texiere	25		

Appendix 1d   The account of Gasparo Pacchierotti at Coutts & Co. (1779–1784)

1779–1780

Debits			£	s	d
Jul	21	To Cash paid for £664–14–11. 3% Consolidated Annuities at 68%			
			398	17	0
		Brokerage		16	6
		Power of Attorney		6	6
Jan	31	To Cash paid himself	9	19	5
		Total	409	19	5

Credits					
Jul	20	By cash recd	400		
Jan	31	By Christmas Dividend on £664–14–11. 3% Consolidated Annuities	9	19	5
		Total	409	19	5

1780–1781

Debits			£	s	d
Jul	5	To Cash paid 64 days discount on £604–9–0			
			5	5	10
	21	To Cash paid for £1000. Consolidated 3% Annuities at 61⅝%			
			616	5	0
		Brokerage	1	5	0
Feb	1	To cash paid for £28–11–11. Consolidated 3% at 57⅞%			
			16	11	0
		Brokerage		1	0
		Total	639	7	10

Credits			£	s	d

Jul 5 By cash received R. B.Sheridan's bill on Jon. Garton Discd.

			604	9	0

     19 Midsummer dividend on £664–14–11. Consolidated 3%

			9	19	5

Jan 29 Christmas dividend on £1664–14–11. Consolidated 3%

			24	19	5

		Total	639	7	10

1781–1782

Debits

Jul 31 Cash paid for £44–5–5. Consolidated 3% @ 57¼%

			25	6	11
		Brokerage		1	1

Jan 29 Cash for £46–8–8. Consolidated 3% @ 56%

			26	0	0
		Brokerage		1	3

Apr 24 Cash for £856–16–0. Consolidated 3% @ 57⅝%

			498	18	4
		Brokerage	1	1	8

May 15 Cash for £672–5–5. Consolidated 3% @ 59½%

			399	3	2
		Brokerage		16	10
		Total	951	9	3

Credits

Jul 19 Midsummer dividend on £1693–6–10. Consolidated 3%

			25	8	0

Jan 24 Christmas dividend on £1737–12–3. Consolidated 3%

			26	1	3
Apr	22	By cash recd	100	0	0
	23	Of Laubier & Co per rect	400	0	0
May	13	Received	400	0	0
		Total	951	9	3

1782–1783			£	s	d

Debits

			£	s	d
Jul	24	Cash paid for £616–14–10. Consolidated 3% @ 56⅝%			
			349	4	7
		Brokerage		15	5
Aug	27	Cash for £87–4–6 ditto @ 57%	49	14	4
		Brokerage		2	3
Oct	4	For noting W. Taylors Note £100		1	6
	7	79 days discount on £300	3	5	0
	8	Cash for £509–8–10. Consolidated 3% @ 58⅛%			
			296	2	3
		Brokerage		12	9
	26	For noting W Taylors note		1	6
Nov	11	Himself	150	0	0
	16	ditto	100	0	0
Feb	3	60 day discount on £100		16	5
	4	For £246–6–10. Consolidated 3% in our name @ 67¾%			
			166	17	10
		Brokerage		6	4
	10	43 days discount on £200	1	3	6
	11	For £291–17–0. Consolidated 3% in our name @ 68%			
			198	9	2
		Brokerage		7	4
Apr	8	For £372–8–9 ditto @ 67%	249	10	9
		Brokerage		9	3
		Total	1568	0	2
May	22	For £595–18–5. Consolidated 3% @ 67%			
		Brokerage	399	5	4
				14	8

Credits

			£	s	d
Jul	23	Cash	350	0	0
	29	Midsummer Dividend on £3222–2–4. Consolidated 3%			
			49	16	7
Oct	7	W. Taylors bill on Messrs Grant disc'd	300	0	0

1782–1783			£	s	d
Nov	8	Ditto note pr £150 & charges	150	1	6
	15	Ditto £100 ditto	100	1	6
Jan	17	Christmas dividend on £4026-1-8 Consolidated 3%			
			60	7	9
		Ditto £509–8–10 ditto in our name	7	12	10
Feb	3	W Taylors bill on W Jewell Discd	100	0	0
	10	Ditto on Messrs Grant Discd	200	0	0
Apr	7	Recd per rect	250	0	0
		Total	1568	0	2
May	21	By cash recd p rect	400	0	0

1783–1784

Debits

Jul	9	To cash paid for a power of attorney from the Bank		6	6
	19	To cash W Taylors bill on W Jewell £100 & charges	100	2	6
	22	For £157–18–6. 3% at 61¼%	96	14	6
		Brokerage		4	0
Aug	6	To cash Lady Mary Duncans account	83	6	8
	8	His bill to Danoot & Company	100	0	0
Oct	16	Himself	100	0	0
Dec	17	Ditto	93	5	0
Feb	9	Himself	93	0	0
		Total	666	19	2

Credits

Jul	19	By cash recd of Lady Mary Duncan's account being the amount of Mr Sheridan's debt	483	6	8

1783–1784			£	s	d
24	Midsummer dividend on				
	£5503–17–8		82	11	1
	Ditto on £583–3–10 in our name	8	1	5
Jan 13	Christmas dividend on				
	£6200. 3%		93	0	0
	Total		666	19	2

(Pacchierotti's account at Coutts & Co. continues well into the nineteenth century. One payment of note on 17 March 1787 is £131. 12s. 6d. to John Broadwood.)

Appendix 1e   A page of opera payments and receipts in the Salt MSS (1780)

SMS.343 ('Sheridan Letters')

1780		Expenditure	£	s	d
Feb	29	Bal[ance] due to Mr Harris	6029	15	3
Mar	30	To Cash	30		
Apr	9	To Ditto	3	3	
	13	Paid Mrs Holloway	26	7	
	16	To Cash	20		
Aug	2	To Samprions Bill	50		
	9	To Le Bruns d^o	52	10	
	19	To Hind's d^o	11		
	31	To Cash	4	4	
Sep	3	To D^o his Serv^{ts}	2	2	
	11	To D^o Mr Wood	105		
Oct	15	To Heavisides Bill	100	2	3
	16	To Colomba's D^o	81	14	8
	31	To Mountford's D^o	100		
Nov	7	To Cramer's D^o	50		
		To his own Bill	30		
		To Ditto	30		
	13	To Bernasconi's D^o	116	13	8
	21	To Crawford's D^o	100		
		To Guirdelli's D^o	80		
	23	To His own Bill	102		
		To Ditto	127		
	28	To D^o	200		
Dec	4	To Le Bruns ditto	200		
	5	To His own Bill	100		
		To Pacchierottis d^o	608	13	2
	21	To His own Bill	100		
		Total	8460	5	

1780		Receipts	£	s	d
Feb	3	By 3 D Lane Shares 10 Years to Mr Leake	450		
Mar	2	By 3 d^o to d^o	450		
	16	By 2 D^o to D^o	300		
		By Opera Acc^t for 78 & 79 Ballance in Hand	926	11	4
Apr	12	By D^o Subscriptions 1779 & 80	462	3	6
Aug	31	By Cash of Mr Tusle	150		
Sep	14	By 1 D Lane Share 21 y^{rs} to Viviratti	230		
Oct	11	By 1 D^o to Spurrier	232	5	
	16	By 1 D^o for 10 years to Hoss	140		
Nov	1	By D^o to Jos Gibbs	140	3	6
	3	By D^o to Crane	140		
	6	By D^o to Lickbarrow	131	16	9
		By D^o for 21 years to James Gibbs	240		
	14	By 1 Opera Share to Stephenson	230		
		By 1 Opera Share to Hosse	200		
	23	By 1 D Lane Share for 10 y^{rs} to Cooke	130		
		Total	4553	0	1/4

Appendix 2a   Petition to the Lord Chamberlain (c.1770)

Considerations on the State of the Stage

As an Act of Parliament passed in the Reign of His late Majesty restricting Theatrical performances, it is proposed to examine into the Cause, as 'tis not impossible it may be understood to have its rise from a presumption that the Number existing at that time was prejudicial to Society in general: but this was not the Case – for its affects are directly contrary, as can easily be proved from various instances & Reasons – but prior thereto it is fit to shew whence the restriction took its rise, – about the year 1738 a Theatre was opened in Goodmans feilds W^h for some time performed Theatrical Peices unmolested – their success encouraged a Broken Wit (says Cibber) to collect a 4th Comp^y in the Hay market; who soon finding the best Plays ill performed turned to a bad Acco^t, thought it necessary to give the Public some extraordinary peices, of such a Specie that no bad Acting coud Spoil; and that from their Nature, shoud, if not draw the attention of the Judicious, at least attract that of the Million (the Mob): under this distress he became Intrepidly abusive and licentious & in several Frank and free Farces, he pelted his Superiours and seemed to Aim at the destruction of every Idea of distinction in Mankind, both on the Heads of Religion, Governm^t, Priests, Ministers & Judges; all were leveled by this Draw-cancer in Witt, who Spared neither Friend nor Foe till at last by his own Poetic Fire (like a second Erostratus) he consumed his own Stage, by writing up an Act of Parliament, for the purposes before recited – thus farr *Cibber* who wrote at the time the Act passed: but it was suspected that this Adventurer was hired to do this dirty business by the Patentees, who possibly were apprehensive if some Check was not given their Emolum^{ts} woud soon decrease. if 'twas so, no price was too high for the purchase of so invaluable a privilege – from hence tis Evident 'twas the licentious use & abuse of the Stage that was the real Cause of the Restraint by w^h only Two Theatres were from that time permitted, and those under ye immediate Inspection of the Ld Chamberlain, whose licence must give Sanction to every peice before it can appear: this restriction has totally suppressed every abuse nay it has even banished every indelicacy; so that there is now nothing left that can Shock the Ears of an Audience. The good Effects of this part of the restriction is further Evident as it has been the Cause of rooting out the Indelicacies of Old Authors as well as refining the Modern – the Stage at this day is so Chaste, that it is become a School of Morality – and considering the strong effect theatrical representations have on the Heart where is there so good a Master – no Lecture on Lawless Ambition can ever operate on the Mind with equal power to the Animated Scene of a *Macbeth*; nor will any sermon on the relative duties sink so deep in the young Heart, as those inculcated by a *Barnwall*: and it is further to be observed that since frequenting the Theatres has become general, that the manner and Conversations of the people in this kingdom is become more delicate more refined; for what woud have been received as Wit in 1675 woud in this Age be deemed obscenity.

If in the year 1737 Two Theatres were thought necessary, how inadequate will they appear in 1770 – when the population is so immensely increased in this Metropolis: tis but to examine those vast Spaces of Ground which from Bond S^{tr} were so lately green fields, and are now Covered with almost Numberless buildings, forming the New Squares and Streets extending even to Mary-Le-Bon, to be Convinced of the vast disproportion there is in the two periods; and if to this we add that there is in every part of London an increase of Play goers in proportion as 20 is to 1: since the time the Act passed: should general observation not bring conviction – another Test can be produced amounting to a greater certainty – tis about 20 years since drury Lane House did not contain when full £180 – and then but Seldom subject to an overflow: and that every House is at this day generally inaccessible for the greatest part of the Season, though it is enlarged so as to contain £280 – and the same observation holds good at the other House, can there want a Stronger proof that 3 Houses now is not more in proportion than *one* was at the period referred to.

That it does not, nor ever has been looked upon as an amusem^t that Infringes too much upon the time and attention of a Trading People, or as being too expensive to them, is a fact; the Law was framed to Correct the language not to restrain the frequenters of the Theatre; nor was any Arguments used upon that occasion that had that tendency – but solely turned upon the Insolence, Malice, Immorality and seditious Calumny which was at this time propogated by Theatric peices: nor did it then pass without a Vigorous opposition; and leaving in His Majesty an indiscriminate power at any time to extend by his Royal Letters patent this prerogative whenever, he in his Wisdom should think fit to grant such an Indulgence; within 10 Miles of his usual Residence – Relaxations are necessary, they will they must dissipate; Men do it now at the Theatre, instead of the Tavern, by this means excess is avoided, the mind improved & domestic society is promoted; nay tis economy, for tis less expensive to pay for a Place in the Pit or Gallery than a Tavern bill – the Mistress of a familey in this Age has not a less propensity to relax, if so, tis surely better to lead her to an amusem^t that will edify – than to see those Hours spent in Visiting and being Visited, the general apendage to which is the Card Table, – and tis too well known that every Mimicker of Fashion is too well bred to play low: of w^t importance is it then to divert them from a Gameing Table, and lead them to the much more moderate expence of a rational Evenings entertainm^t at the Theatre – Nay so farr is it from being deemed an Amusement prejudicial to the Minds or Interest of a Trading people there is many, the most Consequential Corporations in this Kingdom, have, *as bodies Corporate* applied to parliam^t and obtained Royal Patents for Theatres, thinking such amusem^{ts} absolutely necessary to keep the Active mind well and soberly employed, by which they continue Industrious;

As there is at present with all the increase of population with all the Thirst among all ranks of people for this usefull amusem^t no more than 2 Theatres which was only thought Sufficient 33 years ago, thousands are excluded and fly to more expensive and less edifying scenes of Pleasure, – and these have no choice – they attempt to get to a Play – find no Access Night after Night, the House is full; tis so true that many Women of fashion give up sending for places, many a Tradesmans familey is drove into more dangerous pleasures. Admitting there is any truth in the preceeding observations 'tis humbly hoped his Majesty will graciously condescend to use his prerogative in Granting a 3^d Patent for a Winter Theatre, but sh^d any doubts arise in respect to the influence it may have upon the propperty of the present Patentees it may with deference be urged, that as to the proprietors of Drury Lane, they have by a Continuation of Royal Indulgence Made princely Fortunes, one of them without Heirs to Inherit; the other having only an Illegitimate Son – the other Patentees possess by purchase; but to any argum^{ts} in their favour, the following observations may tis hoped with Justice be opposed – tis certain they Clear communibus Annis £10,000 – for which they have invested a Capital of £60,000 – which after deducting the Interest at 5 P C^t leaves them a Clear proffit of £7000 P Ann: with their patent (wch being perpetual always retains its value) – so that admitting a 3^d Patent shoud be granted as it cannot be presumed to rival them, no oppressive disadvantages can arise, – let it be admitted some division of the proffit shoud be made, it woud not be unjust; their gain is great – it will bear a Reduction – and if 'tis tried in the Scale of Justice it will not preponderate in their favor – 12 P C^t is more than a proffit to the Man of Trade who gives a Credit, and runs the Risk of bad Debts for his Goods – what then may it be called in a Business – where the money is paid dailey? clear of every Risk – Clear of every deduction – admitting this it allows a drawback upon them – of £3000 – leaving them a Clear proffit of about 12 P C^t – but it is by no means certain they coud suffer even that deduction –

This monopoly of Royal Favor ties up even the Hands of Government from extending its influence for we find in History it has been no uncommon thing to reward the faithfull services of distinguished Characters by this Mode of Grant, which Created a new place a Sine Cure well worth the Acceptance of any Gov^t whose merit wethor in parliamentary or other Capacities intitled them to solicit such marks of favor – being no less then £2000 p^r Ann: among which were – Collier Esqr MP.

Sr Wm Davenant	Mr Congreve
Henry Killigrew	Sr Jno Vanbrugh
Sr Tho. Skipwith	Sr Richd Steel M.P.

who obtained the Grant often in favor of persons who conducted the undertaking paying them the stipulated allowance.

(Reprinted from: Sir John Fortescue, ed., *The Correspondence of King George the Third from 1760 to December 1783*, vol. II, London, 1927, 194–7.)

Appendix 2b Petition to the Lord Chamberlain (c.1775)

The Managers of the Opera to the Lord Chamberlain

The managers of the Opera beg permission to solicit the Lord Chamberlains protection, and to lay before his Lordship a real state of the hardships under which they suffer.

They beg leave to represent to his Lordship that it is impossible for the Receipts of Italian Opera's only to support the necessary expences.

That the Salaries of the first Singers and Dancers being so enormous they are at a larger yearly expence than the other Theatres, and instead of six Nights in a Week have in effect only one as on the Tuesdays they constantly play to great loss.

That the Subscription Saturday Nights are only twenty five and the few nights after the Subscription scarce worth taking, as the People of fashion are out of town.

That the Kings Theatre was originally a play house under his Majestys immediate protection and that of the Lord Chamberlain and continued such till Mr Collier came into a compromise with the Managers of Drury Lane to suspend giving plays at the Opera House on condition the Managers of Drury Lane engaged not to play on Opera Nights and to allow the Directors of the Opera as a further compensation Two Hundred Pounds a Year: an Agreement which has not been fulfill'd on the side of the Patentees of the other Theatre for many years: on the contrary, they have given the strongest pieces they possibly cou'd at both houses, on Opera Nights, and given both comic and serious English Operas with Italian Music, to the great detriment of the Managers of the Opera.

That the Salary of even one capital Performer at the Opera House, is more than equal to those of three at the Playhouse: tho the latter play six times a Week and the Opera House but twice, and one of those Nights a certain loss.

That his Lordship has been so good in consideration of the impossibility of supporting Operas without some indulgence to allow the Managers two

Masquerades but from their being become so common, and given every where, they do not pay the expences, and therefore they have this year been obliged to decline them and have only given one tho' his Lordship was so good to allow them two.

That besides the above disadvantages the Pantheon a new undertaking, establish'd since the present Managers came to the Kings Theatre in the manner it is now carry'd on, is to the utmost degree ruinous to the Opera, as they not only divide the Musical audiences, but by offering the most exorbitant terms to Italian Singers make it almost impossible for the Managers of the Opera to engage any Performers, except at prices which even the utmost success can never enable them to pay. This they can easily do as they are a numerous body fifty persons at least divided amongst whom the salaries are but trifles, and many of whom, being (as we are inform'd) tradesmen find their account in furnishing refreshments, as well for the common nights, as for Masquerades &c.

That the present Managers have embark'd a large Sum in the purchase which must be sunk with perhaps much more, unless his Lordship has the Goodness to grant them an extension of their present licence.

That in the days of Shakespear London contain'd no less than seventeen play houses a circumstance to which we probably owe that immortal writer. That the present number of Theatres in this Capital being so very inadequate to the amazing encrease of its inhabitants since the act of limitation, the Nobility and Gentry, continually refus'd places, and weary'd out by repeated disappointments have to the great discouragement of dramatic genius, almost left off frequenting the theatres.

That if there are any solid objections to an additional theatre, they cannot affect the Opera House, originally built and licens'd for a play house, and honor'd with the name of the Kings Theatre.

That the present Directors encourag'd by the general wish of the Nobility and Gentry to have plays at a Theatre so conveniently situated, humbly entreat that the licence for the Opera House, now confin'd to Italian performances, may be extended on the intermediate Nights to theatrical entertainments in the English language also.

If a licence for plays is absolutely impossible that his Lordship will be so good to permit English Operas on the intermediate nights, or if that cannot be had, a summer licence in the nature of Mr Foote's patent but on different nights.

If it shou'd be urg'd that the present Managers of Drury Lane and Covent

Garden House purchas'd at a great expence, the Managers of the Opera have done the same, and have ever since play'd to loss, whereas the profits of the other theatres, even with a third wou'd be immense: it is also to be considered that the law restraining the number of theatres expressly gives Power to the Lord Chamberlain to licence more at his pleasure, and therefore the purchases of Drury Lane and Covent Garden have been always made under the supposition that more might, and probably wou'd be granted.

Nor was the Act of Limitation intended to limit the number which is still in the Lord Chamberlain's power but to restrain the licentiousness of the theatres: Nor wou'd such an extension of their licence as the Managers of the Opera humbly solicit, add to the number of theatres, which wou'd be still the same: a consideration which has encourag'd them to ask his Lordships protection.

(Reprinted from: Sir John Fortescue, ed., *The Correspondence of King George the Third from 1760 to December 1783*, vol. II, London, 1927, 191–4.)

Appendix 2c   Draft petition to the Lord Chamberlain from Sheridan and Harris (1777)

Gentlemen

According to your desire the Plan of the proposed *Assistant Theatre* is here explained in Writing for your further consideration.

From our situations in the Theatres Royal of Drury Lane and Covent Garden, we have had opportunities of observing many circumstances relative to our general Property which must have escaped those who do not materially interfere in the management of that Property – One point in particular has lately weigh'd extremely in our Opinions which is an Apprehension of a new Theatre being erected for some species or other of Dramatic Entertainment. Were this Event to take place on an opposing Interest in all probability the contest that would ensue would speedily end in the absolute ruin of one of the present Established Theatres, – We have reason it is true from His Majesty's gracious Patronage to the Present Houses to hope that another Patent for an opposing Theatre is not likely to be obtained – but the motives which appear to call for one, are so many and those of such nature as to encrease every day – that we cannot on the maturest consideration of the subject divest ourselves of the dread of such an event. With this Apprehension before us – We have naturally fallen into a joint consideration of the means either of preventing so fatal a Blow to the present Theatres or of deriving a general advantage from a Circumstance which might otherwise be their ruin –

Some of the leading motives for the establishment of a third Theatre are as follows –

1st: The great extent of the Town and encreased Residence of a higher class of People who on account of many inconveniences seldom frequent the Theatres –

2d: The distant situation of the Theatres from the Politer Streets – and the difficulty with which Ladies reach their Carriages or Chairs.

3d: The small number of side Boxes, where only by the uncontroulable influence of Fashion Ladies of any Rank can be induced to sit.

4th: The earliness of the hour, which renders it absolutely impossible for those who attend Parliament, live at any distance, or indeed for any Person who dines at the prevailing hour to reach the Theatre before the Performance is half over –

These considerations have lately been strongly urged to me by many leading Persons of Rank – There has also prevailed, as appears by the number of private Plays at Gentlemen's seats an unusal Fashion for Theatrical entertainments among the politer Class of People – and it is not to be wondered at that they finding themselves, (from the causes before enumerated) in a manner excluded from our Theatres, shou'd persevere in an endeavour to establish some Plan of similar entertainment on Principles of superior elegance and accomodation –

In proof of this disposition and the effects to be apprehended from it we need but instance one fact among many which might be produced, and that is the well known circumstance of a subscription having actually been begun last Winter, with a very powerfull Patronage for the importation of a French Company of Comedians – a scheme which tho' it might not have answered to the undertakers would certainly have been the Foundation of other Entertainments whose opposition we shou'd speedily have experienced –

The Question then upon a full view of our situation appears to be whether The Proprietors of the present Theatres will contentedly wait till some other Person takes advantage of the prevailing wish for a third Theatre or having the remedy in their power profit by a turn of fashion which they cannot controul –

A full conviction that the latter is the only line of conduct which can give security to the Patents of Drury Lane and Covent Garden Theatres and yield a probability of future advantage in the exercise of them, has prompted us to endeavour at modelling this Plan which we conceive the Theatres may unite in the support of a third to the general and mutual advantage of all the Proprietors.

Proposals –

The proprietors of the Theatre Royal in Covent Garden appear to be possessed of two Patents for the Privilege of acting Plays etc. – under one of which the above mention'd Theatre is open'd – the other lying Dormant and useless. It is proposed that this dormant patent shall be exercised (with his Majesty's approbation) in order to licence the Dramatic Performances of the New Theatre to be erected –

It is proposed That the Performances at this New Theatre shall be supported from the united establishments of the two present Theatres – so that the unemploy'd part of each company may exert themselves for the advantage of the whole.

As the object of this assistant Theatre will be to reimburse the proprietors of the other two at the full season for the expensive establishment they are obliged to maintain when the Town is almost empty, it is supposed that the scheme of Business to be adopted in the New Theatre shall differ as much as possible from that of the other two and that the Performances at the New House shall be exhibited at a superior price and shall commence at a later hour –

If a Theatre for these purposes is hired or to be built (being the Property of the Builder or Builders) it must be for an agreed on Rent with security for a Term of Years, in this case the Proprietors of the two present Theatres shall jointly and severally engage in the whole of the risk and the Proposers are ready on equitable Terms to undertake the Management of it – But if the proposers find themselves enabled either on their own credit or by the Assistance of their Friends on a plan of subscription, the mode being devised and the security given by themselves to become the Builders of the Theatre, The Proposers will in that case undertake that no Rent shall be demanded for the Performances therein to be exhibited for the mutual advantage of the two present Theatres – Reserving to themselves any profit they can make of their Building employ'd in purposes distinct from the Business of the Theatre and towards which the Privilege of the Patent does not contribute.

The proposers undertaking the management of the New Theatre shall be entitled to a Sum to be settled by the Proprietors at large or by an equitable arbitration.

Then it is proposed that all the Proprietors of the two Present Theatres Royal of Drury Lane and Covent Garden shall share all profits from the Dramatic entertainments as above specified exhibited at the New Theatre – that is each shall be entitled to receive a Dividend in proportion to the shares he or she shall possess of the present Theatres – First only deducting a certain nightly sum to be paid to the Proprietors of Covent Garden Theatre as a Consideration for the licence furnished by the exercise of their present dormant Patent.

Should the above Plan be carried into execution it is evident that there will be a more extensive Field for the encouraging and rewarding of Theatrical Performers as well as greater scope for the Talents of Dramatic Writers – so that the Proprietors instead of being compell'd to lower the

Drama by diminishing their present establishments, (which they are sensible must be the case) will be enabled by enlarging the circle of Audiences, to support all their entertainments with additional Lustre.

The Proposers have only to add that they are so entirely convinced of the general Advantage and Equity of the Plan now offered that they do not hesitate to join the following Proposition to the execution of it viz. They will severally undertake to any Proprietor with whom they are now in Partnership who shall be apprehensive that his or her Present Property may be impaired instead of benefited by the establishment of the New Theatre, they will with such Proprietor undertake to Purchase at a Proper Notice his or her share any time within the period of two Years from the commencement of the Plan – The Price to be fix'd at the full present Value and estimation of their Property – Or if any Proprietor shall prefer a certain Dividend from the whole they are ready in manner as before to Rent the share of such Proprietor for any desired Term at an Estimated Sum to be fix'd on an Average Profit of any number of past Seasons – But if the Proprietors of Covent Garden Theatre do not think it expedient to Prefer the exercise of their present Dormant Patent in the Proposed Theatre – The Proposers are ready to listen to any other Plan which they or any other Proprietor shall think more for the advantage and security of both Theatres.

(Signed by Sheridan and Harris; dated in another hand 25 November 1777.)

(Reprinted from: Cecil Price, ed., *The Letters of Richard Brinsley Sheridan*, 3 vols., Oxford, 1966, I, 116–21.)

Les Sieurs Piccini, Paésiello, Trajetta, & d'autres grands maitres d'Italie, ont occupé cette année le théatre de Londres, les opéras de *Germondo*, d'*Astarto*, de *Telemacs*, de *Pyramo & Thisbeea*, ceux de la *Fraschetana*, de la *Buona Figliola, il Geloso in Cimento, la Schiava* etc etc. & mardi 20 May, *I Capriccii del Sesso*, ont été représentés depuis le commencement de l'hiver. Nous parlerons seulement de ceux qui ont paru faire le plus de sensation.

En général l'Opera Comique a été plus gouté que l'Opera Sérieux, & il est certain qu'il le méritoit davantage. La musique de Télémaque cependant est remplie de choses sublimes, & fait le plus grand honneur à son compositeur *Mr Trajetta*. On a essayé d'y introduire des Ballets analogues au sujet, mais c'est un bien petit pas qu'on a fait dans cette carriere.

Je ne craindrai pas de dire mon avis à cet égard. Je suis toujours fort étonné que le compositeurs des ballets, qui sont François, qui ont pris les leçons de leur art à l'Academie Royale de Paris, n'ayent pas essayé plûtot de suivre l'exemple de l'Opéra François. Je leur crois assés de gout me persuader qu'ils ne demanderoit pas mieux qu'on leur en donnat les moyens. Comment est il possible que le premier spectacle d'une des prémiéres Capitales de l'Europe, d'une des nations les plus éclairées, & les plus célébres, puisse languir si longtems dans cette anarchie du bon gout. J'avouerai que je n'ai pas vu de pais où le public fut aussi complaisant, aussi indulgent, & aussi bon. Il pardone tout, & avec cette liberté de trouver mauvais ce qui l'est, & de le témoignes de maniére à obtenir quelque chose de mieux; il souffre qu'on lui donne *l'aimable Vieillesse*, qui est bien une preuve qu'on n'en meurt pas, ou la *force de l'amour*, pendant tout un hyver; ce n'est pas assurement que mon intention soit de dénigres ces deux ballets, ils sont jolis, la pantomime en est agréable; il y a un pas dans *l'aimable Vieillesse* ou le Sieur Valouy, danseur charmant, plein de graces, & de sentiment, fait toujours le plus grand plaisir; mais cela n'empeche pas qu'il ne soit souverainement ridicule de donner ce ballet depuis le 1ʳ Novembre jusqu'au mois de Juin. On me dira à cela; *mais il est toujours applaudi*. Sans doute, quand le Sieur Valouy vient danser son joli *Noël*, il n'est pas possible de n'en pas être content, & de ne pas témoigner sa satisfaction par des applaudissemens, mais il le seroit autant & plus dans un Ballet

nouveau, que dans l'aimable Vieillesse, qui cesse *d'être aimable* par la monotone & fatiguante répétition qu'on nous en donne. Voila ce qu'on éviteroit, si
les Ballets étoient toujours analogues aux sujets des Opéras, & envérité cela
seroit bien plus naturel. Je crois bien que les Directeurs font de leur mieux;
leur interet personel les y engage autant que le motif des plaisirs du public. Je
sais qu'ils ont de grandes dépenses à faire. Un opera Italien sérieux & un
opera comique, demandent de grands fraix. Des premiers sujets qui auroient
de gros appointemens dans leur pays, veulent en avoir de plus considérables
pour s'expatrier & venir dans un pays fort cher pour les Etrangers, aux
risques de leur santé & de leur talent, ce climat étant peu favorable à la voix.

Ne seroit il pas possible d'établir une petite Académie d'enfans de chaque
sexe, qui par la suite pouroient fournir d'excellents sujets, & qui mettroient
à même de se passer des Etrangers. Mlle Davies & M ^lle Prudom sont
Angloises, & cela suffit pour prouver qu'il seroit très possible de se dispenser
de faire venir ici des Virtuoses Italiens. Si absolument on ne pouvoit se passer
de ces Messieurs, il vaudroit mieux assurement en faire venir, que d'en
établir ici une manufacture, mais on en seroit quitte pour un ou deux
soprano, ce qui ne couteroit pas les fraix de deux Operas, qui sont immenses,
& qui empechent nécessairement les Directeurs de faire ce qu'ils
voudroient. Je serai donc le premier à les excuser à cet égard, mais je ne sçau-
rois m'empecher de leur reprocher un peu de négligence dans certain détails
absolument nécessaires aux représentations. Est il décent de voir arriver à la
suite de Calypso, une douzaine de petits Polissons des rues, plus mal
peignés, plus mal propres, plus dégoutans, couvert d'une espéce de tunique
d'un ligne sale, & on apelle cela les nymphes assurement si elles eussent
ressemblés à ces ridicule Pantins, Télémaque n'eut pas eu besoin de Mentor.
Ces petits détails qui ne paroissent pas d'une aussi grande conséquence
qu'ils le sont en effet, font beaucoup à la représentation, & demandent au
moins à être rendus d'une maniére décente; mais dans cette occasion ainsi
que dans beaucoup d'autres ils ne le sont pas, & par conséquent on droit
songer à y faire attention.

L'Opéra comique qui a obtenu le plus d'aplaudissements cette année est
sans contredit, La *Fraschetana*. Il est certain qu'il y a des morceaux de la plus
grande beauté. Les deux choeurs qui terminent le premier & le second acte
sont d'un genre de Musique absolument neuf. Il seroit à desirer que ce genre
obtint la préférence, quand ce devroit être un peu aux dépens de l'ariette si
monotone, communément si déplacée & en général si peu naturelle. Ces
deux morceaux au contraire, sont composés chacun d'une suite de plusieurs

scènes qui se succedent; le musicien habile a sçu y adapter des mouvemens analogues, aux différentes situations de ses acteurs, point de ces tristes *da capo*, point de répétitions fastidieuses, tout va, tout marche, la parole, le jeu, la musique, tout est ensemble, l'interet se propage, l'action se soutient, continue, & conduit l'attention du spectateur également occupé de ce qu'il voit & de ce qu'il entend à une réunion générale de tous les differences sentimens, qui exprimés dans les choeurs pleins de force, d'energie & d'élegance font éprouver tout à la fois, le charme de la plus heureuse harmonie, par la beauté de leurs accords; le plaisir de l'interet par la variété des situations, & ont pour effet certain d'entrainer tous les applaudissemens.

Voila ce que j'apelle de la Musique *Pictive*, voila celle que je voudrais qu'on employat plus souvent. Je suis bien éloigné de rejetter l'Ariette, toutes les fois quelle se trouvera bien placée, je serai enchanté d'entendre une jolie voix, m'étonner & me ravir par une grande légéreté dans les passages les plus difficiles, par des cadences, bien martelées, & bien justes; ou les sens harmonieux d'un bel organe, guidé par la meilleure manière de chanter; mais toutes les fois que je ne trouverai que ce genre de perfection, le plaisir n'ira jamais jusqu'à mon ame, c'est du sentiment qu'il faut pour en exciter en moi, & le sentiment n'appartient qu'à la nature. Il sera détruit toutes les fois que je la verrai violée outrageusement par des non convenances, qui sont si souvent multipliées dans nos spectacles. Ceci me conduiroit trop loin, si je voulois mettre au jouer les idées que j'ai sur l'art dramatique en général. Je trouverai l'occasion de les placer dans le cours de cet ouvrage.

Nous allons parler maintenant des acteurs de l'Opera de Londres. Nous mettrons dans nos observations toute la justice & la vérité nécessaires pour qu'ils puissent s'en raporter à nous sur nos avis quand ils nous paroitront en avoir besoin, & sur nos éloges quand nous croirons devoir leur en donner, n'ayant d'autres motifs, que le bien de la chose, & leurs plus grans succès.

Le Sieur Rauzzini a sans contredit un talent supérieur, il a la voix agréable, un joli gout de chant, & en tout une charmante maniére. Il joint à ces avantages, du talent pour la déclamation, mais il devroit se défaire de cette habitude nationale des gestes déplacés qui ne disant & n'exprimant rien, sont toujours fatiguans pour les spectateurs. Avec cette petite attention, & du travail, il peut devenir un des meilleurs acteurs d'Italie. Communément ils s'occupent de leur chant, de préference à toute attention pour leur jeu. C'est ce qui rend en général les grands Opéras si monotones, & si insipides. Tout doit engager le Sieur Rauzini à se distinguer de la foule de se ses confréres, ayant deja tout ce qu'il faut pour y réussir.

Les Acteurs de l'opera comique en Italie sont en général outrés & gri-
maciers. Le Sieur Trebbi a beaucoup moins ce défaut que ne l'ont ordinairement ses compatriotes, cependant on pourroit lui reprocher de faire encore
trop de gestes. Il a dailleurs une très belle voix, & on peut dire avec vérité
qu'il est difficile de chanter plus parfaitement que lui. Nous devons croire
que c'est pour se rendre utile qu'il a accepté les roles de l'Opera Sérieux. Il
est beaucoup mieux placé à tous égards dans ceux de l'opera comique. Mais
on doit lui Savoir gré de son Zêle pour l'amusement du public.

Quant au Sieur Savoi, on peut dire que son organe est un des plus beaux
& des plus purs qu'on puisse entendre. Lorsqu'il se donne des soins pour
bien chanter, il fait assés de plaisir pour l'inviter à en prendre plus souvent la
peine.

Les Sieurs Fochetti & Micheli ont l'air d'avoir envie de plaire, & ce desir
suplée quelque fois à de plus grands talens; à plus forte raison doit il réussir
dans des acteurs qui, sans être de la prémière classe, ne laissent pas de faire
plaisir dans les roles dont ils sont chargé. Le Sieur Fochetti joue bien les
jaloux. Nous conseillerions au Sieur Micheli de s'en tenir aux roles bouffons
pour les quels il a un excellent masque. Il met de la gäité dans son jeu, qui
seroit dailleurs assés naturel, s'il ne chargeoit pas quelque fois ses roles.

La Demoiselle Davies a certainement un des plus grands talens pour le
chant qu'on puisse avoir. Elle est une preuve, qu'en prenant du chant Italien
tout ce qu'il a de charmant, on peut faire le plus grand plaisir, sans en avoir
absolument l'idiome national. Il est dailleurs flatteur pour la nation de voir
une Angloise remplis avec succès le role de prémière chanteuse sur son
théatre Italien.

La demoiselle Sestini a de l'élégance, de la gäité, une figure fort agréable,
mais toujours un peu du défaut national. Si on vouloit sentir combien cet
excès de gestes est choquant on en feroit beaucoup moins. Elle chant
dailleurs avec une grande facilité. Peut être devroit elle ménager un peu plus
sa voix dans les sons hauts, mais en tout c'est une actrice fort amiable.

La Demoiselle Prudom qui avoit débuté avec de grands succès, paroit se
ralentir un peu dans ses progrès. Elle a pourtant tout ce qu'il faut pour
réussir, une voix agréable, une jolie manière de chant, une figure interessante. Il ne lui faudroit qu'un peu de travail. Comme elle est fort jeune, elle
s'imagine pouvoir réparer le tems perdu. Mais on peut prendre dans cet
intervalle de mauvaises habitudes qu'il est difficile de perdre. Nous lui
paroitrons peut-être un peu séveres, mais nous ne lui donnerions pas ce
conseil, si nous n'apercevions en elle les meilleurs dispositions possibles

pour en profiter, & dailleurs en nous montrant aussi vrais à l'égard d'une jeune persone, jolie & intéressante, c'est bien faire nos preuves d'impartialité.

Il nous reste à parler des Demoiselles Farnese. La Cadette a montré dans le role de calypso de véritables dispositions pour sa scène. Avec de bons conseils, elle pouroit devenir Actrice. L'ainée n'a joué que de petits roles & les a assés bien remplis.

Passons à la danse, nous avons dit ce que nous pensions du Sieur Valoui, & nous n'avons été que l'Echo du public. Nous devons témoigner des regrets d'avoir été privés, des talens de Mme Valouï par la maladie qui l'a empéché de danser cet hyver. Mais nous devons faire compliment à la D^{lle} Baccelli qui fait tous les jours de nouveaux progrès, & qui deviendra surement avant peu une des premiéres danseuses qui existent.

Le S^r & la D^{me} Simonet connoissent bien la danse, & justifient la réputation qui les avoit précedé dans ce pais ci. Une des perfections de Madame Simonet est la maniére dont elle a la tête & les épaules placées. Elle danse parfaitement le demi caractére joue le Pantomime, la noble surtout, avec beaucoup d'expression. Dans le ballet d'l'epouse Persane, il seroit difficile de desirer mieux.

Le Sieur & la Dame Zucchelli dansent avec beaucoup de légéreté. La Dame Zucchelli a la jambe tres brillante.

Le Sieur *Valouï* le cadet, annonce des dispositions à suivre les leçons de son frére. Il ne sauroit choisir un meilleur modele.

Terminons ce morceau par quelques réflexions sur l'ensemble de l'Opéra. Ne seroit il pas possible de remédir à des inconvénients principaux qui détruisent absolument toute espece d'illusion. Je pourrous citer pour prémier exemple, cette negligence que les acteurs ont d'aprendre leurs rôles. Je ne connois rien de plus ridicule que d'entendre perpétuellement la voix fort discordante d'un souffleur qui récite très haut & mot à mot toutes les paroles de l'Opéra. Je conçois bien que le peu d'attention qu'on y accorde, n'engage pas les acteurs à se donner des soins particuliers à cet égard. Mais s'ils ont sçu secouer vis-à-vis du public le joug auquel tout acteur est soumis, ils devroient au moins reconnoitre cette indulgence, en apprenant leurs roles assés superficiellement, pour n'avoir besoin que de tems en tems des secours du souffleur, qui de son coté devrait avoir l'attention de parler de maniére à n'être entendu que de l'acteur. Voila comme on prouve au public le respect qu'on lui doit, mais que malheureusement on lui rend moins que jamais. Je le répete, il est beaucoup trop bon ce Public, & par cette excessive douceur, il perd le droit qu'il a aux égards des gens faits pour l'amuser. Il seroit plus sensible à ces sortes de soins qui annonceroient le desir de lui plaire, qu'à ces plattes & révérences, que les acteurs ont la puèrile attention de faire, à chaque coup de main qu'on leur accorde. Y a t'il rien d'aussi ridicule que de couper ainsi toute espece d'intéret. Cela va jusqu'à interrompre une ariette, quand ils ont fait quelque passage assés bien pour obtenir des applaudissements. Je ne puis pas cacher mon étonnement de voir souffrir des chose aussi absurdes. Ce n'est pas la faute des acteurs, ils s'imaginent par là plaire au public, & l'effet les justifie, puis que toutes les fois qu'ils quittent la scène en se soumettant à ce ridicule usage, il y a toujours quelqu'un qui applaudit. Mais cela n'empéche pas que cela no [?] soit très déplacé. Je dirai plus, c'est que le respect dû au Public est compris dans cette sorte de familiarité. Il seroit bien mieux annoncé par une contenance modeste, qui marqueroit en même tems la reconnoissance.

Un acteur très aimé du Public, qu'on n'auroit pas vu depuis quelque tems, à qui on témoigneroit des bontés particuliéres par des applaudissemens multiplés, pouroit, avant de commencer son rôle, se dépouiller pour ainsi dire du caractère qu'il est chargé de représenter, redevenir lui, & alors témoigner le plus respectueusement qu'il lui sera possible la sensibilité mais du moment qui son rôle est commencé, il ne peut jamais en suspendre l'éxécution sans détruire toute espece d'illusion & de vraisemblance.

Le détail des machines mériteroit un peu plus d'attention qu'on ne lui en accorde. Le Décorateur, qui lui même est machiniste le Sr. COLOMBA à sans contredit du talent. L'Orage qui est dans l'Opera de Télémaque en annonce beaucoup, & cette nouvelle maniére d'imiter les Eclairs est une invention fort heureuse. En tout ce qui s'apelle représentation, toutes les fois qu'on se rapprochera de la nature, on sera sûr de faire un pas vers la perfection.

Quoique l'Orchestre rassemble d'excellents sujcts, chacuns dans leur genre, & qu'il soit dirigé par un homme de talent superieur, & comme violon, & comme compositeur, nous ne pouvons nous empêcher de nous plaindre que souvent il y manque cet ensemble si nècessaire pour l'exécution. Souvent même les instrumens à vent pechent par le défaut de justesse, & dans les accompagnemens du chant surtout, ce défaut est insupportable. Il seroit à desirer que l'Orchestre de l'Opera de Londres, dirigé par le Sieur GIARDINI, dont le nom seul fait l'éloge méritat la même réputation que lui.

Nous ne pouvons terminer cet article sans dire un mot du nouvel Opéra de *I Capriccii di Sesso*. Cet ouvrage fait autant d'honneur au Sieur Trajetta que ses précédentes productions. Le prémier acte surtout est parfait. Il y a dans le troisiéme un *duo* de la plus grande beauté. Le Rondeau, *il mio cuore* est aussi d'un chant tres agréable. La scene d'yvrogne du second acte est beaucoup trop longue. Il faudroit nécessairement retrancher la plus grande partie du récitatif que chante le Sr. Trebbi. En général le plan, les paroles de cet Opera n'ont pas l'ombre du sens commun. Est il possible qu'un nation qui se vante d'avoir un METESTASE, puisse faire & entendre des Opéras qui sont si loin de ces chef d'oeuvres.

On annonce un Opera de Mr. Back. Le nom seul suffit pour en donner d'avance l'idée la plus favorable.

JOURNAL ETRANGER, NO. 10 (NOVEMBER 1777), 148–55.

Spectacles de Londres

. . . Mais, pour la musique, l'article essentiel de la musique! il faudra que
l'Opera de *Paris* baisse pavillon devant l'Opera de *Londres*, malgré ses *Gretry*,
ses *Gluck*, ses *Piccini* même, qui assurement, est un bien grand homme, mais
qui avec son génie, ne poura jamais faire chanter de la musique Italienne à
des macheoires qui n'ont jamais que crié de la musique françoise. Nous
avons les oreilles, nous pouvons même dire l'ame tout fraichement affectés
des chefs d'oeuvres que nous avons eû le plaisir d'entendre hier & aujour-
d'hui, aux répétitions de l'Opera serieux de *Creso* du Sieur *Sacchini* & de celui
des deux *Contessi*, opera Bouffon dont presque tous les airs & surtout les
prèmiéres finales des trois actes sont du Sieur *Paesiello*. Il nous seroit bien
difficile de rendre compte de celle qui nous a donné plus de plaisir. Ces deux
musiques sont si analogues à leurs sujets, l'une est si majestueuse, si tendre,
si brillante, l'autre, si gaïe, si aimable, si variée, si plaisante même, enfin elles
sont toutes deux si bien ce qu'elles doivent être, qu'il faut nécessairement
partager la couronne qu'on voudroit accorder à toutes le deux.

   Parlons, maintenant, du choix qu'on a fait des nouveaux acteurs nous ne
pouvons encore rendre compte de leur jeu, mais comme malheureusement
pour la chose, ce n'est pas ce qui paroit de plus interessant, nous serons à
tems d'en juger à la répresentation. Rendons seulement compte, de ce que
nous avons entendu, & essayons de dévancer le jugement du public.

   La Demoiselle Dantzy, chargée des prémiers rôles sérieux, a un genre de
voix qui est une des choses les plus extraordinaires qu'il soit possible d'entendre: une étendue incomprehensible, & surtout, une grande justesse. Elle
chante dans le second acte de *Creso* un air de *Bravoura*, qui est de la plus
sublime composition, & qui réunit de difficultés qu'aucun auteur n'auroit
osé écrire, n'imaginant pas qu'il fut possible de les rendre. Elle a d'ailleurs,

une figure agréable qui sera, surement, tres bien au théatre; elle paroit avoir beaucoup de timidité, deffaut dont on poura la corriger en la rassurant par les applaudissemens que surement elle méritera.

Le Sieur *Ronkalio* qui succede au Sieur *Rauzzini* ne permettra pas qu'on regrette aussi longtems ce charmant acteur, il a une voix beaucoup plus agréable, un gout parfait et en tout une maniere de chanter beaucoup plus intéressante, n'ayant aucune espece d'affectations, qui sont toujours des grimaces. Quant à la figure, il a la taille fort élancée & paroitra peut être un peu grand au théatre, il a d'ailleurs, la phisionomie fort noble & fort distinguée, nous verrons s'il surpasse en fait de jeu son prédecesseur qui étoit un des moins mauvais acteurs qu'il-y-eut dans ce genre: mais s'il joüe comme il chante ce sera un acteur parfait.

Nous ne detaillerons pas aussi particulièrement les acteurs du second ordre de l'opera sérieux, nous dirons seulement que le Sieur * * * qui remplace le Sieur *Savoy* paroit connoitre bien, le chant, mais, il seroit difficile á qui que ce fut de le remplacer dans son organe: Le Sieur *Savoy* ayant, sans contredit, une des plus belles voix que l'on puisse entendre.

Quoique le Sieur *Trebbi*, ne fut pas destiné originairement à remplir le rôle de *Tenore* dans l'Opera serieux, & que sa phisionomie, naturellement comique, se prétat peu a jouer les rôles de Rois, de Tyrans, & d'Empereurs Romains, la perfection de son chant & agrément de sa voix faisoit passer sur l'improbabilité de sa tournure nous craignons qu'il ne soit pas remplacé dans cette partie. Le Tenore chargé de ces rôles a dit-on, beaucoup de mérite comme chanteur, il est extrêmement bon musicien, connoit parfaitement le chant, mais sa voix nous a paru nazale & désagréable; il a d'ailleurs une bien petite figure, nous désirons nous tromper, & que l'illusion du Théatre puisse pallier un peu, ces imperfections, nous serons les prémiers, à revenir sur notre jugement, si celui du public n'y répond pas; mais nous craindrions de perdre sa confiance, si, par complaîsance, ou prevention, nous lui annoncions des talens superieurs, dans des sujets qui ne repondroient point à l'ésperance que nous lui en aurions donné.

La Demoiselle *Prudhomme* & le Sieur *Micheli*, sont de vieilles connoissances, l'une a un talent qui a déja été souvent accueilli par le public; l'autre a de la bonne volonté, & fait son possible pour plaire: effort dont on doit toujours savoir gré & qui mérite quelqu'indulgence.

Passons aux détails de l'Opera Bouffon. *Le due Contessi*, est le titre de l'Opéra qu'on prépare dans ce genre, c'est une espèce de *pasticcio*, comme la *fraschetana* & fort bien arrangé par le Sieur *Giardini*; presque tous les airs, les finales surtout, sont comme nous l'avons dit, de *Paësiello*, il-y-a seulement deux ou trois airs ajoutés, composés par les meilleurs maitres d'Italie, dont le choix fait honneur au Sieur *Giardini*: enfin nous ne serions pas étonnés, que cet Opéra fit autant de plasir que la *fraschetana*, & assurément c'est beaucoup dire.

La Signora Todi, qui remplace *la Signora Sestini*, a la voix plus douce & plus agréable, elle a d'ailleurs une manière de chanter qui sera, surement, aplaudie par les connoisseurs; sa figure sera fort bien pour le Théatre, autant qu'on en peut juger dans le deshabillé d'une répétition; nous ne pouvons donner aucune idée de son jeu, qui est pourtant un article Beaucoup plus essentiel, dans l'Opera Bouffon, que dans l'Opéra sérieux: mais, s'il répond à son chant, nous n'aurons point à nous plaindre.

Nous avons dit que le Sieur *Trebbi*, ne seroit pas remplacé dans l'Opera sérieux, mais nous ne pouvons annoncer qu'il le sera parfaitement dans l'Opéra Bouffon; une voix charmante, beaucoup de gout, une manière de chant eccellente que nous pouvons, pour en donner une idée, comparer à celle du Sieur *Piozzi*, une figure fine, & agréable, voilà ce qu'on trouvera dans le Sieur *Germoglio*, il faut encore le voir jouer, mais à quelques gestes échapés à la répétition, dans la vivacité du chant, nous avons lieu de croire que son talent à cet egard, ne démantira pas l'idée avantageuse que nous en avons conçue.

Sa femme la *Signora Germoglio* est chargée des second rôles, comme elle a fort peu de choses à chanter dans cet Opéra, nous n'avons pas été à même de juger de l'étendue de sa voix; mais on sait que ces seconds rôles ne sont jamais donnés qu'a des chanteuses du second ordre, & il ne faut pas s'attendre à trouver des talens pareils à ceux qui remplissent les prémiers.

Il nous reste à Parler du Sieur *Rossi* chargé de l'emploi de *Buffo Caricato*. Sa phisionomie prévient en sa faveur, à le voir passer dans la rue, on jureroit que cet homme est un excellent comique, & surement il tiendra parole, il est d'ailleurs, excellent Musicien, chose encore fort essentielle dans cette espèce de rôle. Il chante dans cet Opéra deux ou trois airs qui sont charmans, un surtout, dans le second acte, dans lequel il fait parler tous les instrumens les uns après les autres. Cette idée est neuve, & la musique est admirablement adaptée aux paroles. D'ailleurs il chante ces airs avec une gaïté qui, soutenue par la caricature de son visage, fait un effet très comique & très plaisant.

Enfin, prononçons que l'Opéra est parfaitement monté cette année, en chanteuses, chanteurs, & surtout, compositeurs. Moyennant cette certitude, nous pouvons compter sur une excellente musique, supérieurement exécutée. Le Sieur *Cramer* à la tête d'un orchestre qui paroit fort bien composé ne nous laissera rien à désirer à cet égard, nous devons ésperer que les ballets y répondront. Le Sieur & la Dame *Simonet*, la D^lle *Bacelli* nous le promettant. Et les fraix que les Directeurs viennent de faire pour repeindre toute la salle dans un trés bon genre, nous annoncent qu'ils ne veulent rien négliger pour satisfaire le public, & pour obtenir l'approbation générale.

JOURNAL ETRANGER, NO. II (NOVEMBER 1777), 142–8.

Opera de Londres

Le compte que nous avons rendu de l'Opera de Londres dans le précédent N° nous paroit avoir été approuvé par le témoinage du public, & nous sommes flattés de voir que notre jugement, quoique anticipé, a été analogue au suffrage général.

Rien de plus charmant que la voix & le chant du sieur *Roncaglia*, it est inutile d'entrer dans aucun détail à cet egard: tout ce que nous pourions dire ne donneroit qu'une foible idée de sa supériorité, il faut l'entendre pour en juger.

Rien de plus étonnant que l'étendue de la voix de la D^lle *Danzi*, si on étoit enthousiasmé des petits cris aigus de la Signora *Aguïari*, lorsqu'elle passoit la portée ordinaire de la voix, combien doit-on être admirablement surpris d'entendre une voix naturelle & agréable, passer de cinq tons, cette portée la plus étendue, avec une justesse étonnante & la netteté la plus incompréhensible. Nous avons appris, que la D^lle *Danzi* est engagée pour être la prémière chanteuse de l'Opera de *Milan*, l'année prochaine; malgré les regrets que nous aurons de la perdre, nous la verrons, avec plaisir, passer dans un païs où elle ne poura pas manquer d'acquerir cette perfection de chant qu'on n'obtient que dans cette charmante Italie, la mère patrie de tout ce qui s'appelle musique; avec des moyens aussi étonnans que ceux que la nature a accordé à la D^lle *Danzi*, nous pouvons annoncer, qu'après quelques années de séjour dans une aussi parfaite école, la D^lle *Danzi* sera la plus étonnante cantatrîce qui ait jamais été entendue; son age de dix neuf ans, sa figure qui est trés agréable, & vraîment théatrale, & son jeu dans lequel nous avons découvert de grandes dispositions, doivent faire croire aussi, qu'avec du travail, elle peut devenir une excellente Actrice.

Nous esperons qu'on ne nous saura pas mauvais gré annoncé le Sr.

Jermoli, comme un des plus parfaits *Tenore* qu'on puisse entendre; nous pouvons ajouter que son jeu ne depare pas son chant.

La Signora *Todi*, joüe avec noblesse, & fait, heureusement, beaucoup moins de Grimaces que n'en sont ordinairement les Italiens. Sa voix est douce & agréable, & son chant annonce une *Virtuose* trés consommée dans son art.

Sans répeter, ici, les détails que nous avons déja donnés des autres acteurs & actrices, nous pouvons redire avec plaisir, que depuis longtems, l'Opera n'a été bien composé quant à la musique.

Quant aux Ballêts, Mlle *Bacelli*, qui fait tous les jours de nouveaux progrès, & la dame *Simonet*, sont deux danseuses charmantes.

Le Sieur *Banti* avoit à vaincre la prévention bien juste que nous avions pour le Sr. *Vallouis*, & quoiqu'il soit un joli danseur, il n'atteint pas à cette supériorité que nous sommes dans le cas de regretter.

La D^{lle} *Banti* a du brillant & de la gaïté dans la danse, nous l'invitons cependant, à ne pas avoir toujours la bouche ouverte d'une manière si affectée, & si continue; car, quoiqu'elle ait les plus jolies dents du monde, on auroit bien plus de plaisir à les revoir de tems-en-tems, qu'a ne jamais cesser de les voir pendant tout le tems qu'elle danse.

Nous ne devons pas terminer cet article sans rendre justice à la Signora *Zuchelli* qui a fait, sans contredit, de trés grands progrès depuis l'année derniere, & qui est une danseuse trés agréable.

Le premier ballet remplit son titre; il est annoncé ballet sérieux, & assuré-ment, il l'est fort. Mais il est bien difficile que ce genre ne le soit pas; beau-coup de pirouettes, beaucoup d'entrechats, beaucoup de *Tends* de cuisse, sans plan, ni dessein, par consequent sans intéret. Ces ballêts là ne sont jamais que des quadres pour faire paroître le talent supérieur des danseurs principaux, & alors il faut qu'ils soient trés superieurs pour faire plaisir.

Le second ballet est assés joliment deffiné, le choix des airs charmans de l'Opera du devin du village, caracterise assés bien la pantomime pour les personnes qui connoissent l'Opera, mais nous craignons qu'il n'ait pas le même effet pour ce païs-cy; & c'est une des choses à la quelle un Maitre de Ballets devroit faire le plus d'attention. Il doit toujours Travailler de préfer-ence pour le public qu'il a à satisfaire, consulter ses Goûts & s'appliquer surtour à lui plaire. Nous autres françois, sommes enchantés d'entendre les airs d'un Opera que nous avons toujours aimé, que nous savons par coeur, la pantomime suffit pour nous en rapeller les situations, nous chantons les paroles dès que nous entendons les ritournelles; Mais, à Londres, il ne faut pas avoir envie de plaire aux François, & je deffie que les Anglois, qui ne connoitront point cet Opera, entendent rien à cette pantomime.

Le dernier Ballet est d'un effet agréable, le pas de trois du Sieur *Simonet* des D^lles *Bacelli* & *Simonet* est très bien composé, les airs en sont bien choisis, nous avouerons cependant, que nous n'avons pas conçu bien distinctement l'intention de l'episode dansé par le Sr. & la Dame *Zuchelli* & le Sr. *Vallouis* le cadet, à moins que ce ne soit une pettite leçon qu'on ait voulu adresser en passant aux Maris jaloux, pour les instruire du parti qu'ils ont à prendre en pareille circonstance le Sieur *Zuchelli*, *Calmouck* ou *Cosaque*, Tout ce qu'on voudra, surprend sa femme, ou sa Maistresse, en Tête-à-Tête, c'est à dire dansant un pas de deux avec un autre petit *Calmouck*, le Sieur *Vallouis le tres cadet*, il vient armé d'un poignard pour venger son honneur offensé, la pauvre femme qui a negligé de fermer sa porte, se trouve prise sur le fait, & n'a d'autres moyens à employer que les larmes; elle se jette aux pieds de son mari, & a l'air de lui dire, qu'il est bien cruel de se porter à de pareilles extremités pour deux ou trois entrechats qu'ils ont fait ensemble: le Mari convaincu, sur le champ par d'aussi puissantes raisons, s'apaise, jette son poignard avec une indignation qui prouve combien il est pénétré de l'injustice qu'il alloit commettre, console sa femme, & le petit Monsieur, de la peur qu'il leur a faite, & la scêne finit par un pas de trois qui annonce la meilleure intelligence. Nous avouons que cette petite scêne ne nous a pas paru un grand effort d'imagination, mais, on en est dédommagé par deux entrées seules des dames *Bacelli* & *Simonet*, qui dans tous les païs du monde, seront toujours regardées comme deux danseuses du premier ordre.

Nous aurions à nous reprocher de finir cet article sans rendre au Sieur *Cramer*, le tribut d'éloges qu'il mérite. Il est absolument impossible, qu'un orchestre soit mieux conduit que sous la direction de ce grand Maître, & nous croyons pouvoir prononcer qu'il n'y a personne capable d'occuper cette place avec autant de supériorité.

JOURNAL ETRANGER, NO. 12 (DECEMBER 1777), 142–3.

On a redonné un ballet qui avoit déja été exécuté l'année dernière, il est intitulé le *Clochette*, il a paru faire plus de plaisir que le ballet polonnois, les airs en sont bien choisis, & trés dansans, Mlle *Bacelli* & M^de *Simonet* y dansent chacune un pas, qui quoique d'un genre different fait le plus grand plaisir, &

laisse quelquefois dans l'incertitude quand on veut prononcer sur le talent comparé de ces deux charmantes danseuses.

On continue de donner les operas de *Creso* & *di due Contesse*: tous les deux, comme nous l'avons déja dit, superieurs pour la musique, nous croyons pouvoir annoncer, que plus on les entendra & plus ils seront de plaisir.

On prépare un grand Opera de la composition de Mr. *Sacchini*, célébre à si juste titre, & certainement un des prémiers compositeurs de l'Europe. Cet Opera a pour titre *Eriphile*.

Nous ne nous occuperons plus des détails ce Spectacle que quand il-y-aura des Nouveautés.

JOURNAL ETRANGER, NO. 13 (DECEMBER 1777), 161.

Spectacles de Londres

Nous avons eu à l'Opéra un nouveau ballet qui, quoique serieux, a fait le plus grand plaisir. La D^lle *Bacelli* y danse deux pas charmants, le S^r & La D^me *Simonet* y sont égallement très bien.

On doit donner, Mardy prochain, un Opéra nouveau, intitulé, la *Vittorina*; les paroles de *Goldoni*, & la musique du fameux *Piccini*, préviennent d'avance en sa faveur; mais nous pouvons ajouter que l'un & l'autre tiennent parole à leur réputation; il y a des choses charmantes dans la musique, on y reconnoitra facilement l'auteur de la *Buona figliuola* & des autres excellents ouvrages qui lui ont assigné la place d'un des premiers compositeurs de l'Europe.

JOURNAL ETRANGER, NO. 14 (JANUARY 1778), 144–5.

Opera de Londres

La Vittorina, opera nouveau, soit disant comique, composé par *Goldoni* & *Piccini*, auroit du remplir l'attente que les Spectateurs devoient naturellement concevoir d'après la réputation méritée de ces deux grand auteurs: cependant cet intermede n'a pas eu tout le succès qu'on esperoit; un seul air dans le second acte, chanté par la Signora Todi a été généralement applaudi. Il est pourtant vrai qu'il-y-a d'autres morceaux de musique réellement interessants dans cet Opera. Mais, soit qu'on n'ait pas voulu se préter au genre de sensation que cette représentation devoit produire, puisque bien loin d'étre comique, le drame est très sentimental, & même du genre Larmoyant, soit que les situations n'ayent pas paru satisfaisantes, ou qu'on n'ait pas trouvé la musique heureusement adaptée, enfin, on a prononcé généralement qu'il étoit triste. Quelques personnes plus sévères ont ajouté qu'il étoit ennuyeux, Mais pour y suppléer on a donné un ballet nouveau de la composition des Sieurs *Zuchelly* & *Banty*, qui est fort agréable; le sujet, la pantomime, les habits, la décoration, le choix des airs tout y est bien, & d'ailleurs le plaisir de voir danser dans les autres ballets la D^{lle} *Bacelli*, qui fait tous les jours de nouveaux progrès, doit dédomager des momens où on ne trouveroit pas toute la satisfaction qu'on auroit droit d'attendre.

JOURNAL ETRANGER, NO. 18 (MARCH 1778), 123–8.

Spectacles de Londres Opera

La vera Costanza, & *Eriphile* sont les deux operas nouveaux qui occupent le Théatre. Nous ne nous étendrons pas prodigieusement sur le detail de ce Spectacle, nous rendrons seulement justice au mérite des Compositeurs. Il n'est pas possible d'ajouter à la réputation de Mr. *Sacchini*; pour peu qu'il manquat un Laurier à sa couronne, *Eriphile* le lui donneroit; il y a des choses de la plus sublime composition dans cet opéra, les coeurs sont presque tous des chefs-d'ouvres, celui surtout des prisonniers.

> *O Tu che siedi in Cielo*
> *Arbitro de' mortali*

Et celui de

> *Morte funesta, morte etc*

Devroient faire l'impression la plus profonde s'ils n'étoient dénués de toute espéce de vraisemblance, & détestablement éxécutés par cinq ou six vilains enfans qui chantent faux, qui partent les uns apres les autres, & qui violent même la décence, en se poussant, en riant, en poliçonant de la manière la plus révoltante. Mais n'entrons point dans ces détails, nous aurions trop à dire, & dans la circonstance ou nous sommes, on pouroit nous soubçonner de prévention. Bornons nous donc à rendre justice à qui la mérite. Mlle

Danzy, déja tres étonnante dans l'Opera de *Creso*, nous a fait voir qu'elle approchoit à grands pas du but de la perfection. Nous le répétons avec plaisir, & nous verrons accomplir notre prédiction, quelqu'années de séjour d'Italie, & cette charmante cantatrice sera sans contredit, *la prima Dona* de l'Europe entiere. L'ariette qu'elle a chanté dans l'Opéra d'Eriphile accompagné par Mr le *Brun*, est en vérité une chose étonnante de part & d'autre: aussi a-t-elle été recue les transports de l'admiration. On a-beau dire, le vraiment beau entraine, tout esprit de parti est obligé de ceder, devant ce qui s'apele sublime . . . La circonstance ou se trouve ici Mr *Le Brun* est réellement tres délicate, il court la même carriere que Mr *Fischer*, qui jouit d'une réputation bien méritée, il a affaire à un auditoire, conséquement prévenu, d'autant plus que la nation Angloise s'attache volontiers aux sujets supérieurs à qui elle a donné, une fois, son aveu, les protége de manière à paroitre même jalouse des succès étrangers. Nous avons été temoins de preuves répétée de cette partialité exclusive qui seroit inexcusable si elle n'avoit pas d'aussi excellens motifs; sans chercher à diminuer en rien le merité reconnu de Mr *Fischer*, dont nous avons toujours été les plus grands admirateurs, nous oserons accorder, cependant, quelques éloges à Mr *le Brun*, & nous croyons le pouvoir sans nous compromettre, le jugement du public qui l'a entendue avec ravissement, & qui le lui a Temoigné, suffiroit pour nous y autoriser; Mais si nous avions besoin d'autres titres, nous pourions ajouter, qu'un homme qui entre en lice avec le fameux *Bezzosi* le premier hautbois de toute l'Italie, & pour qui on est obligé de partager la couronne qu'on destinoit au vainqueur, mérite un peu d'être distingué. Osons donc le prononcer, Mr *Fischer* & Mr *le Brun* sont deux hautbois admirables, applaudissons les tous deux, & sans chercher à élever l'un en abaissant l'autre, jouissons de la supériorité de leurs talens & accordons, leur tous les succès, & les éloges qu'ils méritent.

Le Sieur *Roncaglia* a chanté comme à son ordinaire, ce qui veut dire parfaitement. Son jeune âge ne lui permet pas d'avoir, encore, une grande habitude du Théatre, il paroit embarassé dans les scènes d'éxécution, mais malheureusement, on ne s'occupe gueres du charme de la représentation, on néglige si cruellement le plaisir des yeux, on le sacrifie si despotiquement à celui des oreilles, on se soucie si peu de ce qui pouroit affecter l'ame, & amuser l'esprit, enfin on fait si peu de cas ce qui feroit le plus de plaisir, qu'il suffit qu'un acteur soit supérieur dans le *Cantabile*, Brillant, étonnant dans les *Bravoura*, qu'il fasse avec adresse un joli passage; qu'il se tire bien d'une cadence, on n'en veut pas davantage, l'on est bien satisfait de lui & de soi même; quel aveuglement! quelle barbarie! nous sommes bien dans l'enfance du bonheur, en fait de plaisir, & nous avons l'air d'y rester encore longtems.

La *Vera Costanza* opéra comique de la composition du Sieur *Anfossi* est tres agréable, il y a des choses charmantes dans la musique, la finale du second acte est un chef-d'oeuvre. La Signora *Pozzi* y a chanté le prémièr rôle. Elle a un joli Organe, si elle ouvroit un peu plus la Bouche en chantant, & si elle s'attachoit à mieux prononcer, à varier un peu ses passages, à mieux terminer ses phrases musicales, à changer un peu ses gestes qui sont servilement, & malheureusement, toujours les mêmes, elle pouroit devenir interessante; elle a une figure agréable, une voix douce & flexible; elle est fort jeune; avec du travail, & de bons maitres, elle a tout ce qu'il faut pour réussir.

Nous ne devons pas terminer cet article, sans rendre justice au Sr *Rossi*, qui dans cet opéra a fait ses prémières preuves de talent; it est réllement bon *caricato* quoique exagéré, comme le sont tous les Italiens dans ce genre. Mais l'éloge le plus vrai que nous puissons faire, & le mieux merité est celui de la *Signora Jermoly*, particulierement dans son jeu qui est à tous égards tres agréable, beaucoup de finesse, de la vivacité, de l'esprit, de la grace, point, ou tres peu d'affectation, enfin nous sommes tres persuadés que ce Spectacle seroit tout autre si tous les acteurs y jouient comme elle.

JOURNAL ETRANGER, NO. 19 (MARCH 1778), 143–6.

Opera de Londres

On a donné à ce Théatre, un Opéra comique nouveau, intitulé *l'amore artigiano*; la musique de feu [Sieur?] *Gasman* est d'une trés agréable composition, cependant l'ensemble de l'Opéra n'a pas paru plaire prodigieusement. Les deux finales du premier & du second acte & surtout celle su second, sont deux excellens morceaux de musique. On nous a assuré que cet Opéra avoit eu le plus grand succès en Italie, mais que, d'après les changemens considérables, & les retranchemens qu'on avoit été obligé d'y faire, de plusieurs morceaux, par l'impossibilité de les éxécuter, il n'étoit plus reconnoissable. On a taché d'y suppléer par deux ballets nouveaux; dans le premier, le Sieur *Simonet* & la D^lle *Bacelli*, dansent le menuet de la Cour, & surtout la gavotte parfaitement bien. Quoique nous soyons fort empressés à rendre justice aux talens du Sieur & de la D^lle *Banti* qui ont un genre de danse agréable, nous ne pouvons pas être de l'avis de ceux qui ont fait répéter la soi disante *allemande Strasbourgeoise* qu'ils ont dansée dans ce ballet: nous n'y avons pas trouvé, la gaïté, la vivacité, qui sont ordinairement, le charme de cette danse nationale. La lenteur de l'air, la pésanteur des pas, la difficulté & la gêne des passes Nous ont paru bien différentes de cette légèreté, de cette pétulence, de cette ame du plaisir qui vivifie les bals de la *Robert's house*, & de la *Vassersone*, je pourois en appeler à tout *Alsacien*, & passer condemnation s'il s'en trouvoit un seul qui ne fut pas de mon avis. Né dans cette charmante partie de la France, je ne dois pas souffrir qu'on altère & qu'on diminue les avantages que la nature semble nous y accorder. Nous savons joindre les choses aimables a des parties plus essentielles, à notre amour pour notre roi, dont nous avons donné des preuves bien sures dans les occasions les plus intéressantes, à notre dévouement *Athenien* pour notre patrie. Nous unissons le goût des arts, nous naissons presque tous musiciens, traversez les rues de *Strasbourg*, & vous entendrez presque tous les ouvriers, former des concerts naturels, & chanter en partie avec autant d'exactitude & d'accord que s'ils avoient appris les règles de la composition, nous avons au moins autant de gout pour la danse, depuis la classe du plus bas peuple jusqu'aux gens le plus distingués, tout est fou de cette espèce d'amusement. Les servantes, avant de s'engager, mettent dans leurs accords, avec leurs maîtres, qu'on les laissera danser, les unes deux, les autres trois fois par semaine. Nous dansons pour ainsi dire avant de venir au monde, puisque nos méres sortent du bal pour aller accoucher: & le pilier des poèles Allemands, autour duquel on danse, est toujours entourée de nourrices qui donnent à tetter à leurs enfans en suivant la cadence, nos airs sont d'une extréme gaité, il est bien difficile de se refuser à la démangeaison qu'ils donnent de danser. Nous pouvons assurer que nous n'avons rien vu à *Strasbourg* ni dans ses environs qui ressemble à la danse du Sr & de la D^lle *Banti*, nous sommes trop bons patriotes pour laisser prendre une idée aussi défavorable des agrémens, & des plaisirs de notre *mère Patrie*.

Le second ballet, intitulé le sérénade interrompue, est d'une tres agréable composition & fait beaucoup d'honneur à M. *Simonet*. C'est sans contredit, le plus joli ballet qu'on ait vu, depuis longtems sur le Théatre de l'Opéra. Les détails en sont variés & charmans, la Demoiselle *Bacelli*, y danse mieux qu'a son ordinaire, par la raison que ses progrés vont toujours en augmentante. Le choix des airs est trés heureux. Ceux éxécutés par le Sieur *Nofferi*, sur la guittare, sont charmans. Enfin nous le répétons avec grand plaisir, en rendant justice aux talens du Sieur *Simonet*, il est très adroit à lui d'avoir su mettre au Théatre un ballet aussi agréable avec aussi peu de sujets, & d'aussi petits moyens qu'on lui en accorde.

JOURNAL ETRANGER, NO. 21 (APRIL 1778), 129–30.

Spectacles de Londres

On a donné à l'opera la prémière représentation *de la clemenza di scipione*, la musique est de Monsieur *Bach*, ce mot suffit pour en faire l'éloge; il-y-a des morceaux de la plus grande beauté, mais surtout, celui du second acte, avec accompagnement obligé du *Hautbois*, du *Violon*, du *Violoncel*, & de la *Flutte*, executé par Mrs *le Brun*, *Cramer*, *Cervetto*, & *Florio*, est au dessus de tout éloge, & Mlle *Danzy* la chanté sa superiorité ordinaire.

Le dernier ballet, analogue au *denouement* de cet opera, fair honneur à la composition du Sieur *Simonet*.

NOTES

INTRODUCTION

1 Beinecke Library, Osborn MSS 3, box 13, folder 984; Gasparo Pacchierotti to Charles Burney, 2 May 1785.

2 Curtis Price, Judith Milhous and Robert D. Hume, *Italian Opera in Late Eighteenth-Century London*, vol. I, *The King's Theatre*, Oxford, 1995; vol. II, *The Pantheon*, forthcoming.

3 *Ibid.*, 53.

4 Daniel Heartz, 'From Garrick to Gluck: the Reform of Theatre and Opera in the Mid-Eighteenth Century', *Proceedings of the Royal Musical Association*, 94 (1967–8), 111–27.

5 Price, Milhous and Hume, *Italian Opera*, vol. I, 194.

6 Lorraine McMullen, *An Odd Attempt in a Woman: The Literary Life of Frances Brooke*, Vancouver, 1983.

7 *The Remarkable Trial of the Queen of Quavers*, London, 1778.

8 The two central works of reference are: George Winchester Stone, Jr, *et al.*, *The London Stage 1660–1800: A Calendar of Plays, Entertainments and Afterpieces*, 5 parts, Carbondale, Ill., 1960–8; Philip H. Highfill Jr, Kalman A. Burnim and Edward A. Langhans, eds., *A Biographical Dictionary of Actors, Actresses, Musicians, Dancers, Managers and Other Stage Personnel in London 1600–1800*, 16 vols., Carbondale, Ill., 1973–93.

9 Curtis Price, Judith Milhous and Robert D. Hume, *The Impresario's Ten Commandments: Continental Recruitment for Italian Opera in London 1763–64*, London, 1992.

10 Elizabeth Gibson, 'Italian Opera in London, 1750–1775: Management and Finances', *Early Music*, 18 (1990), 47–59.

11 Elizabeth Gibson, 'Earl Cowper in Florence and his Correspondence with the Italian Opera in London', *Music & Letters*, 67 (1987), 235–52.

12 Curtis Price, 'Italian Opera and Arson in Late Eighteenth-Century London', *Journal of the American Musicological Society*, 42 (1989), 55–107.

13 Judith Milhous and Robert D. Hume, 'Opera Salaries in Eighteenth-

Century London', *Journal of the American Musicological Society*, 46 (1993), 26–83.

14 Price, Milhous and Hume, *Italian Opera*.

15 Charles Sanford Terry, *John Christian Bach*, 2nd edn, London, 1967.

16 Frederick C. Petty, *Italian Opera in London, 1760–1800*, Ann Arbor, Mich., 1980.

17 McMullen, *An Odd Attempt*.

18 Patricia Howard, 'Attempting to Reconstruct Gluck's 1773 Orfeo', *Musical Times*, 137 (1996), 13–15; 'Guadagni in the Dock: a Crisis in the Career of a Castrato', *Early Music*, 27 (1999), 87–95; Sheila Hughes, 'Gasparo Pacchierotti', *The Music Review*, 55 (1994), 276–92.

19 *Music for London Entertainment 1660–1800*, series E, vol. II, *Antonio Sacchini: Il Cid*, introduction by Dennis Libby, London, 1996.

20 Charles Burney, *A General History of Music from the Earliest Ages to the Present Period*, ed. Frank Mercer, 2 vols., London, 1935.

21 Alvaro Ribeiro, ed., *The Letters of Charles Burney: Volume I (1751–1784)*, Oxford, 1991.

22 British Library, Add. MSS 39929.

23 Fanny Burney, *The Early Journals and Letters*, ed. Lars E. Troide, Oxford, vols. I and II, 1988 and 1990.

24 British Library, Eg. MSS 3691. Extracts from Susan Burney's letter diary were first published by Constance Hill, *The House in St Martin's Street: Being Chronicles of the Burney Family*, London and New York, 1907, chapters 19, 21, 22, 24, 25, 26 and 27.

25 Petty, *Italian Opera*, 149.

26 Wilmarth S. Lewis, *et al.*, eds., *The Yale Edition of the Correspondence of Horace Walpole*, 48 vols., New Haven, Conn., 1937–83.

27 James A. Home, ed., *The Letters and Journal of Lady Mary Coke*, 4 vols., Edinburgh, 1889–96.

28 James Harris, ed., *A Series of Letters from the First Earl of Malmesbury*, 2 vols., London, 1870.

29 Ian Woodfield, 'New Light on the Mozarts' London Visit: A Private Concert with Manzuoli', *Music and Letters*, 75 (1995), 187–208.

30 British Library, Althorpe MSS, F series, unbound.

31 Royal Academy of Arts, Ozias Humphry MSS, HU 2 / 12, 13, 17, 18, 21, 22, 33, 36, 37, 40–1, 63, 67.

32 Bodleian Library, Montagu MSS d.6, fol. 239.

33 Johnson Miscellanies, vii, 192.
34 Beinecke Library, Osborn MSS f.c.80.
35 Beinecke Library, Osborn MSS c.4.
36 Frances Brooke, *The Excursion*, 2 vols., London, 1777.
37 *Town and Country Magazine*, London, September 1777, 460–3.

1 THE HOBART MANAGEMENT

1   Hertfordshire Record Office, Panshanger Collection, D/EP, F 252.
2   *A General History of Music*, II, 855.
3   Panshanger Collection, D/EP, F 252.
4   Burney, *A General History of Music*, II, 856.
5   *Ibid.*, II, 860.
6   *Ibid.*, II, 865.
7   British Library, Althorpe MSS, F 130.
8   Paget Toynbee and Leonard Whibley, eds., *Correspondence of Thomas Gray*, 3 vols., Oxford, 1935, II, 374.
9   Burney, *A General History of Music*, II, 878.
10 Ian Woodfield, 'New Light on the Mozarts' London Visit', 187–208.
11 *A General History of Music*, II, 868.
12 Mrs Harris reported to her son: 'The opera next winter is to be managed by Mr G. Pitt and Mr. Hobart – they talk of having the the [sic] Guadagni, and the Amicci, but I have lived long enough to know that spring talk and winter performances are not always the same.' Harris, *A Series of Letters*, I, 180; 21 April 1769. The identity of Pitt is not known. In a letter to Lady Spencer dated 23 December 1769, George Bussy Villiers wrote: 'The Opera has produced little more than numberless Enquiries after you from Mrs Pitt.' British Library, Althorpe MSS, F 103.
13 Richard G. King and Saskia Willaert, 'Giovanni Francesca Crosa and the First Italian Comic Operas in London, Brussels and Amsterdam, 1748–50', *Journal of the Royal Musical Association*, 118 (1993), 246–75.
14 Price, Milhous and Hume, *The Impresario's Ten Commandments*, 56–7. Lord Clive wrote to Lady Clive from Naples on 21 January 1774: 'The Opera House is the largest I ever saw; it will contain 3000 People. The singers are very indifferent and the Dancers shocking. The principal Singer is Amici who sang some Years ago in England in the Barlettas. She is now become a serious Performer and if you believe the English

she is greatly improved.' National Library of Wales, Aberystwyth, Powis 1990 Deposit, uncatalogued box marked 'Clive of India'.

15 In a letter from the Earl of Carlisle to George Selwyn dated 10 February 1768, Hobart was reported as passing through Turin 'in pursuit of March's old flame the Zamperini'. See John Heneage Jesse, *George Selwyn and his Contemporaries*, London, 1882, II, 251.

16 British Library, Althorpe MSS, F 103. The *London Magazine*, 60 (1771), 93, confirms the incident, condemning Hobart for having on one occasion introduced 'military power upon his benefactors the public'.

17 Lewis *et al.*, eds., *The Correspondence of Horace Walpole*, XXXII, 39. Both singers appeared in Piccinni's 'Le contadine bizzarre', which opened at the King's Theatre on 7 November 1769.

18 *Ibid.*, XXXI, 144; 14 December 1769.

19 British Library, Althorpe MSS, F 103.

20 Burney, *A General History of Music*, II, 876.

21 *London Magazine*, 40 (1771), 93–7.

22 Patricia Howard, 'Guadagni in the Dock', 87–95.

23 *London Magazine*, 40 (1771), 93–7.

24 Mrs Delaney wrote to Viscountess Andover on 27 December 1770: 'The Opera dismal, but a spirit of opposition has arisen, which may mend matters, and a new opera planned by the supporters of Mrs Cornelly, which, as it is *Lawless* (and that you know gives a zest) is to be called the *Harmonick Assembly*!' Lady Llanover, ed., *The Autobiography and Correspondence of Mary Granville, Mrs Delaney*, 3 vols., London, 1862, I, 319.

25 'Giardini's opera at Mrs Cornelly's really fills, and undoubtedly will greatly injure that of M. Hobart's in the Haymarket.' Harris, *A Series of Letters*, I, 211.

26 Lewis *et al.*, eds., *The Correspondence of Horace Walpole*, XXXI, 151.

27 Harris, ed., *A Series of Letters*, I, 212.

28 *Ibid.*, I, 216.

29 Lewis *et al.*, eds., *The Correspondence of Horace Walpole*, XXIII, 271–2; letter of 22 February 1771.

30 Howard, 'Guadagni in the Dock', 91.

31 *London Magazine*, 40 (1771), 97; Harris, *A Series of Letters*, I, 219.

32 Lewis *et al.*, eds., *The Correspondence of Horace Walpole*, XXIII, 278–9.

33 Terry, *John Christian Bach*, 122.

34 Lewis *et al.*, eds., *The Correspondence of Horace Walpole*, XXXI, 164; letter of
    11 December 1771.

35 Charles Burney, *An Eighteenth-Century Musical Tour in France and Italy*,
    ed. Percy A. Scholes, London, 1959, 245.

36 Lewis *et al.*, eds., *The Correspondence of Horace Walpole*, XXXV, 343–4.

37 Harris, ed., *A Series of Letters*, I, 235; letter of 27 July 1771. Monnet wrote
    to Garrick on 4 July 1771 that he had seen the contract ('engagement')
    that Heinel had been given by Hobart. It was worth 1,100 Louis plus a
    benefit, for the period from November to May. See James Boaden, ed.,
    The Private Correspondence of David Garrick, London, 1831–2, II, 585.

38 *A General History of Music*, II, 878.

39 Beinecke Library, Osborn f.c.80.

40 British Library, Althorpe MSS, F 104. See also the letter of 30 April 1773.

41 Madame du Deffand wrote to Horace Walpole on 27 February 1772:
    'Vous ne me parlez plus de notre danseuse; on dit qu'elle va revenir, et
    qu'elle est en dispute avec les directeurs de votre théâtre sur l'argent
    qu'on lui a promis.' (You do not tell me anything more about our
    dancer. It is said that she is returning, and that she is in dispute with the
    managers of your theatre, concerning the money she was promised.)
    Lewis *et al.*, eds., *The Correspondence of Horace Walpole*, V, 195.

42 *Ibid.*, XXIII, 403.

43 Fanny Burney, *The Early Journals and Letters*, I, 221. General
    Cunningham, however, wrote to Lady Spencer on 29 April 1772 (the
    letter is mis-dated 1771), a few days after Millico's debut: 'The new singer
    Millico is admir'd.' British Library, Althorpe MSS, F119.

44 Burney, *A General History of Music*, II, 878.

45 *Public Advertiser*, 6 and 20 May 1773.

46 John Williams, *A Pin Basket to the Children of Thespis*, London, 1797, 172.

2 THE NEW MANAGERS TAKE CONTROL

1 British Library, Althorpe MSS, F 104. A plan of the theatre drawn up in
   1777 (see F. H. W. Shepphard, ed., *Survey of London*, vols. XXIX–XXX,
   London, 1960, XXX, plate 27a) depicts what the editors describe as
   'proscenium doors or boxes on the stage'. See Price, Milhous and
   Hume, *Italian Opera*, I, 43.

2 Public Record Office, LC 7/88, 11 January and 7 February 1773.

3 *Public Advertiser*, 13 September 1775.

4 Public Record Office, LC 7 / 88, 5 February 1774.

5 *Ibid.*, LC 5 / 16, 10 November 1773, 182.

6 Michael Kelly, *Reminiscences of Michael Kelly, of the King's Theatre, and Theatre Royal, Drury Lane*, 2 vols., London, 1826, II, 359.

7 British Library, Althorpe MSS, F 104.

8 James T. Kirkman, *Memoirs of the Life of Charles Macklin*, 3 vols. London, 1799, II, 57.

9 Boaden, ed., *The Private Correspondence*, I, 505.

10 British Library, Althorpe MSS, F 104. In fact opera singers were being engaged. An advertisement in the *Public Advertiser* on 6 May 1773 listed some of the performers already hired.

11 David M. Little and George M. Kahrl, eds., *The Letters of David Garrick*, 3 vols., Cambridge, Mass., 1963, II; letter 791, dated 6 August.

12 Fanny Burney, *The Early Journals and Letters*, II, 55–6.

13 *Ibid.*, 4–5.

14 Madame d'Arblay [Fanny Burney], *Memoirs of Dr Burney*, 3 vols., London, 1832, I, 334–5.

15 See McMullen, *An Odd Attempt*, chapter 4, for an account of this episode. See also, K. J. H. Berland, 'Frances Brooke and David Garrick', *Studies in Eighteenth-Century Culture*, 20 (1990), 217–30.

16 Brooke, *The Old Maid*, 18, 105; 6 March 1756.

17 Little and Kahrl, eds., *The Letters*, II, letter 361.

18 McMullen, *An Odd Attempt*, 196. Photocopies of the Brooke–Gifford correspondence are in the British Library, RP 1012.

19 *Ibid.*, 197.

20 Sir John Fortescue, ed., *The Correspondence of King George the Third from 1760 to December 1783*, 6 vols., London, 1927–8, II, no. 873.

21 McMullen, *An Odd Attempt*, 133.

22 *Ibid.*, 198.

23 *Ibid.*, 156. See Highfill *et al.*, eds., *A Biographical Dictionary*, XVI, 327–8 for further details of the very public quarrel between Colman and Smith and Yates.

24 McMullen, *An Odd Attempt*, 157. The reference here is given as *Newspaper Cuttings on London Theatres 1772–1775*, British Library. I have not been able to find the original. See *The London Stage*, 4 (1841). The *London Magazine* 43 (1774), 407, confirms the epilogue: 'the important

station she [Mary Ann Yates] filled as empress of the Italian signors and signoras, was laughably described, and her having quitted the throne to *serve* in Drury Lane well conceived and expressed with some wit and humour'. Compare this with the *Hibernian Magazine*, 4 (November 1774), 675: 'The important station she filled as Empress of the Italian Signors and Signoras, was laughably described; and her having resigned her Opera Sceptre to "Richard King of Quavers" to *serve* in Drury Lane, was well conceived and expressed with some wit and humour.'

25 Highfill *et al.*, eds., *A Biographical Dictionary*, xvi, 317.

26 Fanny Burney, *The Early Journals*, i, 236.

27 *Ibid.*, 238.

28 British Library, Althorpe MSS, F 119.

29 *Ibid.*

30 'The New Opera composed by Sacchini seems to be universally liked.' British Library, Althorpe MSS, F 43; 22 January 1773.

31 Llanover, ed., *The Autobiography*, iv, 493; 30 January 1773.

32 British Library, Althorpe MSS, F 118.

33 Lewis *et al.*, eds., *The Correspondence of Horace Walpole*, xxxii, 89.

34 *Ibid.*, xxii, 117.

35 Fanny Burney, *The Early Journals*, i, 257.

36 *Ibid.*, 234–6.

37 Charles Burney, *An Eighteenth-Century Musical Tour in France and Italy*, 202. Fanny Burney first mentions him in her journal for 4 May 1772, when he led the band at a concert. See *The Early Journals*, i, 218.

38 Fanny Burney, *The Early Journals*, i, 238. For further details on Celestino, see Simon McVeigh, *The Violinist in London's Concert Life: Felice Giardini and his Contemporaries*, New York and London, 1989, 72.

3 SACCHINI AND THE REVIVAL OF *OPERA SERIA*

1 Charles Burney, *A General History of Music*, ii, 894.

2 Petty, *Italian Opera*, 126–34.

3 Bottarelli's libretto is reproduced in: *Music for London Entertainment 1660–1800*, 'Eccellenza: La nuda Istoria è la Tela sù cui ho disegnato co' miei versi il Quadro favoloso, colorito dipoi dall'illustre *Sacchini*, il quale, sulle orme de'Maestri i più celebri, amatore della bella semplicità, sprezza i rabeschi, non prodigalizza passagi, fà tacere i trilli ove

parlano le passioni, sostiene il senso musicale, entra e rimane nel cuore,
e da in una parola, al linguaggio di Parnasso la vera energìa.'

4 Price, Milhous and Hume, *Italian Opera*, 208.

5 Petty, *Italian Opera*, 99.

6 *Ibid.*, 106.

7 *Ibid.*, 115.

8 *A General History of Music*, II, 687.

9 *Ibid.*

10 British Library, Add. MSS 39929; letter from Thomas Twining to
Charles Jenner; 13 August 1773.

11 *Morning Chronicle*, 20 January 1773.

12 *Westminster Magazine*, 20 January 1773.

13 *The Early Journals and Letters*, I, 258. Sacchini's choruses achieved consid-
erable popularity as concert pieces. John Marsh wrote on 12 June 1778:
'At this concert some new Italian chorusses by Sacchini in the opera of
Eryphile were done with very good effect, being very airy and lively
tho' rather light and something different from those of Handel.' Brian
Robins, *The John Marsh Journals: The Life and Times of a Gentleman
Composer (1752–1828)*, Stuyvesant, N.Y., 1998, 181.

14 Burney, *A General History of Music*, II, 877.

15 Petty, *Italian Opera*, 127.

16 Patricia Howard, 'Attempting to Reconstruct Gluck's 1773 Orfeo', 13–15.

17 *Ibid.*, 13.

18 *Ibid.*, 14.

19 *Ibid.*, 15.

20 British Library, Althorpe MSS, F104.

21 Howard, 'Attempting to Reconstruct Gluck's 1773 Orfeo', 15.

22 Fanny Burney, *The Early Journals and Letters*, I, 264.

23 Robins, *The John Marsh Journals*, 272.

24 Price, Milhous and Hume, *Italian Opera*, 333.

25 Burney, *A General History of Music*, II, 877.

4 RECRUITMENT PROCEDURES AND ARTISTIC POLICY

1 Charles Burney, *The Present State of Music in France and Italy*, London,
1771. See, *An Eighteenth-Century Musical Tour in France and Italy*.

2 Burney, *The Present State of Music in Germany, the Netherland and the*

United Provinces, London, 1773. See, *An Eighteenth-Century Musical Tour in Central Europe and the Netherlands*, ed. Percy A. Scholes, London, 1959.

3 Fanny Burney [Madame d'Arblay], *Memoirs of Dr Burney*, I, 334.

4 Fanny Burney, *The Early Journals*, II, 5.

5 That Davies had not already been hired by Hobart is evident from the advertisement for the forthcoming season in the *Public Advertiser* on 6 May 1773 in which her name does not appear.

6 British Library, Althorpe MSS, F105.

7 Joel Collier, *Musical Travels through England*, London, 1774, 4.

8 Brooke, *The Old Maid*, 3, 29 November 1755.

9 *Ibid.*, 26, 8 May 1756.

10 In a letter to her son dated 24 July 1773, Elizabeth Beaufort Botetourt wrote that Sir Horace Mann had done the singer 'the honor of his Protection'. Betty Matthews, 'The Davies Sisters, J. C. Bach and the Glass Harmonica', *Music and Letters*, 56 (1975), 165.

11 Burney, *An Eighteenth-Century Musical Tour in France and Italy*, 57.

12 *Ibid.*, 173 and 174.

13 *Ibid.*, 257.

14 *Ibid.*, 67.

15 *Ibid.*, 66.

16 *Ibid.*, 69.

17 *Ibid.*, 76.

18 Price, Milhous and Hume, *The Impresario's Ten Commandments*, 23.

19 Burney, *A General History of Music*, II, 871.

20 British Library, Add. MSS 40714, fol.16.

21 Home, ed., *The Letters and Journal*, II, 87.

22 Highfill *et al.*, eds., *A Biographical Dictionary*, VI, 275.

23 The letter is in the archives of Hoare and Co.

24 *Public Advertiser*, 18 and 23 October 1773.

25 Fanny Burney, *The Early Journals*, I, 270.

26 British Library, Althorpe MSS, F105.

27 Lewis *et al.*, eds., *The Correspondence of Horace Walpole*, XXXV, 468; 6 December 1773.

28 Price, Milhous and Hume, *The Impresario's Ten Commandments*, 23.

29 Hoare and Co., ledger 89, fol. 245$^\text{v}$.

30 Fanny Burney, *The Early Journals*, I, 8.

31 *Ibid.*

32 Lady Mary Coke wrote in her journal on 1 February 1774 during a visit to Turin: 'The first Man and the first Woman singers are very good ones; the Man I hear is engaged to go to England next year.' Home, ed., *The Letters and Journal*, IV, 304.

33 Fanny Burney, *The Early Journals*, II, 163.

34 *Ibid.*, II, 54–6.

35 *Memoirs of Dr Burney*, II, 37.

5 THE KING'S THEATRE IN CRISIS

1 Petty, *Italian Opera*, 140.

2 *Ibid.*, 136; *Music for London Entertainment*, series E, vol. II, xi.

3 Burney, *A General History of Music*, II, 878.

4 *The Early Journals and Letters*, I, 257.

5 National Library of Wales, Powis 1990 Deposit, box marked 'Clive of India'.

6 British Library, Oriental and India Office Collections, Eur D546/26.

7 'Miss Davies is the admiration of all London, but of me, who do not love the perfection of what anybody can do, and wish she had less top to her voice and more bottom. However she will break Millico's heart.' Lewis *et al.*, eds., *The Correspondence of Horace Walpole*, XXXV, 468 (6 December 1773); 'Miss Davies has great success. I cannot say she charms me. Her knowledge of music seems greater than her taste; or perhaps it is that I do not like the new taste. Millico is jealous of her, and they make something like parties.' *Ibid.*, XXIII, 547.

8 Historical Manuscripts Commission, *The Manuscripts of the Earl of Carlisle*, London, 1897, 267; 5 February 1774.

9 Fanny Burney, *The Early Journals and Letters*, II, 24.

10 Lewis *et al.*, eds., *The Correspondence of Horace Walpole*, XXIII, 570; 1 May 1774.

11 'Miss Davies (for the honour of our Country) has greatly distinguished her self on our Opera Theatre, both as a Singer and an Actress.' British Library, Add. MSS 42069, fol. 94; letter from James Harris; 15 September 1774.

12 *Hibernian Magazine*, 4 (1774), 275–6.

13 Burney, *A General History of Music*, II, 879.

14 *Ibid.*, 881.

15 On 21 April 1774, Mrs Francis heard the singer at Lady Clive's house. British Library, Oriental and India Office Collections, Francis MSS, E 22.

16 Fanny Burney, *The Early Journals and Letters*, II, 79–80.

17 *Ibid.*, 106; 14 April 1775.

18 Harris, ed., *A Series of Letters*, I, 304.

19 Fanny Burney, *The Early Journals and Letters*, II, 156.

20 Hoare and Co., Account of James Brooke and Richard Yates, ledger 94, 195^v and 196^v.

21 Lewis *et al.*, eds., *The Correspondence of Horace Walpole*, XXXIX, 238.

22 The opening of the Pantheon in 1772 may not at first have concerned the King's management unduly. The more immediate threat was to the Bach–Abel concert series. See Simon McVeigh, *Concert Life in London from Mozart to Haydn*, Cambridge, 1993, 15.

23 Lewis *et al.*, eds., *The Correspondence of Horace Walpole*, XXXIX, 223–4.

24 Fanny Burney, *The Early Journals and Letters*, II, 75.

25 Beinecke Library, Osborn MSS, f.c.80.

26 Burney, *A General History of Music*, II, 879.

27 Little and Kahrl, eds., *The Letters*, III, 921.

28 Frank A. Hedgecock, *A Cosmopolitan Actor: David Garrick and his French Friends*, London, 1912.

29 British Library, photocopy RP 2046.

30 Cecil Price, ed., *The Letters of Richard Brinsley Sheridan*, 3 vols., Oxford, 1966, I, 103.

6 THE RECRUITMENT OF LOVATTINI

1 There are discrepancies between these figures and those given in Petty's annual listings as a result of the following: in the 1767 list, *Il signor dottore* should be listed as a comic opera; in the 1768 list, *La schiava* should be listed as a comic opera; in the 1769 list all the works are correctly listed as comic operas, and I have amended the table accordingly. See, Petty, *Italian Opera*, 376.

2 Lewis *et al.*, eds., *The Correspondence of Horace Walpole*, XXII, 473–4.

3 Home, *The Letters and Journal*, I, 173.

4 British Library, Add. MSS 39929; 20 February 1769. After reading

Twining's lavish but thoughtful praise, the comment of an admirer who extolled the tenor as 'in all probability the best Male singer upon Earth' seems less extreme. See Petty, *Italian Opera*, 121.

5 Home, ed., *The Letters and Journal*, I, 199.

6 Fanny Burney, *The Early Journals and Letters*, II, 263.

7 Burney, *A General History of Music*, II, 872.

8 Writing to Sir William Hamilton on 15 February 1774, Lord Pembroke noted the lack: 'The only two Operas, which were performed during the little time I staid in London, were both serious.' Lord Herbert, ed., *The Pembroke Papers 1734–1780: Letters and Diaries of Henry, Tenth Earl of Pembroke and his Circle*, London, 1939, 43.

9 'They [the operas] are ill attended; and the burlettas are so bad and the dancers so execrable, that the managers are afraid of not being able to go on.' Lewis *et al.*, eds., *The Correspondence of Horace Walpole*, XXIII, 547, 19 January 1774.

10 Fanny Burney, *The Early Journals and Letters*, I, 267.

11 Lord Clive wrote to Lady Clive from Rome on 12 January 1774: 'The first night of our arrival we went to the Barletta Opera where the music was very fine. After we had sat some time a great noise of Applause ran all over the Theater upon the appearance of a certain Performer and to my very great surprise he turn'd out to be Senior Lovatini who is a great Favorite.' National Library of Wales, Powis 1990 Deposit, box marked 'Clive of India', uncatalogued.

12 Kelly, *Reminiscences*, I, 25. On 12 April 1774, Sir William Hamilton recorded the imposition and removal of a quarantine. See British Library, Egerton MSS 2636. Two to three weeks was a normal length for a quarantine. See Brinsley Ford, ed., *The Letters of Jonathan Skelton Written from Rome and Tivoli in 1758*, Walpole Society, XXXVI (1956–8), London, 1960, 34.

13 The Royal Academy of Arts, Humphry MSS, HU 2/12. Romney had travelled to Italy with Ozias Humphry. James Paine, the architect and sculptor, was already in Rome in 1774.

14 *Ibid.*, HU 2/13.

15 Lipparini eventually made it to London, appearing in the 1790–1 season at the Pantheon and the Little Haymarket. His salary was still only £600. See Milhous and Hume, 'Opera Salaries', 54.

16 The Royal Academy of Arts, Humphry MSS, HU 2/21.

17 *Ibid.*, HU 2/22.

18 Gibson, 'Italian Opera', 59.

19 Reproduced by permission of the Hyde Collection, Four Oaks Farm, New Jersey, Johnson Miscellanies, VII, 192–5.

20 Note by Ozias Humphry: 'At the same time I deliver'd to Sig^r Barazzi the Letter of Credit dated Naples, Oct 1st 1774 from Messr^s. Hart and Wilkins for one thousand and eighty Neapolitan ducats payable to Mr James Butler upon wch Letter F. Barrazzi had given Mr. Bu[t]ler a re[ceipt] under for the said sum.'

    Note by Francesco Barazzi: 'Rec^d this 17th day of Decemb^r 1774 from the Hands of Ozias Humphry a Letter of Credit dated Naples Oct 1 1774 from Messr^s Hart and Wilkins for one thousand and eighty Neapolitan ducats payable to the late Mr James Butler deceas'd upon wch letter I gave Mr Butler a rec^t for the said sum.' The Royal Academy of Arts, Humphry MSS, HU 2/18.

21 'Sig^r: Francesco Barazzi in cont^o delle lire duecento sterline, che sono in sue mani, espettanti alla b.m. di James Butler, sì compiacerà farne pagare all'ordine di me sotto scritto Zecchini duecento Romani, in Bologna, obbligandomi nella più ampla forma all R. camera apostolica di rilevarlo in tutto e per tutto al propino, quando degli eredi del med:^{o} James Butler, non venisse approvito e ratificato questo pagamento volendi essere tenuto in tutto, e per tutto come sopra.' Rome 19 October 1774. *Ibid.*, HU 2/17.

22 British Library, Add. MSS 42069, fol. 94.

23 Hampshire Record Office, 9M73/G468/2.

7 THE ENGLISH COMMUNITY IN ROME

1 Lesley Lewis, *Connoisseurs and Secret Agents in Eighteenth-Century Rome*, London, 1961.

2 A. P. Oppé, ed., *Memoirs of Thomas Jones*, Walpole Society, XXXII (1946–8), London, 1951, 70–1.

3 Kelly, *Reminiscences*, 71.

4 Brinsley Ford, 'Thomas Jenkins, Banker, Dealer and Unofficial English Agent', *Apollo*, 99 (1974), 422.

5 Burney, *An Eighteenth-Century Musical Tour in France and Italy*, 205.

6 Ford, 'Thomas Jenkins', 417.

7 Algernon Graves, *The Society of Artists of Great Britain 1761–1791: The Free Society of Artists 1761–1783*, London, 1907, 45–6.

8 Roger Fiske, *English Theatre Music in the Eighteenth Century*, Oxford, 1973, 425–6.

9 Piccinni and his pupil crossed the path of the artist Thomas Jones, who noted in his diary: 'While we were waiting, the *Procaccio* from *Rome* to *Florence* arrived – and among the Company that belonged to it – were *Piccinni* the famous Composer and Young Butler his pupil – both on their way to *Paris* where *Piccinni* was engaged for the Kings Opera.' Oppé, ed., *Memoirs of Thomas Jones*, 52. Butler was felt not to have benefited from his years with Piccinni. The author of *A.B.C.Dario Musico*, Bath, 1780, pointedly commented: 'This gentleman will tell you that he studied three years in Italy under Piccini. If he did, (which is not universally credited) we are astonished that his improvement did not follow.'

10 Brinsley Ford, 'Sir Watkin Williams Wynn: A Welsh Maecenas', *Apollo*, 99 (1974), 436.

11 Burney, *An Eighteenth-Century Musical Tour in France and Italy*, 206.

12 Historical Manuscripts Commission, *The Manuscripts and Correspondence of James, First Earl of Charlemont*, 2 vols., London, 1891, I, 185.

13 Burney, *An Eighteenth-Century Musical Tour in France and Italy*, 291.

14 Burney, *A General History of Music*, II, 442.

15 British Library, Add. MSS 56235.

16 Burney, *A General History of Music*, II, 446 and 447.

17 Burney, *An Eighteenth-Century Musical Tour in France and Italy*, 245.

18 The Royal Academy of Arts, Humphry MSS, HU 2/63.

19 It was apparently the custom for opera stars to congregate in northern Italian cities to await engagements for the following year in England. See Price, 'Opera and Arson', 64.

20 Ribeiro, ed., *The Letters*, I, 248.

21 Elizabeth Banks (wife of Thomas Banks, sculptor) wrote to Ozias Humphry in Rome on 1 April 1778: 'I suppose you have heard poor Wiseman is dead, his wife is very Ill a Bed, and in great distress as you may suppose, The English here have made a collection for her.' The Royal Academy of Arts, Humphry MSS, HU 2/67.

22 Gibson, 'Earl Cowper in Florence'.

23 The Royal Academy of Arts, Humphry MSS, HU 1/fol.33. This source was not used in the Linley articles in *A Biographical Dictionary*.

24 Oppé, ed., *Memoirs of Thomas Jones*, 53.

25 *Ibid.*, 54.

26 Brooke's letter to Ozias Humphry on 11 November 1774 was addressed thus: 'au Caffe Anglois a Rome'.

27 George Grant wrote to Ozias Humphry on 13 December 1794: 'It is above a month since Mr Taylor the sole proprietor of the Opera House set your name down (in all the Books belonging to it) on the free list – You have only therefore to announce your name, which will obtain admission at any door for Pitt or Gallery. Inclosed you will find four Tickets for this evenings amusement – I will thank you to send your friends to the Pit, to support the undertaking – You are now one of us – Mr Taylor intends paying his respects shortly to you and Banti will accompany him and me.' The Royal Academy of Arts, Humphry MSS, HU 4/105. Beckford wrote to him in 1796 to ask for his assistance in obtaining a good box at the opera house. Lewis Melville, *The Life and Letters of William Beckford of Fonthill*, London, 1910, 244–5.

28 Price, Milhous and Hume, *The Impresario's Ten Commandments*, 83.

29 Oppé, ed., *Memoirs of Thomas Jones*, 79.

30 During his Italian tour, Garrick instructed Colman to 'direct your next, as I desir'd before, A Monsieur Fran[cesc]o Barazzi Banquier a Rome – or rather to Me chez Monsr Franco Barazzi etc'. Little and Kahrl, eds., *The Letters*, 1, letter 321, 24 December 1763.

31 British Library, Add. MSS 47791, fol.40.

32 Oppé, ed., *Memoirs of Thomas Jones*, 56.

33 Jonathan Skelton wrote to William Herring on 11 January 1758: 'The Merchant's Name that I intend to receive the Mony of, is Barazze, he was so kind the last night as to offer me the Mony but I did not chuse to receive it till I had your Order and knew who to draw upon. This Gentleman was strongly recommended to me by an English Merchant at Leghorn, and I to him. I frequently visit him.' Ford, ed., *The Letters of Jonathan Skelton*, 35.

34 Price, Milhous and Hume, *The Impresario's Ten Commandments*, 66. See also J. E. Norton, ed., *The Letters of Edward Gibbon*, London, 1956, 1, letters 63, 64 and 66.

35 Hart was another English banker in Naples. When Lord Herbert was about to leave the city in September 1779, he went to 'Mr Hart's the Banker to gett changed what money I had by me'. Herbert, ed., *The Pembroke Papers*, 253. Hart and Wilkins were also regularly used by Sir

William Hamilton for payments to musicians and others. See British
Library, Add. MSS 40714.

36 Otto E. Deutsch, 'Lady Hamilton', *Notes and Queries*, 192 (1952), 540 and
560. A letter from General Cunningham to Lady Spencer, 23 November
1772, confirms that whilst visiting Vienna, Lady Hamilton was asked to
play on the harpsichord. British Library, Althorpe MSS, F119. Lady
Hamilton's talent was highly regarded in diplomatic circles. Sir Horace
Mann wrote to Sir William Hamilton on 11 April 1769: 'The Great
Dutchess asked after Mrs Hamilton's health, spoke of her inimitable
execution on the Harpsichord and said she hoped the Emperor had
heard her.' British Library, Eg. MSS 2641, 11 April 1769.

37 The British Library, Althorpe MSS, F117. Another instance of Sir
William's establishment at Naples as the focal point for musicians is to
be found in Add. MSS 41197, Lisbon, 8 April 1772. Robert Walpole recommends to Sir William 'Mr Baron . . . a Scholar of Sir Joshua Reynolds
for Painting, and Giardini for Musick'.

38 British Library, Althorpe MSS, F117.

39 British Library, Eg. MSS 2640, 20 October 1767.

40 *Ibid.*, 10 November 1767: 'I told the de Amicis how much Mrs Hamilton
and you esteemed her and that that gave her a fresh title to everything
that I could do for her service. You will have heard that she has chosen
an husband for herself without consulting her mother, who however
knew her inclinations but thought that she could watch her so closely as
to prevent her putting them into execution. Nothing could exceed the
rage she was in when she found herself disappointed . . .'

8 LUCREZIA AGUJARI AT THE PANTHEON

1 *The London Stage*, IV, 1856.

2 *Ibid.*, 1764 and 1766.

3 Petty, *Italian Opera*, 142.

4 Fanny Burney, *The Early Journals and Letters*, II, 67.

5 *Ibid.*, 79.

6 Burney, *A General History of Music*, II, 881.

7 Petty, *Italian Opera*, 142.

8 In November 1776, Thomas Jones attended a performance of Anfossi's
L'avaro at Turin. The attendance was poor: 'Went to the *Opera Ill Avaro* –

25 sous – thin house – Audience noisy – English Country dances and a Hornpipe introduced – Incantations and Pantomime – felt cold – sup'd in our Appartments.' Oppé, ed., *Memoirs of Thomas Jones*, 46.

9 Harris, ed., *A Series of Letters*, I, 290.

10 British Library, Althorpe MSS, F43.

11 Lewis *et al.*, eds., *The Correspondence of Horace Walpole*, XXXIX, 211.

12 Petty, *Italian Opera*, 142.

13 Lady Mary Coke wrote: 'Everybody admires the first singer. I thought him when I heard him at Turin the most pleasing I had ever heard.' Home, ed., *The Letters and Journal*, IV, 426.

14 British Library, Althorpe MSS, F119.

15 Brooke, *The Excursion*, I, chapter 9.

16 Burney, *A General History of Music*, II, 881.

17 *Music for London Entertainment 1660–1800*, series E, vol. II, *Antonio Sacchini: Il Cid*.

18 Introduction, *ibid.*, XIII.

19 William Bingley, *Musical Biography*, London, 1814, II, 315, recalled that the actor had been greatly impressed with Rauzzini in this part.

20 Beinecke Library, Osborn Collection, f.c.80; entry for 1776.

21 Brooke, *The Excursion*, I, chapter 11.

22 Margaret L. Marc and W. H. Quarrell, *Lichtenberg's Visits to England*, Oxford, 1938.

23 Harris ed., *A Series of Letters*, I, 292.

24 Fanny Burney, *The Early Journals and Letters*, II, 154.

25 *Ibid.*, 156.

26 *Ibid.*, 155. After Gabrielli's debut, Burney is reported to have expressed the view that the rivalry between the two singers was so strong that it would be impossible to invite them both to a social gathering. *Ibid.*, 172.

27 Harris, ed., *A Series of Letters*, I, 297.

28 Burney, *A General History of Music*, II, 882. 'At this time, there was no male singer, *di gran grido*, in England, except Rauzzini, who more frequently pleased than surprised his audience.'

29 *Ibid.*, 883.

30 Fanny Burney, *The Early Journals and Letters*, II, 155.

31 Little and Kahrl, eds., *The Letters*, III, letter 908.

32 *Ibid.*, letter 949.

33 Kelly, *Reminiscences*, I, 120.

9 CATERINA GABRIELLI

1 Burney, *An Eighteenth-Century Musical Tour in France and Italy*, 249.

2 Oxford, Bodleian Library, Montagu MSS, d.6, fol. 239.

3 The Royal Academy of Arts, Humphry MSS, HU 2/33; 'Sono stata ad un Oratorio dove era Cantato, Manzuoli, Guarducci, e il Tenore della Opera, la Musica era bellissima e acquistava piu essendo cantata da si bravi Professori.'

4 *Ibid.*, HU 2/40–1; 20 January 1776; 'Il Primo uomo si chiama Rubinelli ed è un Contralto, la sua figura non si può lodare abbastanza essendo la più bella che abbia mai veduto, se La Prima Donna e bella il Primo uomo è più, la sua voce e la piu bella che si possa sentire, egli non a crudezza nella voce come aveva Milico, ma una così Dolie e unità che dà piacere a tutti il sentirlo, la sua Maniera di cantare è molto buona e di buon gusto egli canta molto nella maniera di Mr Parson, non lo posso preferire a Milico per il cantabile, ne a Aprile per le variazioni, ma lui a un poco di tutte due tra la sua bella figura la buona voce e la molto bella maniera di cantare e impossibile trovar meglio.'

5 *Ibid.*; 'Il medesimo Traetta disse che era la meglio che lui aveva composta.'

6 *Ibid.*; 'fa buona figura nei recitatavi che gli Canta con molta espressione ed e applaudita molto, ma al'Arie ella perde tutto l'aplauso'. On 11 December 1778, Carara's husband wrote to Garrick asking for help in obtaining an engagement for his wife at either the King's Theatre or the Pantheon. Boaden, ed., *The Private Correspondence*, II, 323–4.

7 Beinecke Library, Hilles, Box 6; 'La musica e bellissima specialmente l'overtura, il Duo, il Terzetto e un Aria dell'Tenore che e accompagniata da i Clarinetti e corni da caccia, questa e la meglio Musica che abbia sentito. Milico non fa meglio figura in questa che nella passata, perche la sua parte mi pare che fosse nel'altra opera almeno la Prima Aria era meglio che ressuna di queste ... Se lei avesse piacere di avere il libro io lo mandero alla prima occasione ... Ma Milico fa brutta figura in tutto.'

8 Lewis *et al.*, eds., *The Correspondence of Horace Walpole*, xxv, 646.

9 Price, Milhous and Hume, *Italian Opera*, I, 97.

10 Alfred Morrison, *The Collection of Autograph Letters and Historical Documents formed by Alfred Morrison: Second Series 1882–1893: The Hamilton and Nelson papers: Vol. I: 1756–1797*, 1893, printed for private circulation.

Whether Hodges was the William Hodges who failed as a scene-designer at the Pantheon is unknown. See Price, Milhous and Hume, *Italian Opera*, I, 143.

11 Petty, *Italian Opera*, 147.

12 Ribeiro, ed., *The Letters*, 192; 15–16 (?) November 1775.

13 Burney, *A General History of Music*, II, 881, see also 891.

14 British Library, Egerton MSS, 3691, fol. 68ᵛ.

15 Beinecke Library, Osborn MSS, f.c.80; the Diary of Edward Pigott, n.d., before April 1776.

16 British Library, A Collection of Cuttings [1757–1829], XLI, (1774).

17 British Library, Add. MSS 40714; 28 March 1775.

18 British Library, Althorpe MSS, F106.

19 Fanny Burney, *The Early Journals*, II, 159–60.

20 The Royal Academy of Arts, Humphry MSS, HU 2/37; 5 November 1775.

21 Fanny Burney [Madame d'Arblay], *Memoirs of Dr Burney*, II, 37.

22 Fanny Burney, *The Early Journals*, II, 165–6.

23 *Ibid.*, 167.

24 Beinecke Library, Osborn MSS f.c.80.

25 Richard Mount-Edgcumbe, *Musical Reminiscences of an Old Amateur Chiefly Respecting the Italian Opera in England for Fifty Years, from 1773 to 1823*, London, 1824, 16.

26 Fanny Burney, *The Early Journals*, II, 169.

27 *Ibid.*, 170–5.

28 Ribeiro, ed., *The Letters*, I, 190–1.

29 Fanny Burney, *The Early Journals*, II, 172.

30 *Ibid.*, 168.

31 Lewis *et al.*, eds., *The Correspondence of Horace Walpole*, XXIV, 148.

32 New York Public Library, Berg Collection, Scrapbook 1653–1890.

33 British Library, Add. MSS 39929.

34 *Ibid.*

35 Burney, *A General History of Music*, II, 881–2.

36 Burney, *An Eighteenth-Century Musical Tour in Central Europe and the Netherlands*, 46.

37 Burney, *A General History of Music*, II, 882.

38 *Ibid.*, 881–2.

39 In a letter to Thomas Twining dated 'end of Novʳ 1775', Burney was

optimistic: 'The Gab comes on, I think, in favour.' Ribeiro, ed., *The Letters*, I, 193.

40 Late in the season, Gabrielli again had problems with her voice 'being so hoarse as to be incapable of singing her songs'. She 'went through a song in a kind of *meza voce*', upon which the audience, 'very numerous and brilliant', appeared so irritated that Mary Ann Yates had to come on in 'deshabille' and apologise. British Library, A Collection of Cuttings [1757–1829], XLI (May 1776).

10 RAUZZINI'S LAST SEASON

All Le Texier quotations are translations from Anthoine Le Texier, *Journal Etranger de Littérature*, I (June 1777).

1 Burney, *A General History of Music*, II, 884.
2 British Library, Add. MSS 39929; 29 November 1776.
3 Burney, *A General History of Music*, II, 884.
4 Mount-Edgcumbe, *Musical Reminiscences*, 16.
5 Petty, *Italian Opera*, 149.
6 *Hibernian Magazine*, 6 (December 1776), 821.
7 The review in the *Westminster Magazine* (January 1777), 44, which is perhaps a 'puff', stated: 'Signora Davies . . . performed her part with that taste and judgement for which she has been so justly admired. She was received with uncommon applause by one of the fullest and most brilliant houses we have ever seen.'
8 British Library, Althorpe MSS, F106; 2 November 1776.
9 *Ibid.*; 4 November 1776.
10 *The Morning Chronicle and London Advertiser*.
11 Hedgecock, *A Cosmopolitan Actor*, 267–74.
12 Earl Spencer and Christopher Dobson, eds., *The Letters of David Garrick and Georgiana Countess Spencer*, Cambridge, 1960, 37.
13 Burney, *A General History of Music*, II, 880.
14 Fanny Burney, *The Early Journals and Letters*, II, 187.
15 *Hibernian Magazine*, 6 (December 1776), 821.
16 Burney, *A General History of Music*, II, 894–5. The plagiarism controversy is dicussed in Price, Milhous and Hume, *Italian Opera*, I, 265–6.
17 Petty, *Italian Opera*, 146.

18 Jno Leland Hunt, *Giovanni Paisiello: His Life as an Opera Composer*, New York, 1975, 15.

19 Petty, *Italian Opera*, 149.

20 *Ibid.*, 151.

21 Burney, *A General History of Music*, II, 877.

22 He may indeed already have published on the subject. *Idées sur l'opéra* printed anonymously in 1764 is attributed in the Bibliothèque Nationale catalogue to 'Le Texier de Forge'.

23 Little and Kahrl, eds., *The Letters*, III, 1093.

24 Heartz, 'From Garrick to Gluck, III–27.

25 The English translation of Algarotti, *An Essay on the Opera Written in Italian by Count Algarotti F.R.S. F.S.A.* (London, 1767) seems not to have provoked much response.

26 Little and Kahrl, eds., *The Letters*, I, 395.

27 *Ibid.*, 400.

28 W. A. Mozart, *Briefe und Aufzeichnungen*, ed Wilhelm A. Bauer and Otto Erich Deutsch, 7 vols., Kassel, 1962–75, II, 426.

29 Burney, *A General History of Music*, II, 876.

30 *Ibid.*, 877.

31 Howard, 'Guadagni in the Dock', 87.

32 *Ibid.*, 92.

33 *Ibid.*, 88.

34 During his brief period as manager, he attempted to promote this idea. Probably at his behest, Sacchini (unusually) incorporated ballet music by Stamitz *within* Act II of his *Enea e Lavinia*. The merits of this case were developed at greater length in his later pamphlet *Ideas on the Opera*, London, 1790.

35 Diary of Samuel Quincy, *Proceedings of the Massachusetts Historical Society*, 19 (1881–2), 216–23.

36 Roger Lonsdale, *Dr Charles Burney: A Literary Biography*, Oxford, 1965, 150–3. It should also be noted that the establishment of an academy was the central proposal of *Idées sur l'opéra avec un projet d'établissement d'une véritable Académie de Musique* in 1764, attributed to Le Texier de Forge.

37 Le Texier seems to be in error about the nationality of Prudom. See Highfill *et al.*, eds., *A Biographical Dictionary*, XII, 193–4.

38 See Daniel Heartz, 'The Creation of the Buffa Finale in Italian Opera', *Proceedings of the Royal Musical Association*, 104, 1977–8.

39 Ribeiro, ed., *The Letters*, I, 309.

40 British Library, Althorpe MSS, F106; 4 November 1776; 'The dancing is very poor for Mad^me Vallovy has lost her gentility and grace by an unfortunate Grossesse [pregnancy], that she is not to get rid of these four months.'

41 Beinecke Library, Osborn MSS, c.467, vol. IV, 7 August 1786.

42 Price, Milhous and Hume, *Italian Opera*, I, 185.

11 THE KING'S THEATRE FLOURISHES

All Le Texier quotations are translations from Anthoine Le Texier, *Journal Etranger de Littérature*, 10 and 11 (November 1777); 12 and 13 (December 1777); 14 (January 1778); 18 and 19 (March 1778); 21 (April 1778).

1 Burney, *An Eighteenth-Century Musical Tour in Central Europe and the Netherlands*, 32.

2 Terry, *John Christian Bach*, 129–30.

3 Burney, *An Eighteenth-Century Musical Tour in Central Europe and the Netherlands*, 34.

4 'The celebrated Dantzy sung and Le Brun played upon the Hautboy, who is equal if not superior (as they say) to Fischar. As to Dantzy she has a prodigious compass and a surprising facility and sings most naturally and agreeably. She is engaged to sing at the Opera next winter.' Herbert, ed., *The Pembroke Papers*, 96.

5 Beinecke Library, Osborn MSS files 'B' 707.

6 In the *Queen of Quavers* satire, reference is made to Adamberger's 'dismal tone of voice'.

7 This redecoration predated a major renovation by only one year. See Price, Milhous and Hume, *Italian Opera*, I, 43.

8 Harris, ed., *A Series of Letters*, I, 398.

9 The young Mozart noted down several passages sung by Agujari in 1770, one of which ascended to an astonishing c''''. Further details on these singers are given in John A. Rice, *Antonio Salieri and Viennese Opera*, Chicago, 1998, 259–67.

10 Burney, *A General History of Music*, II, 865.

11 British Library, Additional MSS 39929.

12 Price, Milhous and Hume, *Italian Opera*, I, 197–8.

13 *Ibid.*, I, 200–2.

14 British Library, Egerton MSS 3700A, fol. 69.

15 Petty, *Italian Opera*, 154.

16 *Morning Post*, 9 February 1778.

17 Burney, *A General History of Music*, II, 885–6.

18 Mount-Edgcumbe, *Musical Reminiscences*, 20. Although Roncaglia had the misfortune to be compared regularly with Pacchierotti, he did not, as Lady Clarges reported in 1780, 'seem intimidated by Pac's success, which I wondered at'. British Library, Egerton MSS 3700A, fol. 69.

19 Petty, *Italian Opera*, 155.

20 For a detailed account of the season as a whole, see Price, Milhous and Hume, *Italian Opera*, I, 193–202.

21 Terry, *John Christian Bach*, 157.

12 THE *QUEEN OF QUAVERS* SATIRE

Quotations throughout this chapter are from the *Town & Country Magazine* (September 1777), 460–3, and *The Remarkable Trial of the Queen of Quavers*, London, 1778.

1 Little and Kahrl, eds., *The Letters*, III, 1157.

2 *Ibid.*, 1163.

3 *Journal of the House of Commons*, 36 (1777), 316, 454.

4 McMullen, *An Odd Attempt*, 233, n. 7, cites Tate Wilkinson, *Memoirs*, I, 236, on Garrick's 'characteristic stammer'.

5 Brooke, *The Excursion*, II, 35–6.

6 Little and Kahrl, eds., *The Letters*, III, 1172.

7 Boaden, ed., *Private Correspondence*, II, 239. See also 241.

8 Little and Kahrl, eds., *The Letters*, III, 1173.

9 *The Westminster Magazine* (1777), 433.

10 Boaden, ed., *Private Correspondence*, II, 279.

11 McMullen, *An Odd Attempt*, 175.

12 Brooke, *The Excursion*, II, 142–3.

13 *Hibernian Magazine*, 6 (February 1776), 97.

14 Fanny Burney, *The Early Journals*, II, 56.

15 *Town & Country Magazine* (August 1777), 434.

16 Burney, *A General History of Music*, II, 890.

17 In *Musical Reminiscences*, 27, Mount-Edgcumbe recalled that Adamberger had 'a disagreeable nasal voice'.

18 It. 'bubboni' (boils).

19 It. 'crapulare' (to debauch).

20 Giuseppino is an ironical reference to Millico's figure, described by Fanny as 'immense'.

21 Fanny Burney, *The Early Journals*, I, xxii.

22 *Ibid.*, II, 187; 'He looked like an angel – nothing can be more beautiful than this youth: he has the Complection of our Dick – the very finest White-Red I ever saw: his Eyes are the sweetest in the World, at once soft and spirited: All his Features are animated and charming.'

23 *Ibid.*, 15–17.

24 In *An Eighteenth-Century Musical Tour in Central Europe and the Netherlands*, 102, Burney had written 'I could not keep my eyes off his face.'

25 Brooke, *The Excursion*, I, 123.

26 The 'crazy' opera was *Il creso*, first performed, as pointed out by Petty, in 1765, making it only thirteen years old. See Petty, *Italian Opera*, 346.

13 FINANCIAL MANAGEMENT

1 Price, Milhous and Hume, *Italian Opera*.

2 Gibson, 'Italian Opera', 47–59.

3 On 13 May 1783, the *Morning Herald* reported that Simon Slingsby had 'never had less than £400 a year'. Milhous and Hume, 'Opera Salaries', 46.

4 Price, Milhous and Hume, *The Impresario's Ten Commandments*, 27 and 80.

5 Price, Milhous and Hume, *Italian Opera*, I, 248.

6 I am grateful to Patricia Howard for this reference. Johann Christian von Mannlich, 'Histoire de ma vie', MS, Munich Staadsbibliothek, cod. gall. 616–19. Extracts in: Henrietta Weiss von Trostprugg, 'Mémoires sur la musique à Paris à la fin du reigne de Louis XV', *La Révue Musicale*, 150 (1934), 253–4.

7 British Library, Althorpe MSS, F105.

8 Fanny Burney, *The Early Journals*, II, 24.

9 Milhous and Hume, 'Opera Salaries', 44.

10 On Fish Coppinger, see Lewis *et al.*, eds., *The Correspondence of Horace Walpole*, XXIX, 171.

11 British Library, A Collection of Cuttings [1757–1829], XLI (1774).

12 On 31 March 1769 he received a payment from the opera account at Drummonds Bank. See Gibson, 'Italian Opera', 55.

13 According to the *Public Advertiser* on 24 October 1782, Giardini was to receive £400 for leading the King's Theatre orchestra in the 1782–3 season. See McVeigh, *The Violinist*, 185.

14 London, Public Record Office, LC 7 / 88, 201.

15 The published figures for the Drummonds opera accounts are wrong on two counts: the total receipts given are as at 31 December. Further subscriptions were usually received in January and February. The number of subscribers given takes no account of double or triple family subscriptions. See Gibson, 'Italian Opera'.

16 The budget category for the orchestra in a document cited by Price, Milhous and Hume for the 1784–5 season was £1,711. See Price, Milhous and Hume, *Italian Opera*, I, 121, table 4. There is no way of telling how typical the categories in this document were, but, for example, *figurants* (£975), dressers / nightly servants (£561) and guards (£135) give at least a general idea of how much larger the actual budget might have been than the payments made through the Hoare ledgers.

17 The £10,000 income recently suggested for Sheridan's first season may be an underestimate. See Price, Milhous and Hume, *Italian Opera*, I, 107, table 3.

18 *Ibid.*, 110.

19 *Ibid.*, 60.

20 *Ibid.*, 186.

21 *Ibid.*, 61.

22 *Ibid.*, 55.

23 *Ibid.*, 61.

24 *Ibid.*, 58.

25 *Ibid.*, 61.

26 *Ibid.*, 107, table 3.

27 Milhous and Hume, 'Opera Salaries'.

28 In a letter to Twining on 11 May 1780, Burney wrote: 'He [Le Texier] was appointed director and super-intendant of the Opera at a Salary of 300, or 600, I forget which, a year.' Ribeiro, ed., *The Letters*, I, 309.

29 Price, Milhous and Hume, *Italian Opera*, I, 60.

14 OPERA SALARIES

1 Gibson, 'Italian Opera'; Milhous and Hume, 'Opera Salaries'.

2 Burney, *A General History of Music*, II, 887.

3   The Royal Academy of Arts, Humphry MSS, HU 2/63.
4   Mount-Edgcumbe, *Musical Reminiscences*, 20.
5   British Library, Egerton 3691, fol. 69ᵛ.
6   Price, ed., *The Letters of Richard Brinsley Sheridan*, I, 151–2. British Library, Add. MSS 27925, fols. 5–6.
7   The following year, Garton publicised the fact that substantial sums were overdue from unpaid subscriptions. Price, Milhous and Hume, *Italian Opera*, I, 135.
8   *Ibid.*, 248.
9   Hill, *The House*, 224–5.
10 British Library, Eg. MSS 3700A, fol.69.
11 Beinecke Library, Osborn MSS c.4.
12 *Ibid.*
13 *Ibid.*
14 *Ibid.*
15 Ribeiro, ed., *The Letters*, I, 382.
16 Milhous and Hume, 'Opera Salaries', 54.
17 Price, Milhous and Hume, *The Impresario's Ten Commandments*, 27.
18 Milhous and Hume, 'Opera Salaries', 46.
19 Walpole reported the salaries paid to the *primo uomo* and the *prima donna* in the 1741–2 season as £1,000 each. *Ibid.*, 39.
20 *Ibid.*, 44.
21 T. J. Walsh, *Opera in Dublin, 1705–1797*, Dublin, 1973, 92–106 and 317–24.
22 Milhous and Hume, 'Opera Salaries', 44.
23 It is worth noting that Michael Poitier, dancing master for De Crosa's company in 1748–9, was awarded £800 for a season's work. *Ibid.*, 40.
24 *Ibid.*, 44.
25 Price, Milhous and Hume, *The Impresario's Ten Commandments*, 15.
26 Burney, *An Eighteenth-Century Musical Tour in France and Italy*, 245–6.
27 Ribeiro, ed., *The Letters*, I, 382.
28 *Ibid.*, 401.
29 Price, Milhous and Hume, *Italian Opera*, I, 590.

15 THE SALE OF 1778

1   Price, Milhous and Hume, *Italian Opera*, I, 59.
2   Petty, *Italian Opera*, 154.

3 *Morning Post*, 9 February 1778.
4 The complaint from Philharmonicus was that the Italians kept up an 'incessant jabber' during the music, and then paid for their free admission by thundering out indiscriminately at the end of each song '*brava – Ancora, Ancora!*' Brooke replied that on this occasion the noise had been the result of 'two or three French domestics' using their master's subscription ticket without permission, and that free admission was exceptional. Philharmonicus remained unconvinced and noted the 'excess proportion the *paper currency* [i.e. free tickets] always bears to that of *hard money*'. See Petty, *Italian Opera*, 156. Noise was certainly a problem for real music lovers. Intending to visit the opera house with Burney in the autumn of 1776, Twining humorously asked him to ensure 'that no puppies are admitted into the galleries, nor talkers, nor time-beaters, nor soi-disant connoisseurs'. British Library, Add. MSS 39929.
5 Petty, *Italian Opera*, 159.
6 Burney, *A General History of Music*, II, 882–3. According to a heavily scored-out passage in a letter to Greville (December 1776), Burney had been 'carrying on their [the Pantheon's] foreign Correspondence for 3 years' at a salary of £100 a year, the loss of which he blamed on his having abetted Giardini's 'insolent and tyrannical Governm^t'. It is only possible to speculate about whether the Pantheon management felt there to be any conflict of loyalties between Burney's unpaid advisory role at the King's Theatre and his work for them, and whether this played any part in his dismissal. See Lonsdale, *Dr Charles Burney*, 227.
7 Petty, *Italian Opera*, 150.
8 *Ibid.*, 151.
9 Highfill *et al.*, eds., *A Biographical Dictionary*, XVI, 317.
10 *Public Advertiser*, 7 November 1775.
11 Price, Milhous and Hume, *Italian Opera*, I, 57.
12 Walsh, *Opera in Dublin*, 192.
13 Price, Milhous and Hume, *Italian Opera*, I, 54 and 56.
14 *Ibid.*, 57.
15 Price, ed., *The Letters*, I, 97.
16 *Ibid.*, 116–21.
17 A. Dayle Wallace, 'Le Texier's Early Years in England, 1775–1779', *Studies in Honor of John Wilcox*, ed. A. Dayle Wallace and Woodburn O. Ross,

Detroit, 1958, 82.

18 *Ibid.*, 116.

19 *Ibid.*, 82–8.

20 Lewis *et al.*, eds., *The Correspondence of Horace Walpole*, xxvii, 365.

21 *Morning Post*, 24 February 1778.

22 See, for example, the angry correspondence published in the *Hibernian Magazine*, 6 (1776) 816–17.

23 Judith Milhous and Robert Hume, 'James Lewis's Plans for an Opera House in the Haymarket (1778)', *Theatre Research International*, 19 (1994), 191–202.

24 *Ibid.*, 198.

25 Brooke remained in touch with the Burneys. On 31 October 1783, she wrote to Fanny: 'Will you, my dear Madam, tell Dr Burney I am glad he has got Padre Martini's packet? I am much in the dark about opera affairs, they seem an inexplicable maze, but I am told will be clear'd up in a few days. Mrs Yates joins me in best compliments to the Dr and Mrs Burney, and family.' New York Public Library, Berg MSS, Scrapbook, England, 1759–99.

26 McMullen, *An Odd Attempt*, 189.

27 *Memoirs of Dr Burney*, I, 334–5.

BIBLIOGRAPHY

MANUSCRIPTS

British Library
Althorpe MSS

F43	Letters from Mrs Howe
F101 – F106	Letters from George Bussy Villiers to Lady Spencer
F117	Letters between Sir William Hamilton and the Spencers
F118	Letters from Sir William Jones to Lady Spencer
F119	Letters from Hans Stanley to Lady Spencer
F119	Letters from General Cunningham to Lady Spencer
F130	Various correspondents to the Spencers
Add. 39929	Letters from Thomas Twining to Charles Burney
Add. 41197	Letters to Sir William Hamilton
Add. 42069	Hamilton and Greville papers
Eg. 3691	Letter-journal of Susan Burney
Eg. 3700A	Letters from Lady Clarges to Susan Burney
RP 2046 (photocopy)	Letter from Garrick to Sir William Parsons

Royal Academy of Arts, Burlington House, Piccadilly
Ozias Humphry MSS
HU 1, fol.33;
HU 2/ 12, 13, 17, 18, 21, 22, 33, 36, 37, 40–1, 63, 67;
HU 4/ 105.

India Office Library
Francis MSS E22	Letter-journal of Mrs Francis

Bodleian Library
Montagu d.6, fol.239	Letter from Frances Brooke to Ozias Humphry

National Library of Wales
Powis 1990 Deposit, uncatalogued box marked 'Clive of India'

Hyde Collection, Four Oaks Farm, New Jersey
Johnson Miscellanies,VII,

192–5	Letter from Frances Brooke to Ozias Humphry

Houghton Library, Harvard University

British Library RP 1012	Letters from Frances Brooke to Gifford

Beinecke Library, Yale University

Osborn MSS 3, box 1	Letter from Agujari to Burney
Osborn MSS 3, box 13	Letters from Pacchierotti to Burney
Osborn MSS files 'B'	Letter from Thomas Banks to Ozias Humphry
Osborn c.4	Letters from Pacchierotti to Fanny Burney
Osborn c.467	Correspondence of the Reverend Norton Nichols
Osborn f.c.80	Diary of Edward Pigott, 1770–83
Hilles MSS, box 6	Letter from Maria Cosway to Ozias Humphry
Beckford MSS, Gen.102,1	Typescript of letters from William Beckford to Louisa

New York Public Library
Berg Collection

Scrapbook 1759–99	Letter from Frances Brooke to Fanny Burney
Scrapbook 1653–1890	Letter from Elizabeth Allen Burney

Public Record Office
LC 7/88, 11 January and 7 February 1773, 5 February 1774
LC 5/16, 10 November 1773, 182.

Hampshire Record Office

9M73/G468/2	Letter from Sir William Hamilton to James Harris

C. Hoare and Co., 37 Fleet Street, London
Ledgers of James Brooke and Richard Yates 1773–7:

ledger 89: fols. 245^v, 246, 246^v, 247
ledger 91: fols. 324^v, 325, 325^v, 326
ledger 94: fols. 195^v, 196, 196^v, 197, 197^v, 198, 198^v, 199, 199^v, 200
ledger 98: fols. 270^v, 271, 271^v, 272
Letter from James Brooke to Hoare and Co., 2 January 1773

Drummonds Bank (Royal Bank of Scotland), 49 Charing Cross, London
Sheridan and Harris's opera account 1778–9:
1778 R-Z: DR/427/79
1779 R-Z: DR/427/83
1780 R-Z: DR/427/87 (balance only)
Jonathan Garton's account 1778–9:
1778 E-H: DR/427/77
1779 E-H: DR/427/81

Coutts and Co., 440 Strand, London
Pacchierotti's account (opened 20 July 1779)

William Salt Library, Stafford
'Sheridan Letters', SMS 343
1780 (opera payments and receipts)

BOOKS AND ARTICLES

A.B.C.Dario Musico, Bath, 1780.
Berland, K. J. H., 'Frances Brooke and David Garrick', *Studies in Eighteenth-Century Culture*, 20 (1990), 217–30.
Boaden, James, ed., *The Private Correspondence of David Garrick*, 2 vols., London, 1831–2.
Brooke, Frances, *The Old Maid*, 3 (29 November 1755), 18 (6 March 1756), 26 (8 May 1756).
    The Excursion, 2 vols., London, 1777.
Burney, Charles, *A General History of Music from the Earliest Ages to the Present Period*, ed. Frank Mercer, 2 vols., London, 1935.
    An Eighteenth-Century Musical Tour in France and Italy, ed. Percy A. Scholes, London, 1959.
    An Eighteenth-Century Musical Tour in Central Europe and the Netherlands, ed. Percy A. Scholes, London, 1959.

Burney, Fanny, *The Early Journals and Letters*, ed. Lars E. Troide, Oxford, vols. I and II, 1988 and 1990.

(Madame d'Arblay), *Memoirs of Dr Burney*, 3 vols., London, 1832.

Cortese, Nino, 'Una autobiografia inedita', *Rassengna musicale italiana*, 3 (1930), 123–35.

Deutsch, Otto E., 'Lady Hamilton', *Notes and Queries*, 197 (1952), 540–3 and 560–4.

Edwards, Edward, *Anecdotes of Painters*, London, 1808.

Fiske, Roger, *English Theatre Music in the Eighteenth Century*, 2nd edn, Oxford, 1973.

Ford, Brinsley, 'Thomas Jenkins: Banker, Dealer and Unofficial English Agent', *Apollo*, 99 (1974), 416–25.

'Sir Watkin Williams Wynn: A Welsh Maecenas', *Apollo*, 99 (1974), 435–9.

'Sir John Coxe Hippisley: An Unofficial English Envoy to the Vatican', *Apollo*, 99 (1974), 440–5.

'James Byres: Principal Antiquarian for the English Visitors to Rome', *Apollo*, 99 (1974), 446–61.

Ford, Brinsley, ed., *The Letters of Jonathan Skelton Written from Rome and Tivoli in 1758*, Walpole Society, XXXVI (1956–8), London, 1960.

Fortescue, Sir John, ed., *The Correspondence of King George the Third from 1760 to December 1783*, 6 vols., London, 1927–8.

Fothergill, Arthur, *Sir William Hamilton: Envoy Extraordinary*, London, 1969.

Gibson, Elizabeth, 'Earl Cowper in Florence and his Correspondence with the Italian Opera in London', *Music & Letters*, 67 (1987), 235–52.

'Italian Opera in London, 1750–1775: Management and Finances', *Early Music*, 18 (1990), 47–59.

Graves, Algernon, *The Society of Artists of Great Britain 1761–1791: The Free Society of Artists 1761–1783*, London, 1907.

Harris, James, ed., *A Series of Letters from the First Earl of Malmesbury*, 2 vols., London, 1870.

Heartz, Daniel, 'From Garrick to Gluck: the Reform of Theatre and Opera in the Mid-Eighteenth Century', *Proceedings of the Royal Musical Association*, 94 (1967–8), 111–27.

'The Creation of the Buffa Finale in Italian Opera', *Proceedings of the Royal Musical Association*, 104 (1977–8).

Hedgecock, Frank A., *A Cosmopolitan Actor: David Garrick and his French Friends*, London, 1912.

Herbert, Lord, ed., *The Pembroke Papers 1734–1780: Letters and Diaries of Henry, Tenth Earl of Pembroke and his Circle*, London, 1939.

Hibernian Magazine, 4 (1774), 275–6, 675; 6 (1776), 97, 821.

Highfill, Philip H., Jr, Kalman A. Burnim and Edward A. Langhans, eds., *A Biographical Dictionary of Actors, Actresses, Musicians, Dancers, Managers and Other Stage Personnel in London 1600–1800*, 16 vols., Carbondale, Ill., 1973–93.

Hill, Constance, *The House in St Martin's Street: Being Chronicles of the Burney Family*, London and New York, 1907.

Historical Manuscripts Commission, *The Manuscripts of the Earl of Carlisle*, London, 1897.

The Manuscripts and Correspondence of James, First Earl of Charlemont, 2 vols., London, 1891.

Hodges, Sheila, 'Gasparo Pacchierotti', *The Music Review*, 55 (1994), 276–92.

Home, James A., ed., *The Letters and Journal of Lady Mary Coke*, 4 vols., Edinburgh, 1889–96.

Howard, Patricia, *C. W. von Gluck: Orfeo*, Cambridge, 1981.

'Attempting to Reconstruct Gluck's 1773 Orfeo', *Musical Times*, 137 (1996), 13–15.

'Guadagni in the Dock: a Crisis in the Career of a Castrato', *Early Music*, 27 (1999), 87–95.

Hunt, Jno Leland, *Giovanni Paisiello: His Life as an Opera Composer*, New York, 1975.

Jesse, John Heneage, *George Selwyn and his Contemporaries*, 4 vols., London, 1882.

Journal of the House of Commons, 36 (1777) 316, 454.

Kelly, Michael, *Reminiscences of Michael Kelly, of the King's Theatre, and Theatre Royal Drury Lane*, 2 vols., London, 1826

King, Richard G., and Saskia Willaert, 'Giovanni Francesca Crosa and the First Italian Comic Operas in London, Brussels and Amsterdam, 1748–1750', *Journal of the Royal Musical Association*, 118 (1993), 246–75.

Kirkman, James T., *Memoirs of the Life of Charles Macklin*, 3 vols., London, 1799.

Le Texier, Anthoine, *Ideas on the Opera, offered to the Subscribers, Creditors, and Amateurs of that Theatre*, London, 1790.

Journal Etranger de Littérature, 1, 10, 11, 12, 13, 14, 18, 19, 21 (June 1777–May 1778).

Lewis, Lesley, *Connoisseurs and Secret Agents in Eighteenth-Century Rome*, London, 1961.

Lewis, Wilmarth, S. *et al.*, eds., *The Yale Edition of the Correspondence of Horace Walpole*, 48 vols., New Haven, Conn., 1937–83.

Little, David M. and George M. Kahrl, eds., *The Letters of David Garrick*, 3 vols., Cambridge, Mass., 1963.

Llanover, Lady, ed., *The Autobiography and Correspondence of Mary Granville, Mrs Delaney*, 3 vols., London, 1862.

London Magazine, 40 (1771), 93–7; 43 (1774), 407.

Lonsdale, Roger, *Dr Charles Burney: A Literary Biography*, Oxford, 1965.

Marc, Margaret L., and W. H. Quarrell, *Lichtenberg's Visits to England*, Oxford, 1938.

Matthews, Betty, 'The Davies Sisters, J. C. Bach and the Glass Harmonica', *Music & Letters*, 56 (1975), 150–69.

McMullen, Lorraine, *An Odd Attempt in a Woman: The Literary Life of Frances Brooke*, Vancouver, 1983.

McVeigh, Simon, *Concert Life in London from Mozart to Haydn*, Cambridge, 1993.

    The Violinist in London's Concert Life: Felice Giardini and his Contemporaries, New York and London, 1989.

Melville, Lewis, *The Life and Letters of William Beckford of Fonthill*, London, 1910.

Milhous, Judith, and Robert Hume, 'Opera Salaries in Eighteenth-Century London', *Journal of the American Musicological Association*, 46 (1993), 26–83.

    'James Lewis's Plans for an Opera House in the Haymarket (1778)', *Theatre Research International*, 19 (1994), 191–202.

Morrison, Alfred, *The Hamilton–Greville Letters*, 2 vols., 1893–4.

Mount-Edgcumbe, Richard, *Musical Reminiscences of an Old Amateur Chiefly Respecting the Italian Opera in England for Fifty Years, from 1773 to 1823*, London, 1824.

Music for London Entertainment 1660–1800, series E, vol. II, *Antonio Sacchini: Il Cid*, introduction by Dennis Libby, London, 1996.

Nalbach, Daniel, *The King's Theatre 1704–1867*, London, 1972

Norton, J. E., ed., *The Letters of Edward Gibbon*, 3 vols., London, 1956.

Oppé, A. P,. ed., *Memoirs of Thomas Jones*, Walpole Society, XXXII (1946–8), London, 1951.

O'Reilly, Robert Bray, *An Authentic Narrative of the Principal Circumstances relating to the Opera-House in the Haymarket*, London, 1791.

Parke, William, T. *Musical Memoirs*, 2 vols., London, 1830.

Petty, Frederick, C. *Italian Opera in London: 1760–1800*, Ann Arbor, Mich., 1980.

Price, Cecil, ed., *The Letters of Richard Brinsley Sheridan*, 3 vols., Oxford, 1966.

Price, Curtis, 'Italian Opera and Arson in Late Eighteenth-Century London', *Journal of the American Musicological Society*, 42 (1989) 55–107.

Price, Curtis, Judith Milhous and Robert D. Hume, *The Impresario's Ten Commandments: Continental Recruitment for Italian Opera in London 1763–64*, Royal Musical Association Monographs, London, 1992.

  Italian Opera in Late Eighteenth-Century London, vol. I, *The King's Theatre*, Oxford, 1995; vol. II, *The Pantheon*, forthcoming.

The Remarkable Trial of the Queen of Quavers, London [1778].

Ribeiro, Alvaro, ed., *The Letters of Charles Burney: Volume I (1751–1784)*, Oxford, 1991.

Rice, John A., *Antonio Salieri and Viennese Opera*, Chicago, 1998.

Robins, Brian, *The John Marsh Journals: The Life and Times of a Gentleman Composer (1752–1828)*, Stuyvesant, N.Y., 1998.

Rosselli, John, *Singers of Italian Opera*, Cambridge, 1992.

Sheppard, Francis H. W., ed., *Survey of London*, vols. XXIX–XXX, London, 1960.

Spencer, Earl and Christopher Dobson, eds., *The Letters of David Garrick and Georgiana Countess Spencer*, Cambridge, 1960.

Stone, George Winchester, Jr et al., *The London Stage 1660–1800: A Calendar of Plays, Entertainments and Afterpieces*, 5 parts, Carbondale, Ill., 1960–8.

Stanton, Lindsay, 'Hayward's List: British Visitors to Rome 1757–1775', *Walpole Society*, 159 (1983).

Taylor, William, *A Concise Statement of Transactions and Circumstances Respecting the King's Theatre in the Haymarket*, London, 1791.

Terry, Charles Sanford, *John Christian Bach*, 2nd edn, London, 1967.

Town & Country Magazine, (September 1777), 460–3.

Toynbee, Paget, and Leonard Whibley, eds., *Correspondence of Thomas Gray*, 3 vols., Oxford, 1935.

Wallace, A. Dayle, 'Le Texier's Early Years in England, 1775–1779', *Studies in*

Honor of John Wilcox, ed. A. Dale Wallace and Woodburn O. Ross, Detroit, 1958.

Walsh, T. J., *Opera in Dublin, 1705–1797*, Dublin, 1973.

Weiss von Trostprugg, Henrietta, 'Mémoires sur la musique à Paris à la fin du règne de Louis XV', *La Revue Musicale*, 150 (1934), 253–4.

Westminster Magazine (1777), 569.

Williams, John, *A Pin Basket to the Children of Thespis*, London, 1797.

Williamson, George, *Richard Cosway*, London, 1905.

Ozias Humphry, London, 1918.

Woodfield, Ian, 'New Light on the Mozarts' London Visit: A Private Concert with Manzuoli', *Music & Letters*, 75 (1995), 187–208.

INDEX

Abel, Karl Friederick, 16, 99, 179
Adamberger, Valentin, 155, 174, 192, 214, 252–4, 257
Agujari, Lucrezia, 6, 9, 13, 71–2, 77, 107–8, 115–19, 125, 127, 130–2, 134, 156–7, 182, 206–7, 214, 216, 224, 286
Agus, Joseph, 179, 234, 243–4, 246–7, 250
Ailsbury, Lord, 248
Alessandri, Felice, 184
Algarotti, Francesco, 7–8
Aliberti, Teatro di, 154
Allam, Thomas, 236, 238
America, 180
Andrei (Andries), Antonio, 196, 252, 255
Anfossi, Pasquale, 7, 14, 81–2, 85, 106, 153–4, 162, 179, 292; *Il geloso in cimento*, 219; *La finta giardiniera*, 106, 117, 219; *La vera costanza*, 153, 162, 219, 291–2; *L'incognita perseguitata*, 106
Ansani, Giovanni, 179–80, 201, 214
Aprile, Giuseppe, 123
Arne, Thomas, 160, 192
Asselin, John, 234
Astier, 124
Auge, Monsieur, 243, 245, 247, 249

Baccelli, Giovanna, 108, 149, 180, 192, 208, 210, 214, 239–40, 243–5, 249, 257, 280, 286–90, 292–3
Bach, Johann Christian, 10, 13, 16, 20, 28, 41–2, 49, 90–1, 99, 153, 165, 179, 216–18, 220, 294; *Adriano in Siria*, 42; *Carattaco*, 42; *La clemenza di Scipione*,

10, 165, 220, 294; *Lucio Silla*, 153; *Orione*, 20, 42, 152, 220; *Temistocle*, 153
Badini, Carlo Francesco, 188, 196, 242, 244, 253, 255
Baglioni, Rosa, 179
Baini, Cecilia, 103
Banks, Thomas, 100, 153
Banti, Brigida, 160, 206
Banti, Zaccharia, 252, 290
Banti, Felicità, 287, 292
Barazzi, Franceso, 86–90, 102–4, 221, 245, 307
Barbella, Emanuel, 56
Baretti, Joseph, 170–1, 175, 178–9
Barthelemon, François, 179
Barthelemon, Mrs, 73
Bartolomeo, Mr, 234
Bedford, Duchess of, 235, 239, 242
Bellamy & Co., 251
Benn, Margaret, 66
Bernasconi, Antonia, 193, 197, 206–7, 209, 255, 257, 263
Bernasconi, W., 251, 254
Berry, John, 248
Bertoni (Bartoni), Ferdinando, 196, 202, 211–12, 253
Bew, J., 17, 171
Billington, Elizabeth, 206
Bingham, Lady, 71
Bini, Pasquale, 95
Birmingham, 35, 166–7, 170, 180
Bocchini, Signor, 238
Bologna, 52, 83, 85, 87, 96, 98